For my Pal
Jonathan
Enjoy!
Lew

CONFESSIONS OF A CRIMINOLOGIST

Some of my best friends were sociopaths

LEWIS YABLONSKY PH.D.

iUniverse, Inc.
New York Bloomington

Copyright © 2010 by Lewis Yablonsky Ph.D

All rights reserved. No part of this book may be used or reproduced by any means, graphic, electronic, or mechanical, including photocopying, recording, taping or by any information storage retrieval system without the written permission of the publisher except in the case of brief quotations embodied in critical articles and reviews.

iUniverse books may be ordered through booksellers or by contacting:

iUniverse
1663 Liberty Drive
Bloomington, IN 47403
www.iuniverse.com
1-800-Authors (1-800-288-4677)

Because of the dynamic nature of the Internet, any Web addresses or links contained in this book may have changed since publication and may no longer be valid. The views expressed in this work are solely those of the author and do not necessarily reflect the views of the publisher, and the publisher hereby disclaims any responsibility for them.

ISBN: 978-1-4502-1239-7 (sc)
ISBN: 978-1-4502-1240-3 (ebook)

Printed in the United States of America

iUniverse rev. date: 03/08/2010

Table of Contents

Chapter 1. From Newark to the Navy To Rutgers University (1924-1949) 1

Chapter 2. My Life and Times Getting a Ph.D. at New York University (1949-1960) 27

Chapter 3. Directing a Crime Prevention Program and Becoming a Professor (1953-1958) 53

Chapter 4. Ucla, Synanon, Donna and Mitch (1960 to 1965) ... 71

Chapter 5. The Hippie Trip Period (1965-1970) 96

Chapter 6. George Raft and Hollywood (1970 to 1976) 115

Chapter 7. My Research into Extra-Sex (1976-1980) 132

Chapter 8. Divorce & a Father & Sons Book (1980 to 1994) . 145

Chapter 9. Spinoffs: Lectures in the U.S. and Europe (1994 to 2010) 165

Chapter 10. Expert-Witness Work and Gangs 176

PREFACE

This book is not only an autobiography. It delineates how and why I have written several of my 20 published books. In various chapters I reflect on some details on the subjects of my books, and discuss the main concepts in my books. This includes reflections on the sociology, psychology, and criminology of various subjects like gangs, extra-marital sex, the hippie phenomenon of the 1960s, psychodrama and group therapy, and my research into the old Hollywood through one of my favorite vintage actors--George Raft. I also include, where relevant, various media articles and reviews of my books and life situations The spine of the book is my development and growth from a light-weight delinquent into a light-weight intellectual and writer.

At 85, I am working as hard as ever as a criminologist, and am still sought-after by lawyers as an expert-witness in criminal and gang cases. This autobiography is an effort to recollect the experiences that caused me to become a criminologist instead of a criminal--and includes research and selected interviews I have performed with several thousand gangster and criminals for the 20 books I have published. The subjects of the book veers from frivolous incidents I have encountered in my life to hard concepts on crime that I have developed from the foundation of a life intrigued with criminal behavior in its many forms. In this regard, the book, in addition to being my memoirs is a compendium of my the theories and opinions I have developed as a criminologist over a period of 60 years.

This memoir includes disparate stories of incidents in my life that I found interesting. Many are not necessarily related to my role as a criminologist but are personal. My memoirs include interesting people I have met along the way like one of the astronauts who walked on the moon and many old movie stars I have interviewed for my Hollywood biography of George Raft the actor. The Raft book was partly motivated by my interest in early Hollywood and the movie stars of that era.

I have relived my life in writing this book. I have included and stolen segments from other books of mine where I described various situations and my emotions at that time. The some books I have written on various social issues have been most significant for me to recall important periods in my life.

All of my books were intwined with my emotional state, and the crux of my life at the time I was writing them. In relation to some of my books I have included the process through which I gathered data, and came to certain theoretical conclusions based on my research. On various issues that I consider important I have presented segments derived from my books. My research for and writing each book comprises a significant amount of my time, emotions and are entwined with my life. Researching and writing my various books significantly impacted my total viewpoint on life.

For example, in concluding my book THE HIPPIE TRIP I felt it was relevant to present the impact of an LSD trip I experienced in doing the book. In a similar vein, based on my 50 years of directing psychodramas, I believe it was relevant to present how and why I did some of these sessions.

Also, I have written in this book about some people I have interviewed in the process of my work over some 60 years who are celebrities like one of the men who walked on the moon, or actors including George Raft, Edward G. Robinson, Mae West, Jack Lemmon, Walter Mathau, Lucille Ball, and Fred Astaire--people who I believe are of interest to the general public.

It is probably pretentious--however, wherever I thought it was relevant to include media articles that described my life at the time as portrayed by media interviewers and writers. These include articles from Time and People Magazine, the LA Times, the New York Times, and the New York Daily News.

I have found that that getting my thoughts down on paper produces an emotional contentment. And as my life moves towards the inevitable I believe that I have had some unusual experiences. My story will generally unfold in a chronological order. However, when I remember a vignette in a different time frame--it will be included at the time of my memory.

The book details stories about my early years as a borderline delinquent into becoming a crime researcher, author, and a Professor of Sociology and Criminology at several universities including UMass, Harvard, UCLA, Columbia, Texas A&M, and California State University-Northridge where I taught for 30 years.

Over the course of my 60 year career as a criminologist, as mentioned, I have interviewed thousands of criminals and gang members for my books, and in the past decade served as an expert-witness in 300+ gang, criminal, and civil court cases.

My fascination with my hustler and criminal friends from my old neighborhood in Newark N.J. became a significant foundation for my expertise as a criminologist. As the platitude might go, "some of my early and best friends were criminal sociopaths." When I was a teenager, Interacting with them up close on a buddy level taught me more about crime than my several degrees, including my New York University Ph.D.

Chapter 1

From Newark to the Navy to Rutgers University (1924-1949)

The Early Years

I was born November 23, 1924 in a 6 apartment 3 story house on 19th Avenue in Irvington, N.J a small borough of Newark, New Jersey. I had two brother one older and one later on younger. In our families apartment was an icebox and a wood-coal burning stove for cooking. The house was owned by my fathers mother, grandmother Miriam. Bubba Myam, as she was known to me, lived with 2 sons my uncles Izzy, Morris and my Aunt Sadie. My grandfather, who I was named after was dead. My father came to the U.S. from Odessa, the Ukraine at the age of 3. And my mother came over at around 15 from a small town in Romania. They were married around 1920.

My uncles and Bubba were vegetarians. Sometimes when I was around 4 I was left to stay overnight with them for a sleepover. Nobody talked or played with me. After dinner in their apartment, more times than not I would get so bored I would cry to go home-- upstairs with my Mom, Dad, and older brother Morris. I developed very little tolerance for boredom. In my later years, I leave movies, lectures, and people very fast when I am bored.

I am the middle son of Harry, a truck driver and my Romanian Yidishe-Momma Fannie. My older brother Morris became an engineer, and my kid brother Joe

(4 years younger than me) became a distinguished FBI Agent. In brief, when he was in charge of the Las Vegas FBI office in the early 80's was important in kicking the mob out of Las Vegas.

In my early years I was routinely beaten as a child in Irvington at kindergarten school for being Jewish (e.g. "Jewkelberry.") At around 8, when we moved near Newark's Black hood I was beat up for being white. It was during the writing of this memoir that I realized how many times I have encountered stupid anti-semitism.

Lewis Yablonsky Ph.D

The first school I attended in Kindergarten was in Irvington. At that time, in the early thirties the American Nazi Party led by a psychopath Fritz Kuhn had its headquarters in Irvington. Kuhn and his group were admirers of Hitler. They were well known, and even had some mass meetings in New York. We were one of the few Jewish families in Irvington.

Jewish hatred seeped down into young kids. When they found out I was a "Hebe" I would get beat up going home from school on a regular basis. I remember, at around 7 or 8 thinking here they come, and 4 or 5 stupid kids would start beating me up because I was a Jew.

I am a Jew and was BarMitvahed at the age of 13. My preparation for the event in Hebrew School didn't make a lot of sense. The teacher was named H. He would walk up and down the aisle as we studied the Hebrew text, and if we weren't reading intently he would whack us on the back of the head.

An incident at the Hebrew school that helped shape my life as a Jew was the Jewish National Fund drive. We were sent out with the blue boxes with a slit in the top to collect money to plant trees in Israel. Being a conniving and enterprising kid, with a knife, I slid out as I recall around $2. I stole around 50 cents and put the rest back in the can. A Report was posted on how much each kid collected. The Report said I had collected around $1! Apparently Mr. H. took his cut. It somehow affected my belief in religion.

I do recall, however that my Bar Mitzvah speech was well received. My recollection is that after my speech and I was now a "man" bags of stale candy were thrown at me, and the other kids scrambled after the candy. My Jewish identity is more involved with the great Jewish food; and my continuing interest and amazement at the insanity of the German Holocaust. Since my Bar Mitzvah going to Shul has never been a part of my life.

Our family felt the depression in the early thirties. My father had invested a small amount of money, a few thousand dollars credit, in a Savings and Loan Co. They gave our family the balance owed my father in a very low rent free apartment (around $25 a month) in Newark.

A small park called Milford was near our house on Johnson Avenue. During the depression my father, for a time was out of work. I remember walking by him where he was sitting on a park bench with his head in his hands no doubt depressed. The memory is etched in my mind. Gelt, or better said no money was a factor in my life that was significant. (Later in life, after I had worked hard and found myself in a period with little gelt I wrote a book called THE EMOTIONAL MEANING OF MONEY. (1991 Reprinted by IUniverse, 2009)

In Newark I was enrolled in Miller Street school which had a large student population of "Negros" (as African-Americans were called back then) who often beat me up because I was an "Ofay." I remember becoming friends with one Black classmate Eddie Dades, who was sometimes my bodyguard and sometimes my tormenter. I also recall a big fight I had with a black kid named John Kaye after school. Our fight was cheered on by about 50 other students and some older guys. I think I won, and was dubbed the best fighter in the class.

There were some black gangs that operated near the school. During those years, from age eight to twelve, I was victimized many times by the black gangs for both rational and irrational reasons. The rational approach was a form of protection called "tech-taking." This involved the extortion of fifteen to twenty cents a week from me—big money for a kid in those days. The "protection" was that you wouldn't be assaulted if you paid up. (As we know this became a standard for later gangs like the mafiosa.)

The irrational assaults were related to my being an "ofay." As a white minority, I was periodically assaulted for no special reason—other than what I later found out as a sociologist was reverse prejudice. In those days, violence seldom, if ever, involved any lethal weapons. Most fighting was done one-on-one with fists, although on occasion it was a group-on-one.

In my early gang-like violent situations my response involved rolling with the punches, and getting a few punches in here and there as I was being knocked down.

Some fairness prevailed when I was allowed to fight a one-on-one with an adversary in elementary school. There were a few occasions when I actually won in a fair fight. In brief, I learned early in my life the lesson of the sociopathic characteristics of senseless violence—and this understanding has served me well in my later work as a criminologist and gang expert in the judicial process.

In 1942 I graduated as a C-student from Newark, New Jersey's South Side High (now called something like "Malcolm X-Shabazz High School." When I attended, the school was self-segregated, with black students hanging out on one side of the school and whites on the other. I often integrated the black area of the school, largely because I was interested and entertained by male black students who played "the dozens."

The "dozens" was a verbal game, where a group of kids would encircle two main actors who would verbally spar with each other by spontaneously and creatively rhyming nasty poems—that usually attacked the opponent's mother. (A one-liner I recall was, "Fucked your Ma in an alleyway, when I got through she thought she was Cab Calloway.") The adversary would counter with what was called a "backhap." If his retort was strong, the group would chant, "Man what a strong backhap!" Retrospectively, I believe the "dozens" was really the earliest form of what is now hailed as a new musical form known as "hip-hop gangsta rap."

My interest in the "dozens" unfortunately contributed to a violent situation in which I was seriously assaulted by a black gang. The high school "dozen" players were minor leaguers. One classmate and friend of mine told me, "Man, if you dig these guys you should check out the cats on Prince Street."

The corner of Prince and Kinney Streets in Newark was the center for older more expert "dozen" players. One afternoon, after enjoying several hours of their fascinating impromptu entertainment on the corner of Prince and Kinney Streets, I headed home. I apparently was in the wrong place at the wrong time. Several blocks from Prince and Kinney around four black teenagers came walking toward me with a belligerent demeanor. They crowded me off the sidewalk.

As I tried to get out of their way, one of them greeted me with the puzzling query, "Hey, you ofay motherfucker. What did you say about my mother?" Being stupid and nervous at the time, I started to answer the question with something rational to the effect of "I never met your mother." This was, of course, completely beside the point to my attackers.

The next thing I knew, after receiving a punch right on the jaw, was that I was down on the ground in a fetal position trying hard to avoid kicks to my head and body. The beating continued ferociously for several minutes-- after which, bloody and bowed, I wandered home.

To this day, I still think about the senselessness and the raging ferocity of my undeserved beating by this gang. That event, plus other social factors in my teenage years, caused me to carry a switchblade knife for protection during my high school years until I was almost eighteen. In my early years, the platitude that "some of my best friends were juvenile delinquents" certainly applied to me.

Another valuable experience that further introduced me into the world of gangs, delinquency and social problems before I acquired any formal education on the subject was the part-time job I had my my father. His occupation, as I indicated, for most of his life, was driving a laundry truck that picked up laundry in the poorest section of Newark. This almost completely African-American neighborhood was, and to a large extent remains, a kind of socioeconomic third-world country. People sent out their laundry back then because they had no reasonable available facilities for washing their clothes.

During my adolescent years, when I helped my father on his truck, we delivered laundry to poor people, some living in cellars with orange crates for furniture and mattresses on the floor. Experiencing these situations directly, spending time informally talking with our clients when I delivered their laundry, and observing children growing up under these conditions, were among my most emotionally affecting and profound sociology lessons. In a way more profound than my later university education

My two brothers, Morris and Joe, also helped my father with his difficult job. In addition to helping him deliver laundry, an important aspect of our job was, in effect, being security guards in a crime-ridden and often violent neighborhood. Without our presence, laundry would be stolen from the truck. One day, in an unguarded moment, someone stole the truck with a full load of laundry on it. I later recovered the truck--after scouting the hood. I remember being a hero to my father for my investigative work.

Our work in the Newark hood presented our family with some tough firsthand experiences and insights into crime causation, criminological issues, and victimology. This might possibly explain why I became a criminologist, and my brother Joe served as an FBI agent for over thirty years.

At the peak of his career, he had achieved the status of Special Agent in Charge of the Las Vegas, Nevada, office and in this capacity went up against the mob that controlled Nevada casinos. (Joe and I, over the years, have shared a considerable amount of data and theories on crime, the Mafia and youth gangs. Many of his insights on gang behavior, derived from these discussions, are woven into my gang books and my 2 textbooks: CRIMINOLOGY (1990) and JUVENILE DELINQUENCY (2000)

During my 4 years at South Side High School -- in Newark I carried a switchblade knife for protection. My need for self-protection stemmed, in part, from my teenage years as a dice and card hustler. During this phase of my life I hung out with many individuals who I would, later on, after my formal education, characterize as sociopaths. Fortunately, I had the shadow of a moral compass and knew right from wrong. This did not stop me from doing wrong mainly as a card and dice cheater.

I became involved with cheating at dice and cards through my best friend Davie from around age 10 to 17, He lived next door to me. Davie looked like a young Tyrone Power. He launched my early career as a very petty thief and dice hustler.

I became involved with Davie, at around the age of 10. One thing we did together was sell day old cakes that we bought from a bakery for very little money and sold door-to-door for three times the original cost. This enabled us to steal things that were available. In the classical Italian vein we literally became bicycle thieves.

We had a 50-50 partnership in the profits from selling the cakes and bikes. Somehow Davie managed to always wind up with all of our loot. This happened because after we sold a stolen bike--I would shoot dice head-to-head with Davie, and he always won. Not being totally stupid, after always ending up on the short end of our dice game, I asked him how he always won?

One day he told and showed me. This launched by teenage career as a dice hustler. Davie's older brother was a professional dice and card swindler and he taught Davie how to use "Ts"--a crooked form of dice that was misspotted. Ace-trey-five Ts could only make numbers like 4, 9, 10 etc. no seven outs. This was Davies trick for beating me at dice. During our games, he would palm good dice, and switch in the crooked "no-lose" dice.

Strangely, after I found out I was being constantly cheated I recall not getting mad about my victimization. What I wanted to learn from Davie was how to do it. He taught me all about the manipulation of dice, how to switch dice, and to some extent how to manipulate cards. My hustler career was launched.

As a teenager, after school Davie and I hung out at the so-called Newark Recreation Center Bowling Alley. The place was a place to bowl and was infested with small time hoods, burglars, and thieves of various types who hungout at this scene.

A highlight of the bowling alleys was a few days a month when Newark mobster Abner "Longie" Zwillman would walk in with his entourage of bodyguards. Longie was big-time. He knew and did business with such New York mobsters as Meyer Lansky, Bugsy Siegel, and Frank Costello. When Longy walked into the alleys-- it was like a visit from the Pope. Hustlers, including me, stood at attention and in awe of this great "role-model".

Later on I learned Longy was found dead hanging in his closet at his palatial home in the best neighborhood in Newark. The police called it suicide, but we all knew it was a mob-hit. He had done something "bad" to his associates and paid the price.

Davie and I teamed up with some older characters from the bowling alley where we hung out and this began my teenage life as a small time dice hustler. My sociopathic pals were guys with names like "Cueball." "Red" "Dewey," and "Slip." It was an important time for my learning about sociopathic criminal behavior, first hand, from my "friends." This "education" served me well in my later years as a criminologist. As stated, I believe I learned more at a gut level about criminal motivation and causation than I did in my later graduate work at New York University.

Several experiences woke me up to the path I was heading down that would have very likely end up with me in prison. As a matter of fact Davie wound up later on doing a 7 years term at a Federal Prison in an involved hijacking case that he had masterminded. Briefly it involved the hijacking of a Fur truck. It was hijacked in NY, went through the Holland Tunnel and ran out of gas on the Jersey side. Davie and 2 of his henchmen were arrested and convicted of a federal offense.

A wakeup call came to me one day about my veering towards delinquency when I hung out daily at the bowling alley. Many thieves and hustlers, infested the place. One day when I was around 16 I was having a coffee at the counter, sitting along side a guy known as "Harry the Horse." Harry who was around 30 was well known around the place and admired as a talented professional burglar.

Harry leaned over to me and said, "Kid, how would you like to make some money with me this Summer? I was interested. He then leaned closer and quietly said, "You don't have to do anything--just tell me when your friends or relatives are not home or on vacation. I will hit the house, and share any loot I get 50-50 with you."

I was outraged to think anyone would look at me as the kind of a creep who would sell out his friends and relatives. Apparently I transmitted that kind of character to Harry and others.

It struck me full force that I was so involved in the hustling life around the "Alley" and that I had the kind of rep that would allow Harry to perceive me as a potential aid to his dirty criminal activity. I politely said no. However, it was a wake up call to the trip I was on--but it didn't stop me from continuing.

All of my friends at that time were not bad guys. One of them, Jules Rose, who was around 12 when I was 10 was an honest friend. Around that age Jules and I would visit the Sears store that was around 3 blocks from where we lived. I remember returning from a visit to Sears coming up Bigelow St. I turned to Jules and said, "What did you get?" Jules responded, "what are you talking about? I showed Jules 2 toys I had stolen. He gave me a long lecture about "not stealing" and how wrong it was.(Jules and I met years later and reminisced. He had been a hero in WW2 flying around 30 bombing missions over Berlin.)

I was impressed that Jules thought that way; however, it had little impact on me during my teen years because I did become in those years a "lightweight hustler."

Other friends I knew at that time were the Margo brothers. Billie Margo later on made the news when he was busted for dealing cocaine. The story I learned was that Billie had gone to Italy to make a connection for dope with of all people Lucky Luciano. Little did he know that a Newark undercover cop was following him. When Billie got off the boat he was busted, went to federal prison for a long stretch. In those days "your mother" and "motherfucker" were notable words. In the Margo case, when you said, "your momma pushes dope" it was literally true.

The hustler trip I was on involved the following prototypical con. When either Davie or my other partners in crime saw a mark usually betting on bowling we would "clock" him. This meant some analysis of his BR--or bankroll. If he appeared to have enough money for a score, Davie would say to me. "Are you going to the crap game tonight." This would be said loudly in the hearing of the mark. The mark, would then usually inquire about where and when the game was taking place. Of course, he didn't know he was the entire game.

When he arrived at the place of the "game" often in a garage we used, there would be 4 or 5 of us staging a dice game. We would shoot dice for around an hour with the mark involved. Then Davie would give the hand signal (usually brushing his shirt) to wrap it up. With our crooked dice thrown into the game we would quickly "win" all of the marks money.

I remember Davie was really cold. If the Mark tried, as one did, to withhold any money and leave--Davie would do anything like bet even money on a dice object of a ten. Anything to get all of the mark's money.

Davie and I did a lot of these deals, and for those times made a lot of money for kids. When we had a mark the 4-5 guys working the game with us would be given a split up of the take. At the end of the game, when the mark had left, we would give all the money we had to Davie. He would take the hundred he had put into the game off the top and then we would split the take. I must confess, I cheated and at the end withheld ten or twenty. I believed every one cheated. After all we were cheaters.

During my High School years, dice hustling was only one of my activities. I also worked briefly behind the soda fountain at a drug store. I also managed to become a pretty good baseball player. I was South Side High's varsity first baseman--and when I was a senior I made All-City first baseman in the Newark Evening News pick.

Davie never understood why I would play baseball and miss out on some dice scores. At the same time my baseball team friends never understood why I hung out with creeps like Davie.

At the time, in addition to Davie, I did have some good friends. One of them was a kid named Morty Waimon. Morty came from a home broken by a father in prison in Canada. I don't know the whole story but Morty, for a time, was in an orphanage in Newark. Although he never talked about his father it no doubt deeply affected him. He had a very wry sense of humour and was quite intelligent. He later in life became a Professor of Education at Indiana University. We often, for kids, discussed many major issues about life including what is love? I never forgot a conversation we had one day when we were both around 13. Morty said, "You know Lew, you fell in love at an early age and never got over it." I responded, What the hell are you talking about?" He then said something I never forgot (here 70 years later) "Lew, you fell in love with Lew Yablonsky, and you'll never get over it."

A proud moment in my life was my graduation from South Side High. I recall when I was called up by the principal to receive my diploma he said, "Every school needs a star first baseman, and ours is Lew Yablonsky. He then handed me my diploma. To this day, I don't know whether he meant what he said, lauding my athletic skills, or was somewhat sarcastically teasing a C student who happened to be a good baseball player.

Now that I am an old man, and have literally traveled around the world looking back I can say without too many people arguing with me that Newark, New Jersey was and remains a crappy town. Recently, talkshow host Colin O'Brien and the mayor of Newark had a humorous TV controversy and encounter about Newark.

For me, growing up in Newark, had 2 major cultural institutions that I will always treasure. One was the Empire Burlesque Theater. How I was able to get in to see the shows when I was around 16 is an enigma. However, I did get to see, among other strippers, Lily St. Cyr, Georgia Southern, Gypsie Rose Lee, Ann Corio, Tempest Storm, and other legendary strippers do their acts. They performed along with great burlesque comedians in shockingly (for that time) sexy skits that were for me true sexual turnons. In addition, the weird salesmen who took over during the break and sold fake $2 watches and candy were fun experiences.

The other absolutely wonderful cultural musical times I had in Newark was to go to the Adams theater on Branford place and see, along with a usually lousy movie, all of the great bands of that period. The great bands of that era that performed extraordinary shows at the Adams included: The Dorsey brothers, Duke Ellington with singer Jimmy Rushing, Jimmie Lunceford, Cab Calloway, Larry Clinton, Charlie Barnett, Fats Waller, Louis Armstrong, Count Basie, and Artie Shaw. After a movie, the music would start and the band would rise on the stage. Their magical concerts would transport me into the clouds--at least out of Newark. Some of the famous singers of that time like Billie Holiday and Sarah Vaughn also appeared at the Adam's theater. Sara was from Newark and went to Miller St. School.

In summary, Newark wasn't all bad. Growing up on the streets of Newark taught me directly about crime and criminology. The movie houses had great old films. The Adams had wonderful music, and the legendary burlesque queens were great sexual turnons. When I think back on there sexy performances, I can still get sexually stimulated. Despite these positives, one of my standard closing lines, when I am interviewed by any media for my books or work is and will always be: "my greatest achievement in life was getting out of Newark."

1942 To 1943: A Lonely Life at Bama

For some subconcious reason that still eludes me, part of me wanted to leave my teenage dice game way of life--and get away from Davie and my "friendly" gang of hustlers. My father just about graduated elementary school. However, my Uncle Meyer and my older brother

Morris were role-models who had been to college and acquired degrees in engineering.

To me my brother Morris was a genius. He graduated high school at the age of 16, and acquired an engineering degree at 20. He later served heroically as a Lt. Commander in the Navy during World War 2. I looked up to him but he was seldom around--a very busy guy. He never played the role of "older-brother." In fact, many years later, when I became a therapist I helped him with his bad marital problems.

In 1942 when I graduated South Side High I wanted to follow in Morris's and Uncle Meyer's footsteps and on some level wanted to get away from Davie and the gang. I applied, was accepted, and went away to the University of Alabama in Tuscaloosa. At that time it was easy for a C student to get into a southern university.

Picture a hip Jewboy in pegged pants wearing a green velvet shirt with a long D.A. haircut in the deep South. My first rude awakening about racism was the way Negros were treated in the south. They would literally step off a sidewalk onto the street when a white man or woman walked toward them. I found it appalling!

I had brought some crooked dice with me to Bama--and continued my hustling career. I hooked up with a cabdriver named Red. After playing dice with him head to head we both realized we were both cheaters, laughed about it and did a few scores together. Of interest to me was Red told me where I could buy crooked dice. The purveyor of dice in Tuscaloosa was a local dentist who sold mispotted crooked dice.

When I left South Side High for the University of Alabama things changed. I still didn't find too many sexual partners. I did patronize some local hookers who worked in and around Tuscaloosa.

The most interesting scene was a Drive-In staffed by young girl waitresses. I would have a burger and then for about $5 one of the "waitresses would get in my beatup old $100 Chevvy and drive down the road with me for a sexual experience. I recall having spectacular sex with a young blonde--who I believed dug me. I would have 2 or 3 great orgasms with her in one encounter. She also became for me the model for the type of girl I found most attractive. That is--added to my visions of the Empire Burlesque Queens.

The only girl I dated on campus at Bama was a student who looked like my drive in sex partner. Her name was Eva. We were both 18 and in love. Or, at least, I was in love. Once again, when this girl from a small Alabama town found out I was a Jew--right to my face she dropped me. It was very painful. She told me she didn't date Jews. The rejection was not a lot of fun for a lonely kid from Newark.

At Bama, I found out something more disturbing about anti-semitism. Through my classes with them I had made friends with several guys on the Bama football team. One day I came out of class and three of them were standing-apparently waiting for me. I was puzzled. Then one of them said, "You prick, you never told us you were a fucking Jew." I didn't know I had to announce my religion to friends. There was a further interchange which I did not understand. However, I found out that Jews were aliens in Alabama, and according to popular belief some Jews had horns.

I did however, get my revenge on the anti-semitic Southern Jew haters by screwing the Sigma Chi fraternity--the bastion of white southern young bigots. I beat a guy in a crap game. I later found out he was a Sigma Chi Fraternity member named Sonny Burnett. Sonny was a son of the South and he brought me into his fraternity house to run crap games. I recall he gave me an anglo-saxon name. I always won with my crooked and manipulated dice, and split with Sonny. The two of us were screwing his fraternity brothers. I now realize how much I enjoyed my silly revenge of beating these punks. By the way, I later found out Sonny became an important lawyer in Birmingham.

I was lonely and missed my Newark gang when I was at Bama. I would go home via cheap Greyhound Bus on holidays. Davie and I would write letters to me about his continued hustling games and scores. My mom who knew about my involvement with Davie and what I did. (but of course disapproved of my behavior) sent me a small newsclip from the Newark Evening News.

The news article, in summary, reported that Davie was arrested for cheating a mark. The real story was that the mark at a certain point in the game pulled out a gun and took all of Davies' money. Unscrupulous as Davie was he thought he had been cheated out of his expected winnings. He reported the "robbery" to the police who, after hearing the story, arrested Davie.

My association with Davie and the gang literally came to screeching halt when I went home for the Christmas Holidays to Newark in the Winter of 1942.

Davie had an old Chevvy. With him, and 2 other guys Tommy Fox and Lenny Rodberg we were retuning from an evening in New York. We were on the Pulaski Skyway a highway, around 15 mile from Newark. I don't believe the Holland Tunnel between Jersey and New York had been built.

I recall there were 2 girls we had picked up in the car. I was driving Davie's car and it was snowing. All of a sudden on the icey road the car went out of control--and I vividly remember now over 65 years later, as I write this, I crashed and ended up staring at a pole that I had wrapped the car around. I was not hurt. However, Davie had bloody head and the others in the car had minor injuries.

The next day Davie's mother who was a Ma Barker type brought Davies bloody shirt to show my Mom. She cried on cue and threatened to sue my father the poor laundry man. She never pursued a case.

However, for whatever reasons, Davie and the other guys shut me out of the gang. Although I didn't know it then, being shut out of Davie and the gang was a blessing and an important turning point in my life. Lenny and Davie became 4F and couldn't be drafted, and Tommy went into the Army. I heard stories that Tommy had become a thief in the army at a supply base, and Davie, after he did the federal prison time for his fur truck robbery continued his dice hustler career. Later on he was the owner of the Blue Mirror--a night club in Newark.

The Navy in World War 2 (1943 To 1946)

I was shocked, as were all Americans, by the unexpected and horrendous Japanese attack on Pearl Harbor--December 7, 1941. I was 17 at that time, and heard about the war on a radio.

World War 2 in Europe was certainly on in 1943 when I was at Bama. I had joined the ROTC, and I was sure to be drafted. I signed up for a V-12 U.S. Navy Officer Training Program. After a year at the University of Alabama I was inducted into the Navy and sent for my officer training to Georgia Tech in Atlanta.

When I went into the Navy at Tech, I became good friends with a star football player--Eddie Prokop. Later on Prokop became a Pro football player in the then American Football League.

I roomed with another officer trainee Frank Broyles who was the quarterback on Tech's football team. Frank was a straight arrow, and went on to become one of the most famous football coaches in the U.S. at the University of Arkansas.

I found Frank was a very nice guy but a total square. He scrupulously followed all Navy rules. One night several other sailors and me had sex with a local girl who apparently enjoyed screwing sailors. I recall inviting Frank to participate one evening with the young lady. He said, "No."

At that time, at 19, I didn't understood how any young guy would turn down sex. (As a sociologist I have learned I am clearly and have always been a male chauvinist sexist. I recall Gore Vidal saying on the Dick Cavett Show, "Never turn down an opportunity to have sex or appear on a TV show." I have always subscribed to that advice.)

It took me some time to adjust to being ordered around in the Navy. I rebelled against any authority. At Tech I was an engineering major following in my older brothers footsteps. I hated engineering which of course included math, calculus and understanding machinery. These were my least favorite subjects.

I did not, at that time, discover the love I later had for sociology, psychology and criminology. Sort of "behind the barn" I read and enjoyed Freud, Camu, Dosteovsky, Shakespeare, and other writers and philosophers. (At South Side High, in my group, it was unfashionable to do anything "intellectual" like reading beyond any class assignments.).

I wasn't doing that well in my engineering subjects at Georgia Tech. I was at heart a rebel. I took "liberty" in downtown Atlanta when it was not authorized. I would get into trouble a number of times for offenses like coming in after hours taking "liberty", or wearing the wrong uniform. I was arraigned before a Captain's Mast" the equivalent of a Navy trial several times for my offenses.

My dice hustling continued at Tech every monthly payday. It all came to a horrible halt one day when I was called up to stand trial for my final Captain's Mast at Tech. This final offense would get me kicked out of officer training for "unofficerlike conduct" and gambling.

The circumstance for my final dismissal came about in an indirect way. A trainee who was caught stealing money from another officer candidate's locker said in his trial "I just wanted money to get back into Yablonsky's crap game." The dumb thieving sailor somehow assumed every one, including the officers knew about "Yablonsky's crap Game."

At my final trial the Captain in charge said to me, "Seaman Yablonsky do you run a regular dice game on payday"? The answer of course was "Yes." The next question from one of the officers on the panel was "We hear that you always win. Is this true?" I knew they had me cold and my dumb smartaleck answer was. "You know Captain--you win some and lose some."

This remark was no help to my case. Captain Babcock discharged me from the Tech V-12 program for "unofficer like conduct" and I was to be held in custody and sent to bootcamp as a Seaman 2nd class (the lowest Navy rank) in Bainbridge, Maryland.

While awaiting my being dispatched to bootcamp the Captain ordered me "to be locked up in the brig." Another officer pointed out to the Captain that they did not have a brig at the Naval Unit at Georgia Tech University. They created a "prison" for me in a part of the gym. I was locked up for 30 days in the new prison that was exclusively created for me.

(The experience made a good story for me in my acceptance speech around 60 years later when I was in Atlanta to receive the 2003 Honorary Lifetime Achievement Award for my work as a sociologist and criminologist by the American Sociological Association. I opened my acceptance speech by saying "A few miles from here at the Georgia University of Technology I was busted and did 30 days in the Navy Jail." I then went on to gracefully accept the honor from the ASA.)

The main consequence of my being kicked out of Officer training was that I was sent to the boot camp in Bainbridge, Maryland and

CONFESSIONS OF A CRIMINOLOGIST

I was busted down to being a Seaman 2nd Class. At 19, I was not particularly crushed by the demotion. At least, I was not dishonorably discharged and could continue my career in the Navy.

At Bainbridge my stupid dice hustling continued. I won a great deal of money, for that time. In boot camp we were restricted to the base for the 90 days of training. It was like shooting fish in a barrel.

After bootcamp I was assigned to a school in Yellowater Florida to become an aerial gunner and aviation radioman. I did achieve became an Aviation Radio Man with the rank of seaman 1st Class. I did some flying in a PBY plane as a radio man off the east coast.

I was never in any serious combat situation. I don't believe I was a coward; however, I knew of the deaths of many sailors in invasions invasion boats and on carriers in the Pacific. From 18 to 21 I served my country however, I was not anxious to lose my life in combat.

I had some bizarre experiences when I was stationed in Florida. I recall one time winding up on liberty in a weird town--Fernandina Florida. I got drunk at this bar on a lonely highway, and hit it off with a waitress who lived in the back of the bar. Somehow she and her sailor husband, who was also on liberty that weekend, invited me to stay at their cabin in back of the bar. She was a gorgeous blonde and we had eyes for each other.

We were all together Friday and Saturday with some other girl with whom I had sex. However, I was very attracted to the blonde, and she gave me all sorts of cues that the feelings were mutual. On Sunday, without words I felt the same as her and knew I could hookup with her if her husband wasn't around.

On Sunday, after we all went to the beach, and showered she sent her husband out for pizza. When he left and we were alone we both quickly undressed and jumped into her bed. All of a sudden her husband was back at the door--saying he left his money. He clearly saw us and was furious. He was fuming at catching us en-flagrante. I muttered some excuses, put on my clothes, and walked out the door. I then ran down the highway as fast as I could for about 5 miles, and escaped unharmed.

After gunnery school and my time in Florida, I was assigned to CASU-21 in Norfolk Virginia. CASU stands for Carrier Aircraft Service Unit. This involved making sure the radios on Navy planes on carriers worked properly. Some flyers, who were officers, would be rude to us lowly sailors.

I vividly recall discussing this situation with a Petty Officer Radioman with hash mark stripes for his years of Navy service telling me one day about why pilots had to be very nice to sailors who serviced their planes. He said something like, "Of course flying officers need to treat you nicely. You can easily kill a son of a bitch who gives you a hard time by fucking up his plane."

When some officers at the Norfolk base learned I had some officer training (despite the negative outcome of my being kicked out), for reasons that elude me, in I was assigned as a Master At Arms to a CASU barracks. The facility housed many sailors--some returning from combat. In retrospect, it was a terrible thing to do; however the returning servicemen received large paycheck for their time in combat at sea. Many of them were hungry for any kind of gambling action. I became a kind of Sgt. Bilko.

The officers at the CASU appointed me to the position of "M.A." or Master At Arms of the barracks. My duties involved management of the barracks. My duties did not involved running a crap game. However, I would announce on the loudspeaker for the some hundred sailors in my barracks, "Crap game now going on in the MA shack." There was always around 10-15 sailors with lots of money who were trying to get lucky with no chance since the MA me was cutting the game and using crooked dice when needed.

One absurd day, one of my hired assistants who played lookout for my gambling venture came running up to me during a game in action and whispered to me: "there is an inspection team with 3 officers coming to inspect your barracks!" Thinking quickly I ran down the stairs from the 2nd floor where the crap game I had just been running was ongoing. I met the officers coming into the building.

The crap game was still running on the second floor. When the officers and I arrived in view of the game I immediately took charge and said, "What the hell is going on here? I am taking names and all of you guys will be disciplined." The dice players were flabbergasted- but said nothing. I then told the Officers, "I will certainly take care of this situation." When they left, I resumed the game with most of the sailors who wanted to continue the action.

Aside from my various duties as an Aviation Radioman I did enjoy a number of lovely sex partners during my Navy days. I had several girlfriends in Atlanta, Jacksonville, and Norfolk when I was stationed there as an Aviation Radio Man--serving CASU-21. I always enjoyed the opening line of Mobster Johnny Stepanatos book about his romance with Lana Turner. "If I don't have sex every day I get a headache." (Of course, for whatever reasons Lana's daughter Cheryl stabbed him to death.)

My sex life began well before I was in the Navy at around the age of 13 with a hooker--who lived near our neighborhood. I recall it cost me $5. Somewhat turned off by her appearance I masturbated. Unlike sexuality in todays high schools very few girls at South Side High, in the vernacular-- "Put-out." In my early teen year satisfaction was mainly obtained by "feeling up" a girl and masturbation. However, I did enjoy a varied and full sex life in the Navy.

At Tech I had a wonderful girlfriend Rosanne Justus. she was around 20, lived in Atlanta and to me was a knockout. We enjoyed each other sexually and other wise in hotels all over Atlanta. She was best friend with a gorgeous redhead who was Eddie Prokop's girl friend.

Hotel rooms in Atlanta were hard to come by-so several of us sailors would get one room in a hotel. We never changed partners but screwed a lot in groups in various darkened hotel rooms. Looking back, I guess we were having some kind of orgy that preceded more current sexual scenes.

In retrospect, I wonder why I didn't push to get into combat--especially with my hatred of the Nazis. I am a Jew and always hated what they had done in Europe and to my people. My main explanation of why I fiddled--shot dice and was unofficer like was that on some level, I didn't want to die like so many of my Navy buddies did in combat.

During my Navy years I heard many firsthand lurid stories from sailors and wounded sailors returning from Guadacanal and other Pacific Islands about the hell of war. Walking around with dead bodies strewn on the ground. In the harsh combat of Wake Island,

Okinawa, the Philippines and other Pacific Islands around a third of invading American forces died or were maimed.. Although I was only around 20, I was very aware of the impact of war, and I didn't believe it was wrong for me to be glad I didn't die on some remote Island in the Pacific.

My older brother Morris was a Navy gunnery officer in the Pacific. And my brother Joe was in the army and served in Korea. Both of my brothers were "straight arrows" and did their job. Our family was patriotic and served the country that we loved.

If I had received orders to go into combat I certainly would have followed through. In recent years I often think of how President Harry Truman saved my life by bombing Hiroshima and Nagasaki. If this had not happened we were poised to invade the recalcitrant Japan homeland. It was expected that Japan would fight back any invasion, and the war would have caused millions of deaths on both sides. I would certainly have been part of the invasion, and in all likelihood would not be sitting here writing in 2010 about my Navy days or any days beyond my 21st birthday.

As it turned out my days in the Navy were a positive learning experience. I was proud to serve for my country, and I was honorably discharged. Back then, a veteran had many choices for civilian life, and most important for me was the GI bill that paid for most of my education.

Graduating Rutgers University and a Trip to California (1946 to 1949)

I was in the Navy from 1943 to 1946. When I was released from the Navy with an Honorable Discharge in June 1946 I was quite through with the dice hustling era in my life, and for whatever reasons was highly motivated to go to college. The GI bill that paid for college was a big incentive for a laundryman's son. In those days, I recall, I was a member of the 52 20 Club for veterans. This meant for one year after I was discharged I received $20 a month. Big dough in those days.

For a time after I was discharged from the Navy I lived at home with my Mom and Dad and for the first time in my life studied hard. I became a full-time student at Rutgers-Newark on the GI Bill. I had course credits from Bama and Georgia Tech. I graduated Rutgers

University in 1948 with a B.S. At this time I believed education was survival for me.

I found out Davie was still involved with hustling after his time in a federal prison, and I had nothing to do with the old gang. I did meet Davie at some party and we talked briefly. I asked him what he was doing. He said, "same old thing-I run crap games."

I did go down to the bowling alley a few times. The old pals I did meet could not fathom how and more important why I became a college student. They were mostly still bullshiting bums--doing nothing constructive. They all had high hopes for a big score that never came.

Around this time I fell deeply in love with Ruthie Kirshbaum. Ruthie lived 3 doors down from us on Johnson Avenue. She was, next to my later adored wife Donna, the most beautiful woman I ever knew. Dark haired and gorgeous her body was perfection. From Ruthie I learned about sexual ecstasy.

I first met Ruthie, when she wore a badge as a hall monitor "cop" at Miller Street elementary school. We hung out with each other and I was nuts about her--but I was only 12. At high school she was unattainable. She was 13-14 and went out with older guys. She viewed me as a nice kid and friend. I always wanted her, and dreamed day and night about her. Once on a July 4th we watched fireworks in a Newark park and we did what was called in those days--we "smooched."

In the last months of my Navy time I had turned 21. I came home on leave one time to find out that Ruthie's husband a fighter pilot had been killed in Germany. Out of the blue I called her.

That began the greatest love and sex period of my life. We were together day and night when I was on leave. I also recall her coming to a hotel in Baltimore where we made love for 2 days--never leaving the room. When I was discharged from the Navy, went home, and was going to Rutgers we were inseparable.

We especially enjoyed the music of that time around 1947. A block along 52nd Street in NYC was the mecca of jazz and blues music. There were clubs, like the Onyx Club, The 3 Deuces, and others with the best jazz musicians and blues singer of that period or ever playing nightly. An extra treat at the clubs was that on some nights jazz musicians who were playing in the theaters on Broadway would drop in to the clubs after midnight and jam with the musicians who were headlined at the clubs.

Ruthie and I especially dug Billie Holiday who was a regular at The 3 Deuces. In retrospect it was weird that Billie this great singer and star would often sing to Ruthie, me, and around 10 other customers--the only people in the joint. We knew she was great; however, others took her brilliant talent for granted. After a few drinks, and listening to Billie--Ruthie and I would get in a horse drawn carriage, that drove through Central Park and have great sex in the back of the carriage. OY Vey--it was sensational and very memorable.

Ruthies father was some kind of hustler with mob connections. My mother did not like her family. I wanted to marry Ruthie. It was a tragic and no-win situation for Ruthie and me since at that time fresh out of the Navy I had no job or future career. We even went to NY and got a marriage license. Finally my mother's opinion for good or bad prevailed, and we finally broke up. I never forgot Ruthie--my first love.

I bean my course work at Rutgers with an enthusiasm for education I never had in the past. I became an A student--with the exception of a course in statistics that I had to take twice. Although I often came close with a D, statistics was the only course I ever failed in my life. And I recall the feeling I had on taking the course the second time--it was "do or die." I managed with daily studying to get a C. The Professor Reynolds was a brilliant man, and a great teacher. Failing his course the first time and then breaking through and passing was a great learning experience,

California seemed to be calling, and I wanted to get away from Newark. After graduation from Rutgers, I, for whatever reasons decided to seek fame, fortune, and a job in Los Angeles. In post-war America cars were hard to come by. The same car on the West coast went for much more money than on the East Coast. Consequently there were car dealer ads in the NY Times that offered a free trip to the Coast if you delivered a car from NY to LA.

Two Newark buddies of mine and me took the trip in one of those station wagons that had wood on the side. The cross-country trip was fantastic in seeing the grandeur of America. Like the song we traveled on Route 66. I recall one stop for a day in Ohio to visit a Navy buddy of mine. In addition to our reminiscing about our Navy days he took us to a great local whorehouse. We had a terrific time. It was fairly inexpensive, and I had sex with almost every hooker in the place. Also seeing the Grand Canyon for the first time was exciting.

When we arrived in LA we drove the car around what was then (and for me still is) a city of wonders. Hollywood, Beverly Hills, Venice Beach, and Malibu struck me like great art. It certainly was not Newark. My pals went on with their lives, and went back to New York.

I stayed in one room at the Chancellor Hotel on Cherokee one block up from Hollywood Boulevard. It was in the center of Hollywood action up from a great restaurant Musso and Frank. Mitch and I still eat there. The unbelievable rate for my room at the Chancellor at that time was $6 per week, and you could get a steak at Musso for around a buck.

The hotel residents consisted mainly of young people aspiring for movie jobs and life in the fast lane. I recall one gorgeous gal I took to dinner and bed who surprised me. I asked her what she wanted to become--an actress or a model. Her surprising response was "No, I'm a waitress."

The first job I had on this first trip to Hollywood and LA was at the then Dolores Drive-In on Sunset Boulevard. I was a carhop for about a year. Stars came in--because in their cars they were somewhat incognito. I saw and waited on Frank Sinatra, Mickey Rooney, and Gary Cooper among others. It was an exciting experience for a kid from Newark to meet these great stars even though, all I did, was serve them food.

The notorious LA mobster Mickey Cohen had a "haberdashery store" across the Street from the Dolores Drive-In. He carried out his criminal activities from that "office" which everyone knew was a front for his criminal activities. He came in to the drive-in often, and would look out at 4 or 5 parked cars, people he knew and pay their bills with a good tip for me.

One evening at dusk I saw LA gangland in action. I saw a man who had obviously been shot stumbling out of Mickey's shop. He just about made it to his car and then fell down and died. Police came swarming around the Drive-In asking questions. However, no one including me, "saw anything." I was still partially operating on Newark time and wasn't a "snitch."

After a time I decided to utilize my college degree. My second job in LA was based on my Rutgers degree. I became a "junior executive" for the American Locker Company. They owned and serviced lockers in bus and train stations around the U.S. This office covered the west coast.

It was 1948 and I found out in my first interview that the American Locker Company had a policy of not hiring Jews. I only acquired the job by changing my name to Lew Blaine. (Blaine was the name my older brother Morris used to get a job with an engineering company. He too had trouble getting a company job as a Jew.)

My job with the American Locker Company involved checking out the company's lockers in bus and train stations throughout the Southwest. I traveled all over this area for the company on trains and buses (no airplanes). I serviced various cities including San Francisco, Reno, Las Vegas, Salinas, Merced, and Salt Lake City. The job was fun. I met a lot of women in hotels and bars--and had a rich sex life.

I recall when I was working in Salt Lake City I met and shacked up with a beautiful Mormon girl. We spent a wonderful night together in my hotel room. I found out she was a Mormon because the next day, at breakfast, her religious principles kicked in and she refused to drink coffee.

While on the locker job I moved up in the world from the Chancellor Hotel to the El Cortez Hotel in downtown LA. My past came back to haunt me. Two criminals I knew from Newark came to town and looked me up. Red and Dewey were burglars, conmen, and use to be strongarm men for companies that wanted to break-up unions--a lucrative job in the late 1930s.

I would have dinner with them, and they would recount their ongoing hustles. One time I fell off the wagon and joined Red in hustling a crap game involving cab drivers at a taxi garage in LA.

Red was caught cheating with our crooked dice. I of course did not know him as I escaped the garage. Red was beaten up pretty badly by the angry cab drivers.

Red was a pure sociopath. One day during his sojourn on the west coast he called me at my American Locker Co. office and said threateningly, "Lew, I'm broke. A few of the guys are chipping in to fly me back to Newark. I got you down for a hundred." I told him "No." My "good friend" clearly threatened me, "Look Lew, I know where you live--you better fuckin give me the hundred!" I did.

I recall my last meeting up with Red Kugel. It's a ridiculous story. Around 1965, when I had become a married respectable professor in LA, out of the blue, I received a phone call from Red . I hadn't talked to him in around 20 years. I remember a part of the phone conversation. Red said, "Lew are you rich" I responded, "I'm doing OK." He persisted, "tell me are you really rich." To this day I don't know what he was driving at.

He was passing through LA, and invited me and my wife to lunch with him and his then girlfriend. Out of curiosity I had lunch with him and his busty blonde hooker type girlfriend at the Huntley Hotel in Santa Monica.

The memorable story he told me at dinner figuring I understood and would agree with him on the matter was as follows: Red said, "She's married." pointing at his girl friend who partly lived with him in Las Vegas. "I was all set to kill her fucking husband. I had the gun and everything planned. And this cunt talked me out of it. She's a fucking nut case." Red absurd reasoning reminded me of my early life stupidity--of hanging out with guys like Red.

The meeting reminded me of how close I came to becoming a criminal in my teen years. Red, back, in Newark, had been a close hustler buddy of mine. I also realized how guys like Red from Newark up close had taught me more than any formal Ph.D psychology education the mental dynamics of a criminal sociopath. This street education served me well in my later years as a sociologist and criminologist. Most of my later professor colleagues never learned directly and the hard way about the mental dynamics of sociopathic criminals like Red.

I worked at the American Locker Co, in LA for about a year, and I was then transferred to the Philadelphia office. In Philly. I traveled all over the State of Pennsylvania servicing lockers. Pennsylvania was not sunny California. I began thinking about changing jobs and the course of my life.

One memorable incident, at that time, helped trigger my decision to leave the American Locker Company. I traveled with my then supervisor on a business field trip. This trip had me thinking more about the question, "What am I doing on this stupid job."

The supervisor was a totally obnoxious individual. When we were driving home after a 3 day business trip and we were nearing Philly. As we were driving he pointed out a Housing development. He then said with what appeared to me to be a snarl of anti-semitism, "That's Jewkellberry Hill." Lew Blaine restrained his violent emotions and said nothing. However, the incident completed my motivation to get out of that job.

Chapter 2

Getting a Ph.D. at New York University: (1949 to 1960)-

It was in Philly, during a break in my travel around Pennsylvania that I discovered my life-calling in sociology, psychology and criminology. My Rutgers degree was in Business Administration, and at the University of Alabama and Georgia Tech I studied engineering. I always loved psychology and had read a great deal on the subject--but somehow thought it was too easy, interesting and fun. I somehow thought education had to be difficult.

My discovery of the profession, I have come to love commenced on the same Library step that Stallone's Rocky Balboa raised his hands to that melodious song of victory in the later movie-ROCKY.

I lived at the YMCA in Philly, and when not on the road, spent most of my time at the Philly Library reading. I discovered and read my first book on sociology, It was an introductory text on sociology by Cuber. After reading that book I knew that sociology and criminology was the profession for me. Along with my boredom on the American Locker job, and my disdain for my creepy fellow workers I quit my job.

Within weeks, as if by magic, I found myself in NYC standing in front of a New York University building Greenwich Village looking at a sign that read "Graduate Department of Sociology."

I called and acquired an interview with the Department Chairman Wellman Warner. I wanted to be accepted for graduate work in sociology. Dr. Warner was talking to me as if it was a possibility for me to matriculate for an MA and a Ph.D in sociology. My inner thoughts and self image was that I was a dumb kid from Newark and not deserving of entering this fantastic school. Professor Warner accepted me and I will always be indebted to him for his "bad judgment." From that point on I became a totally "hungry for knowledge" student of graduate sociology and criminology. (And at 85 the passion and the beat goes on.}

In 1952 I received my M.A. and in 1958 my Ph.D. in Sociology with a concentration in psychology and criminology from New York University. It was the most fascinating and exciting period of my life!

During this decade of acquiring my degrees,along with my studies at NYU, I was extremely busy and loved my new found wonderful and exciting career. I consider myself a lucky man to have found the profession I love, and pursued my various work with great enthusiasm. Again, I couldn't help thinking that my earlier life, that included my associations with many sociopathic "friends", turned out to be a treasure trove of life experiences that facilitated my university higher education.

I became involved in various research projects at NYU in the Sociology Department; and I had various jobs in my field. During this period of around 10 years (1949 to 1960) I worked in a Newark Jail for Juveniles; taught a number of part-time courses in sociology and criminology at City College of New York Columbia, and Harvard and later fulltime at the University of Massachusetts.

Also during this decade of my life I was very fortunate to became a student and friend of psychiatrist Dr. J.L. Moreno the founder of psychodrama and group psychotherapy. I also became the Director of a Crime Prevention Program for Moningside Heights, Inc. on the upper westside of Manhattan working with gangs. All of these experiences nurtured my wonderful life career as a sociologist, criminologist, and therapist.

Essex County Jail for Juveniles

From 1951 to 1953 I worked as a counselor at the so-called Essex County Parental School, a juvenile jail in my hometown Newark, New Jersey. Many of the locked-up delinquent kids knew me from the neighborhood and I knew some of them from working on my dad's laundry truck.

They trusted me as a homeboy who made good, and I learned a great deal about crime and delinquency from my in-depth interviews with the young prisoners. I could easily interact with them while in custody, learn about their case histories, and go into the Courthouse with them and observe the penalties the Juvenile Court Judges would hand down. I sometimes would run preparatory role-playing sessions with the kids before they would go into court for sentencing. This would help calm them down and better prepare for what they would say in court to the judge for their defense. (The courthouse was in the same building as the jail lockup.)

This valuable custodial work experience went on for over a 2 year period at the same time I was taking my coursework in sociology, delinquency, and criminology in the evenings at NYU. For one Summer, my brother Joe who had also graduated Rutgers worked with me--and then went on to be accepted as an FBI agent. He worked for the FBI for over 30 years.

I had a variety of interesting experiences on the job at the juvie jail. In those days I was still athletic enough to play touch football in the yard with the inmates. I always played back in the safety position because the fence in back of me, although barbwired could be surmounted--even though the escapee would be injured.

One day a detainee who was in custody for murdering his best friend with an axe went over the fence. I chased him for around 15 blocks to learn his getaway had been planned. A car pulled up with 3 of his buddies at a corner. I chased him around the car yelling to the guys inside "You're not in trouble now but if you open the car door you will be arrested." Finally, after a crowd formed, someone called the police and the escapee was arrested. He had lied about his age, and was actually 18. He was quickly transported to the adult Newark jail.

My athletic background was helpful to me on the job. In another incident a totally recalcitrant youth who would not comply with anything was thrown in the so-called "quiet-room." This room was padded, and only used as a last resort when we couldn't control a kid. In the process of physically containing him in the room for about an hour we had the following memorable conversation: He said, "I fucking hate you" many times. I responded with what I thought was a clever line, "How can you hate me. You don't even know me? He said, "Look you prick, I hate my mother, father, brothers and everyone else. Why shouldn't I hate you"? He had a point.

The reason I couldn't just lock him in the room was because my superior Mr. Wallace sat in hall near the room and told me to keep restraining his efforts to leave the room. This was because the 16 year old had threatened to kill himself with a kitchen knife we thought he had acquired. Consequently, we kept the door open. I stood in front of the door to block his escape. He would charge at me and I kept throwing him back into the room.

We called the police to have him transferred to the adult jail because we couldn't control him. During this time, waiting for the police I stood at the open door of the room. He would say, "I'm getting the fuck out of here." And then charge at me. Around 5 times I had to throw him back into the room.

Finally, 2 burly policemen arrived. I tried to explain to the cops that the kid was a problem. One cop said, "Bullshit, we'll take care of him he's just a kid." Very shortly they were down on the ground with the kid--trying to handcuff him. The redfaced cop looked up at me as I stood over the battle and said "help me." I just walked away as revenge for his early self-assurance. They finally handcuffed him and took him away to the City Jail.

While working at the juvie jail I experienced one of the most interesting "sex affairs" I ever had with a co-employee. A lady Marion was the jails social worker, and she was gorgeous. I was around 25 and she was 50. I thought old ladies of 50 didn't have sex. I knew she was interested in the "hunk" who cavorted around with the inmates--playing football and physically restraining kids who were violent.

One day Marion and I were talking. It was around Thanksgiving time and I mentioned that I loved cooked pumpkin with sugar and cinnamon. She quickly took this as an opening and invited me over to her house for pumpkin. I can't resist saying, "the pumpkin was delicious and so was Marion.

Around 20 years later when I was in Europe I learned that Marion had married a famous British sculptor. They lived in London, and it was fun to see her again. At 70 she had the same gleam in her eye that she had at 50; however, her husband was cordial but never left us alone.

I had many interesting learning experiences with the kids at the jail. One I recall involved a 14 year old who was very violent and diagnosed as a sociopath. In some way I considered him as an experiment to test my therapeutic abilities. I spent many hours during my shift talking with this kid in an effort to change him. At first he would hardly talk to me. Then he revealed his terrible family background and abuse that was the foundation for his violent behavior.

I did make some progress with him. However, I recall seeing his face when he after he had been sentenced to the Annandale Reformatory. He was walking out in handcuffs, and he looked back at me with a smile as if to say "Nice try Lew but I"m going on to bigger and better crimes in spite of your efforts." I later found out he did become a career criminal and wound up in the New Jersey State Prison.

During the period **of** getting my degrees at NYU I was extremely busy. I worked days at the Jail, nights in classes for my Ph.D. and I also worked on several Sociology Department funded research projects. Around this time, I also began teaching sociology and criminology at City College of New York. CCNY was at 139th Street on the upper West Side in Harlem. It was a bad hood.

I recall how I integrated my various experiences. One day a student came late to my class at the City University on Amsterdam ave. He was bleeding from the head. He had just been mugged at a subway station. Before he went to the hospital we had a heated class discussion about the dynamics of criminal mugging.

I had proved to my self that my acquiring a Bachelor of Science Degree at Rutgers was no fluke. I had a brain and fancied myself an intellectual. This was something I never thought much about during my dice and Navy days. In my egomania I had discovered in myself, what might sound pompous but a true--"intellectual perspicacity." Morty Waimon was right about me.

When I was first accepted at NYU, on some level, I thought I had fooled Professor Warner and the other NYU faculty into admitting me into the Ph.D. program. I soon found I was an OK almost straight A grad student. The main reason was that I was truly interested, excited and in love with sociology, criminology, and psychology!

At NYU my intellectual juices became manifest. My days were filled with discussions and action in criminology, and sociology. I worked a full 8 hour day at the juvenile jail and became a supervisor.

My prior education to my studies at NYU was a kind of a rote joke. I did what I was suppose to at Miller Street elementary school. I was literally fighting my way through classes at Miller. At South Side High I was a C student more interested in friends like Davie, dice, and becoming a star baseball player. But my education was of no special interest to me back then. Now my education was exciting because my courses dovetailed with my real experiences at the Jail, teaching, and in my community research for an interesting NYU sociology department project.

Nyu Sociology Department Research

In addition to my classes and other activities, during my NYU graduate school days I worked on a Project as a "Research-Assistant" in a Sociology Department project. The project was directed by Dr. Ashley Weeks, a great professor. It was the so-called Highfields Project.

The project was named after the estate in Highfield N.J. that was donated to the state by the world famous aviator Charles Lindbergh. He had lived there before his child was ruthlessly kidnapped and killed by Bruno Hauptman. The Lindbergh murder was one of the most notorious criminal events and trials of the 20th century.

The Highfield Project was directed by Lloyd McCorkle the former Warden of the N.J. state prison. McCorkle lived on the estate premises, that became a small reformatory, with around 15 delinquents sentence for the treatment. These youths were picked to receive special treatment including a form of group therapy McCorkle had previously developed when he was in the Army.

My job on the Project was to interview family, friends and associates of the youths who were incarcerated at Highfield. My research involved around 100 interviews. I wrote Reports on how the kids were perceived by their family and others before and after their 3 months of high-powered therapy at Highfields.

I discovered I was really good at this job---and that I could write. I contributed to the determination of whether or not the project, in fact, helped to change the delinquent subjects. The youths in the research and therapy project did better on release than the control group at the Anandale Reformatory.

Through my work on the project, I learned a great deal about the factors that cause delinquency and the attitudes of people toward them when they are released to the community. For example, I remember a one-liner from a Police Captain in a small Jersey Town who told me about one of my delinquent subjects: "The only way that kid will be straightened out is when he is shot and killed and put in a Pine Coffin."

I worked 15 hour days. Eight hours at the Juvie Jail, evenings at my NYU classes, doing my interviews on weekends and at a later point in my grad work teaching.

My few leisure hours, some evenings after classes, were spent at the San Remo Bar and Grill and coffee shops in Greenwich Village. My grad student friends and I would drink and discuss our Profs, sociology, crime. and our ambitions.

I did have some interesting girl friends and sex partners around that time. I recall a weird and notable evening at the Remo when another guy and I got into a hassle over some girl we were both hitting on. My adversary was a tough, handsome twenty year old. We almost fought but resolved our differences. I later found out he was an aspiring actor--who became the movie star known as Steve McQueen.

While a grad student at NYU I had an interesting brush with becoming a communist. It was fashionable in those days for sociology students to be very liberal. There was a big fat guy named Arnie in my "Race Relations" class at NYU. In class he spouted off and railed against the theories of the adjunct professor Melvin Tumin who also taught at Princeton. He was a rebel with a cause--communism.

I became very friendly with Arnie, mainly because he took me to left-wing parties where I often met girls for one-night-stands after the party. In those days "left-wing" women and communists believed in "free-love." To be succinct going to these parties enabled me to get laid--a lot.

Arnie, I soon discovered was a real member of the communist party, and he wanted to seriously recruit me. I have never forgotten sitting with him in a car, after a party, around 3AM. He became very serious with me. He said: "Lew you agree with our principles. I would like to offer your name for membership, and you can fully join the Party."

I was frightened by his proposal and had no intention of joining any party--especially the Communist Party. All my involvement in the "party" revolved around my interest in "sexual freedom" and getting laid. I mumbled something about "thinking his proposition over." I began to avoid him in our "race-relations" class, and never saw him again after the class and the attempted recruitment experience.

My Mom Fannie and My Nyu Ph.D.

While working on my Ph.D. at NYU and at the Juvenile Jail, for a time, I commuting from my parents house in Newark to New York. Later on I acquired and moved into several low rent apartments on the lower Eastside of New York. This was long before the area became a fashionable and high cost address. My apartments had little heat with the bathtub in the kitchen. I had one for $25 a month near a homeless shelter in downtown NYC.

During my Greenwich Village days and nights I hungout at the White Horse Bar. I never met him, but around that time the famous poet Dylan Thomas was also a habitué of the bar. I never did get to talk with him. He was a serious drinker. Life was fun and exciting.

In 1957 when I had completed the coursework for my doctorate I was required to take 4 full days of written tests; and then a later oral exam to acquire my Ph.D. It was logical to move back for a time to my parents home in Newark to study for my written tests.

It was warm, cozy and my beloved Yiddish Momma Fannie kept the food coming. She was somewhat puzzled by her son Lewie the former problem student who was now obsessed with his education. There were times she told me, "You're working too hard you should go out and have some fun."

All I knew was that my new circumstances not only changed my life from the dice and card nutcase I had been--but education gave me wonderful new and fascinating life experiences. At my parents house, for several months I did nothing but study to prepare for my final Ph.D. exams.

Strangely, and it was unusual, my Mom hardly bothered me as a I plugged away at stacks of books, listened to tapes, read notes and charts about different aspects of sociology, criminology and psychology that were in my room. The charts, I had on the walls of my room covered many aspects of my social science coursework.

One day, I clearly remember was the day my Mom came into my sanctuary and was dusting the room. She did not interfere with my studying however, I heard her muse to herself, "Oy with all the work he's doing, he could have become a real Doctor."

Mentally I fell down and began chewing the carpet.

My wonderful mother had no concept of what a Ph.D. was. She did know what "real Jewish doctors and lawyers" were.

Later on when I published various books and went on various TV shows like Ophra, Donahue, Geraldo, Mike Douglas and other talkshows to plug my book she began to appreciate what I had become and kvelled appropriately about my accomplishments.

She would still nudge me on occasion. For example, after I appeared on the Mike Douglas Show talking about several of my books she called me and said, "You were good. But how come you're not on Johnny Carson?"

With the important help of my my mother's encouragement for me to be a success, and the influence of my fathers steady workaholic approach to life I completed my Master Degree at NYU in 1952 and my Ph.D. in 1958.

Dr. J.L. Moreno and Psychodrama: An Important Part of My Life at Nyu and Beyond

During my deacade of study at NYU In addition to my family, another significant person became a part of my life. Dr. J.L. Moreno was an Adjunct Professor of Sociology in the Department. He helped me complete an important part of my Ph.D. education and became a mentor and friend.

I met him when I became enrolled in his basic course on "Psychodrama and Sociometry at NYU. Moreno, who I later always called J.L was the inventor of psychodrama and group psychotherapy.

He was a charismatic and brilliant psychiatrist. Through Moreno's teachings and friendship I learned the theory and method of psychodrama. The subject significantly influenced my personal and professional life.

Stemming from my course and meeting him was fortunate to work with him at his Beacon, New York Sanatarium for emotionally disturbed patients, and at his Psychodrama Institute at 101 Park Avenue in New York city.

Moreno and his wife Zerka became my second family. Zerka was no understudy to Moreno. She was a brilliant woman who enormously influenced the development of psychodrama. I admired her work and lectures on many occasions. She, and later the Moreno's son Jonathan became my friends. Jonathan is a gifted social psychologist, who has written several books, and is a Professor at the University of Pennsylvania. Zerka recently published her important book on psychodrama.

Psychodrama is a method I have utilized in all of my professional career and life. Consequently in this chapter I will write about Moreno's historic development of psychodrama and group psychotherapy, and my association and friendship with Moreno that began in 1949 when I was a graduate student at NYU, and continued to Moreno's death in 1974.

Professor Warner had hired Moreno in 1949 as an Adjunct Professor to teach a course at NYU in psychodrama. After taking Moreno's course, I was hired as his graduate assistant. I quickly became one of the practitioners of psychodrama at Moreno's Institute of Psychodrama and Group Psychotherapy on 101 Park Avenue in NYC.

To put it mildly becoming a psychodramatist, through Moreno's friendship and training, changed my life by enabling me to become involved and learn directly about the psychological dynamics of the lives of thousands of people. Throughout my life I have directed thousands of psychodramas. It is a method that provides insights into the protagonists life and social issues that produce insights found in no other methodology.

My mentor and intellectual father Moreno became one of the best friends I ever had. After sufficient learning how to direct psychodramas I worked at Moreno's New York Psychodrama

Institute directing sessions on Friday nights, and at his Beacon, NY Hospital which in those days was called a Sanatarium.

My father Harry was a wonderful man and father. Moreno became my intellectual father as a mentor, professor and friend over a span of 25 years. He not only taught me psychodrama but in the intense years of our relationship I had the good fortune to assist him in the revision of his basic book "Who Shall Survive."

The book illuminates psychodrama, however it also provides insights into the continuing conflict between people and their social and physical machines, and how psychodrama can treat this problem. Moreno was a visionary in predicting our contemporary and controversial problem of global warming. (His influence facilitated one of my later books "Robopaths: People as Machines, Bobbs-Merrill, 1972)

Working with Moreno on his book facilitated my ability to write. I also learned how to effectively direct psychodrama, group psychotherapy and become a therapist.

Because of Moreno's influence, later on in my life, beginning in the late 1960s into the 1980s I founded and directed the California Institute of Psychodrama. The Institute was based in a building that formerly was a school or synagogue on Fairfax Avenue in LA. I ran the Institute at the same time I was Professor of Sociology at CSUN. In the process I trained many students and performed therapy with several thousand people who came to my psychodrama sessions and classes.

To understand psychodrama, a requirement, is some understanding of Moreno's history. Psychodrama was a core part of the life history of Moreno. He was born in 1889, became a medical doctor after attending the University of Vienna, and came to the United States in 1924 to practice psychiatry in New York. (Incidentally, as stated I was born in 1924.)

Moreno, in his early years, planted the roots of psychodrama in the rich philosophical and psychological soil of Vienna around the turn of the century. This was around the same time Freud was developing his theories of pscyhoanalyis. During that period, Moreno's goal was to develop a "theatrical cathedral" for the release of the natural human spontaneity and creativity that he believed existed naturally in everyone.

As early as 1910, Moreno was preoccupied with the development of this concept of a humanistic theater of life. In that period, Moreno's "Theatre of Spontaneity" was a place where people in groups had the opportunity to act out their deepest dreams, frustrations, aspirations, moods of aggression, and love-in brief, the range of their human emotions. Moreno's early dreams have substantially materialized into the various psychodramatic form that are practiced today around the world.

In the early period of Moreno's Theatre of Spontaneity in Vienna, he had a limited concern with fostering "therapy" or "mental health." These positive consequences were noted by Moreno only as side effects of the psychodramatic process. His central "idee fixe" as he called it and motivation was spiritual: to free the spontaneously creative self in a theater of life that provided an unlimited opportunity for freedom of expression.

In the many wonderful and educational meetings I had with Moreno he told me about psychodrama's origins in a spontaneous theater group that he formed when he was a young man in his early twenties. There were many illustrious actors in Moreno's Vienna repertory group, including Elizabeth Bergner and Peter Lorre.

The beginnings of psychodrama as a therapeutic method remain fascinating to me. As Moreno told it to me, an actor in his group told Moreno one day about the problems he was having with his wife. In her theatrical performances and in the actors group she was kind and compassionate. However, her husband told Moreno that in their personal life she had a fiery temper that was destroying their relationship. Moreno, with the theatrical group present, put their marriage on stage in a session that was an embryonic psychodrama.

He had the couple improvise key scenes in their life as they happened in their own home. Members of the repertory group helped the couple portray their conflict by joining in various roles. Moreno concluded from the group's intense response that the couple's enactment of their real conflict was more electrifying and productive to the group than any theatrical scene they had ever performed before an audience.

Based on this experience and others Moreno began to more formally experiment with group enactment's. This led to the development of people reversing roles with each other, doubling, and other methods that have become part of the psychodramatic approach since its origins.

Moreno, of course, inspired my contribution to the development of psychodrama. The methodology he taught me is encompassed in my later book PSYCHODRAMA (Basic Books Harper/Collins, 1976.)

Following are the central aspects of the psychodrama methodology derived from Moreno, and according to Yablonsky, derived from my book. In my discussion of these methods I have included summaries of various sessions I have directed that illuminate these methods.

BASIC PSYCHODRAMA METHODS FOR EXPLORING LIFE Psychodrama methods are techniques employed to bring about a maximum of creativity, productivity, and personal growth for the people in a session. Psychodrama tic production techniques have evolved from the experiences of many years. Techniques are applied in the course of the production at the moment when they seem indicated and are usually not planned in advance. It is essential that the director be sensitive to the group production so that his use of these techniques sparks the production, lends support, and produces insight for the protagonist and other members of the group. Timing in the application of techniques is of crucial importance. Following are some of the basic techniques used in psychodrama and the rationale for their use.

ROLE REVERSAL Role reversal is the procedure in which A becomes B and B becomes A. For example, in a mother-daughter session, a protagonist who is the daughter may reverse roles with her "mother" (an auxiliary ego) when indicated in the situation. Roles are reversed for a number of reasons.

1. A protagonist, when playing the role of the relevant other (e.g., the daughter becomes her mother), 'may begin to feel and understand the other person's position and reactions in the situation. This may enhance the protagonist's "telic" sensitivity (two-way empathy). The daughter learns more about how it is to be a mother to herself as daughter.

2. Role reversal may be used to help the protagonist see himself as if in a mirror. The daughter playing the role of mother will see herself through her mother's perception. This instrument has the effect of producing insights for better understanding by the protagonist as she sees herself through the eyes of a significant other. For example, a daughter who reversed roles with her mother better understood her mother's motivation. She commented, "From the vantage point of my mother, I saw for the first time that she feels badly about her age and her looks and is putting me down-because she has begun to compete with me."
3. Role reversal is often effective in augmenting the spontaneity of the protagonist by shifting him out of defenses. In a typical case a protagonist engaged in the same "fight" with a spouse for years. Each adversary had played the same role in a tired script with no solution. The role reversal will often shake up and change the form that the conflict takes and produce new insights. Part of the learning is that the role reversal helps the protagonist to understand others in the situation through being them.
4. Role reversal is often used simply to help an auxiliary ego to better understand how a role is perceived by a protagonist. The auxiliary, although not having been on the actual scene of a situation, attempts to fulfill the requirements as projected by the subject. For example, in a mother-daughter interchange in which the real daughter is the only one present and there is an auxiliary ego playing the mother, if the daughter plays her mother she cues the auxiliary ego into how the role should be played. In general, the role reversal has the effect of taking a person out of himself so that she can get a look at himself from the "others' " point of view.

For example, I recall having a woman in a session reverse roles with her husband, a man to whom she had been married for fifteen years. In the role of her husband, I asked her to soliloquize his thoughts. After five or ten awkward minutes, it became apparent that she had a limited idea of what her husband thought or even said. In the session she manifested a pattern of nonstop talking at her husband. She seldom had any empathy or awareness of his position or emotions. This was precisely the problem with their marriage.

Empathy, or taking the role of another, is at the center of all human interaction and communication. The process of physically and emotionally doing this in a psychodramatic role-reversal enhances more accurate self-other perceptions and facilitates more meaningful communication.

THE DOUBLE In the double experience, the double attempts to actually become the protagonist. If the protagonist is A, the double is A. The double sits close to the protagonist and physically and emotionally tries to assume the protagonist's posture. The double adds a significant dimension to the protagonist's performance.

The protagonist is instructed by the director to respond to his double. For example, a protagonist may be expressing love, and the double senses that the love is real but is also covering up hate. When the double expresses a feeling of hatred for the subject of the session, at the same time the protagonist is expressing love, the protagonist has several alternative responses to his double: (1) if, the double is right, he can simply agree with the double's statement;...(2) the protagonist can disagree with the double and vehemently state his love with such great anger that the group suspects the validity of his protest ("Methinks he doth protest too much"); (3) the protagonist can ignore the double's comment; or (4) the protagonist can disagree in a manner that reveals this disagreement is an authentic feeling.

A double is used to enlarge a situation in order to help the protagonist's performance. When the protagonist is honestly and effectively presenting his point of view, a double is not necessary and may in some case negatively interfere with the protagonist's action. When used properly, a double gives a protagonist much needed support.

For example, in a session with a young man who felt oppressed by his father, the double helped the son gain the courage to talk back to his overwhelming father for the first time.

In one session I directed related to a marital problem, my wife Donna while doubling for the wife, out of the blue exclaimed, "My problem is that I've never had an orgasm with my husband." The protagonist wheeled around to her double, broke into tears, and with amazement said, "How did you know?"

The double thus propelled the protagonist into a more honest portraiture and broke past the false image the subject was trying to project. She began to reveal that beneath her sexual braggadocio, she was a frightened little girl who was really afraid of men and sex.

Often, a double in a role will have an insight that is not apparent to anyone in the group, including the director, and this will open up the protagonist to his or her deeper, more honest feelings. In addition to helping to break through to deeper feelings, the double tends to become the protagonist's friend and helpmate in difficult situations, often providing the necessary support that enables a protagonist to master complex and difficult situations in psychodrama and that facilitates successful behavior later on in his life. I have always thought it would be helpful to have an invisible double at your side when you were confronting a tough situation.

THE SOLILOQUY The soliloquy is a technique that parallels, as one example, Hamlet's soliloquy in Shakespeare's play. It involves the subject reciting his thoughts out loud in the middle of r scene. It is a useful technique for expressing the hidden thoughts and action tendencies of the protagonist to himself and the group.

The protagonist's soliloquy is often parallel to his overt actions. For example, a person overtly expressing love and affection may be feeling love and affection. At other times, however, a person expressing love overtly may be feeling subjective hatred, and this will be expressed in the soliloquy. It is important to have the protagonist express both emotions, and the soliloquy aids in this process. The soliloquy in most respects parallels the process of "free association" in psychoanalysis, with one significant difference: in psychodrama the soliloquy is performed in the contextual fiber of an actual situation. Also in psychodrama, as differentiated from psychoanalysis, the process is utilized not only for analytic purposes but also to facilitate the dramatic action of the session--with the help of a double.

I recall a session with a man who was having sexual problems with his wife. In brief, the husband and wife had become bored with each other's sexual performance. In the simulated psychodrama that he enacted with a female auxiliary ego who played his wife, the man was having intercourse with his wife. Overtly, as he was having intercourse, he made extravagant declarations of ardor and love.

His double began to soliloquize what he felt were the man's covert thoughts. The protagonist soon joined his double in a synchronized soliloquy. "I wish she could come-I want to get it over with. I'm hungry. I wonder what's in the refrigerator. Did we finish that whole roast beef dinner? Is there any left over?, etc." The wife, who was present in the group, remarked, "I know when he's just stabbing me or making love. And if he's off on a trip, I just viciously hold onto him, resist my orgasm, and let him suffer as long as I can."

After several sessions, the husband and wife obtained a deeper understanding of each other's motives and feelings and became more honest and attuned to each other's mood's. This resulted in greater feelings of affection and their relationship improved, including their sex life.

The unstated soliloquy is a part of every human interaction in everyday life. Many times a person's inner thoughts relate closely to the overt spoken words, but too often-particularly in crisis or problem relationships-there is a disparity between what people say out loud and what they think underneath. The soliloquy in psychodrama is a useful tool for bringing these hidden thoughts to the surface. Soliloquized thoughts are vital to understanding conflict and resolving human problems.

FUTURE-PROJECTION TECHNIQUE This method involves having the subject act out, with the support of auxiliary egos and a group, a meaningful situation in which the subject expects to act in the future. The effectiveness of this procedure depends on the significance and importance of the situation for the protagonist and the extent to which the auxiliary egos are able to actually project the protagonist into the future. It is also important that the protagonist really is going to participate in the situation in the future at a given time. An intense, effective warm-up is the essence of the application of this method. As many particulars and specifics or the situation as possible should be emphasized in the warm-up.

This method, like other psychodramatic approaches, rests on the solid foundation that an individual's thought level can be acted out with the help of a group. The "future" is often most detailed on the thought level.

For example, I recall a session using this technique in which a protagonist exclaimed, "He didn't say that" about a situation that he had never lived out. This indicated that he was psychodramatically presenting a situation that was not new to him. It had been "acted out" many times on his thought level. However, psychodramatically the action, with its many added dimensions, was more vivid and productive for the subject through the aid of the method and the group.

The future-projection technique can prepare a protagonist to perform more effectively in a future situation. I recall another psychodramatic session in which the protagonist, a young married man, revealed how he separated from his wife. They had experienced a violent argument three months prior over some complex differences, and had been separated for that period of time. He was, at the time of the session, scheduled to meet with her and his son the following week to discuss either a reconciliation or a divorce.

He was understandably quite anxious about the future event because he was unsure of his feelings and had to make a decision about their relationship. tn the session, he warmed up to the situation by first describing the plane as it came in from where he stood at the airport. Then, with the help of a double, he soliloquized what he was thinking while waiting. He later told me how important the psychodrama had been in the reality of reuniting with his wife, and that at this time their marriage was wonderful.

These are only some of the methods used in psychodrama. Reviewing them, as I have here reminds me of the thousands of sessions I have participated in and directed. The methods have helped me better understand so-called "normal people" but has also been useful in understanding psychotic people and criminals. These insights from psychodrama have been incorporated into my various books.

Moreno introduced psychodrama into the United States when he came to the the U.S. in 1924. He ran sessions at, of all places Carnegie Hall. Psychodrama, early on was looked with great skepticism by other professionals. In recent years, many former dissenters have jumped onto the group therapy and psychodrama bandwagon.

When I began my work in psychodrama In the 1950s psychotherapy was mainly an individually oriented approach. Here was Moreno talking of the importance of the group in producing personality modification and social change. He had already introduced sociometry, psychodrama, and sociodrama, and these ideas were beginning to stir up the minds and guts of all stripes of psychiatrists and psychologists.

Many of them, especially psychoanalysts felt threatened because much of their professional lives centered around the training and practice of an individually oriented psychotherapy. Those who saw the validity of Moreno's social science system and the necessity of having to change their direction so dramatically were often consciously and unconsciously disturbed by this prospect.

I had a blatant experience related to this issue. One Fall evening in 1952, Moreno invited me to accompany him to a lecture on psychodrama and the group method that he was invited to give to a group of New York psychotherapists. The session took place before a group of around one hundred psychoanalysts and psychiatrist of various schools.

To this day, I have not forgotten the hatred and chastisement that Moreno encountered that afternoon in response to his belief in the primacy of group concepts in all types of therapy. He was openly denounced, ridiculed, and even laughed at by members of the group during a brutal question and comment period at the end of his presentation.

Some of the illustrious therapists loudly whispered as we left, "What a nut!" "He [Moreno] is a paranoid schiz." Moreno maintained his cool. As we traveled downtown, I said, "How can you take these insults?" He smiled, "First, Lew, I know I'm right. Secondly, I may be crazy like they say, but I'm making a lot of other people, like you, crazy with me; and each year, as more and more people join our movement, I will be considered less crazy."

Many individually oriented therapists and classical psychoanalysts currently practice. However, many of these therapists have come to recognize the validity and significance of the group process and psychodrama and the use of these concepts and methods as adjuncts to their practice.

It has been a gratifying aspect of my life to witness Moreno's impact, and, in a modest way, through my own involvement, to help change the orientation of so many people, in the brief span of some twenty-five years, to an acceptance of the validity of the group and psychodramatic viewpoint of therapy where people openly discussed their family issues and mutual problems. These days "reality shows" criminal mysteries and Dr. Phil types dominate TV.

Back in the 1950s I directed many sessions at the Moreno Institute. One, among hundreds stands out. This was a session where I invited around 20 NY Police Officer who were taking a course in criminology from me in a program organized by CCNY and the NYPD police Academy. The session involved a cop who had just shot a suspect in Central Park who was running away from him.

He shot the man, a murder suspect, and then caught up with him. He was, as he had in the real situation, standing over an inert body. In the psychodrama I directed the officer was standing over the body of the suspect he had just shot.

He kept looking around. I asked the officer to soliloquize, a standard psychodramatic method. His Hamletlike soliloquy was, "No ones around, should I or shouldn't I finish this punk off." The police in the group argued both sides of the "issue."

In addition to the psychodramas I ran at the Moreno Institute in the early 1950s at that time--I also was hired through the Institute to do psychodrama at the Rikers Island Prison and the Riverside Hospital for drug addicts. Both facilities were populated by tough, violent mainly Puerto Rican and Black prisoners.

At Rikers I use to open my session with the comment: "I make more money out of crime than all of you put together. This was a shocker that got the groups attention. I would then go around the room--point to a guy and say, "What was your last score--$30 from an old lady" etc. We would then mix it up and I would get one of the men to have a session about his plight in life that the others could identify with. The sessions in addition to aiding the prisoners see some light in their life's was very valuable for m in learning how to do therapy and especially psychodrama.

Later on I directed psychodrama therapy sessions for patients and training sessions for the staff at a number of psychiatric hospitals.

The hospitals I worked at included Camarillo State Hospital, Van Nuys Hospital, Westwood Hospital (where I had Marlon Brando's daughter in one of my groups Metropolitan State Hospital, and Atascadero State Hospital for the so-called criminally insane.

I recall many of the sessions but several stand out because of their bizarre nature. One I directed at Atascadero involved a 20 year old patient who had committed a murder. He was gay, and in one scene in the session he was outing himself to his parents. He became very distraught and ran out of the room. The Chief psychiatrist was in the group. He ran out after the young man. I sent my wife who helped me with sessions to go get them. She found the chief doctor and the patient crying and commiserating about how difficult it was to be outed to parents. Back then "outing" was a much more emotional happening then today.

I recall one strange session involving a man in my group at Metropolitan State Hospital who had some kind of palsey where his body kept uncontrollably writhing. Of course he volunteered for what I knew would be a tough session. The session involved his applying for a job. As he presented himself to his potential employer his body would not stop moving. During the session I asked him to role-reverse and play the role of the employer. His body and speech were normal in the role of the employer! When he went back to himself the body movements began again. Later on thinking back on the session--I thought maybe I am making this up--it's not believable that he would stop the body motion.

At a gathering around 15 years later, a nurse who had been at the session at Metro approached me. I checked my memory. And she said, "yes that's the way the psychodrama happened."

To me that session was a very weird experience: however psychodrama introduced me to many strange and unbelievable aspects of life and relationships. I have always been grateful to Moreno for teaching me the method--an important part of my life. My overall life like most people's experience has involved 3 different areas: reality, dreams, mass media, and the addition one for me psychodrama.

MORENO'S DEATH: THE DEPARTURE OF MY MENTOR AND FRIEND The last time I saw Moreno was shortly before he died in 1974. I had traveled to his home and training center in Beacon, New York, to say goodbye. His death was a fitting departure for the man who invented psychodrama; for Moreno, in a sense, directed his own rites.

At that time, the American Society of Group Psychotherapy and Psychodrama, which Moreno had founded, was meeting in New York City. I had become President of the ASGP&P. Over 2,000 professionals from all over the globe had traveled to attend the conference, and many of them had come explicitly to say goodbye to Moreno. At first, he consented to see only a few close friends. But finally he told his beloved colleague and wife, Zerka, "Let's not be negative. Say yes to everyone who wants to come to Beacon to see me."

When my dear friend Moreno's wife and partner in psychodrama Zerka called me a few weeks before the Meetings to tell me that her husband might soon die. Moreno had been able to talk to me briefly on the phone. We joked a bit, I entreated him to stick around until I could come to Beacon to say goodbye in person. He said matter-of-factly, "Lew, I'm ready to die, but I will wait a few weeks to see you when you come to the meetings in April."

When I arrived in April, life at Beacon was going on as usual. The peaceful New England atmosphere at Moreno's wooded country estate belied the activity in the buildings that served as a powerhouse for psychodrama training and publications. Some twenty students, who lived in a dormitory residence, were training as psychodrama directors. In another building, an office of secretaries worked on correspondence and publications of Beacon House, Inc., which had published almost all of Moreno's writings, as well as various journals of group psychotherapy and psychodrama founded by him.

When I walked into Moreno's bedroom, he had a smile of welcome on his face. We embraced and kissed, and I could feel a sob rising in my chest. "This is no time for sadness, Lew," Moreno whispered in my ear. "I've lived a full life. I've done my job. It's time for me to go on to something else."

Although he was prone, he was still my director and I was the protagonist. According to his plan-one that I more than welcomed-I spent the afternoon in the dining room, right off his bedroom, reading his as yet unpublished autobiography.

Most of the episodes in Moreno's autobiography were not new to me. I was familiar with my friend's life history, since, over the years, he had told me many stories-over dinner or on the train when we traveled between New York and his Beacon sanatorium. We had long talks during summer vacation, when I sometimes stayed at the Beacon Center directing workshops and sometimes assisting him with revisions of his articles and books. Still, reading this panorama of events and insights was an overwhelming experience for me, especially when the hero of the odyssey was ten steps away. I read for five hours, stopping only to laugh with him over some humorous episode or probe a point with him.

As I approached the end of reading the autobiography, I was fascinated by a vignette related to Freud that we both especially enjoyed. In Moreno's creative megalomania, he wrote how he had died and, of course, had gone to heaven. As part of Moreno's heavenly reward, along with other philosophers, he was allowed to participate in an eternal dialogue with some of the brilliant minds of history. On this particular day, Moreno was the subject of an intellectual trial that involved a grand rap session between Spinoza, Einstein, Hegel, Christ, Freud, and several other luminaries. The subject, of course, was the relative merits of psychodrama versus psychoanalysis.

After several hours of brilliant debate, the group had reached a stalemate. One "celestial" member, noting that Freud had been strangely silent in defending his position on psychoanalysis, asked him what he thought of Moreno's psychodrama. A silence fell on the group, as they anticipated a powerful and eloquent diatribe that would elevate the merits of psychoanalysis far above those of psychodrama. Finally, Freud acknowledged stoically, "If I had lived longer, I too would have most certainly become a psychodramatist like Moreno."

Moreno and I laughed over his vision of "the trial" and paradise as I sat by his bedside for the last time. It was early evening, find I was preparing for my ride back to

New York City with some students then in residence at Beacon. Even now, I see that final farewell as less of a definite separation and more of an evolutionary step in my relationship with Moreno. We embraced, and I left the room feeling that he was still with me.

Based on my work with Moreno, my Psychodrama Institute experiences, my psychodramas with a variety of people, including criminals in directing several thousand psychodramas I was very grateful to the man who helped me live a more fulfilling life. Many years later, I published my book PSYCHODRAMA: RESOLVING EMOTIONAL PROBLEMS THROUGH ROLE-PLAYING (Basic Books Harper/Collins, 1976)

I was delighted when I received many positive reviews on my psychodrama book. The one I liked best was published in the Los Angeles Times (May 20, 1976) by the senior critic of the Times Robert Kirsch. He really understood the meaning of psychodrama to me personally and professionally and my relationship with Moreno when he published the following review entitled "All The Worlds a Psychodrama"

"Psychodrama is a theater of life in which human scenarios can be raised to a higher level of consciousness and I comprehension for the purpose of enlarging humanistic · communication and compassion," Dr. Yablonsky writes near the end of this unusual book-part memoir. part tribute to Dr. J.L. Moreno, founder of psychodrama and with whom the author I worked as a student and later as colleague, and part textbook,'

Another way of describing this bundle of approaches is to cast it in psychodrama terms: Dr. Yablonsky is living out are a repertoire of roles in writing this book-pupil, disciple, teacher, therapist, innovator and many more. His debt to the late Dr, Moreno is eloquently acknowledged: I When I realize the freedom that psychodrama has given me and so many others. the ability to play many roles in life with a wide range of emotions and a broader intellectual perspective, I feel a closeness, not a separation, from the wonderful man who founded the movement."

In these pages. Dr, Yablonsky can go from the vivid evocation of a psychodrama scene to a somber and abstract lecture "An awareness of the group's structure is fundamental knowledge to a psyched. paychodramatist in directing a session," From succinct and personal experiences setting up a special course in psyI chodrama in 1968 to defuse the explosive student situation at Cal State Northridge [in the 1960s] where Yablonsky teaches to such rolling generalizations as: "In brief, psychodrama In its foundations and evolution has been eclectic in attempting to use any or all concepts that help people to reduce psychic ! pain, obtain greater insight. enlarge their perspectives on lie and enhance their life performances."

This variation of, styles and approaches is in contrast !with the greater unity of Dr. Yablonsky's other books including "The Violent Gang," "Sienna: The Tunnel Back," and Robopaths: People as Machines. That doesn't detract from the strength of the book. It is 'probably the most effective discussion of psychodrama and its techniques yet written...

It is obvious that psychodrarna has been a crucial instrument in Yablonsky's life and work. His recent PBS psychodrama series, "The Family Game," has aroused new interest and attention. He is by tcmperamcnt a searcher and innovator rather than

an evangelist. Psychodrama suits him because it occupies a special place among the new approaches. It is an instrumentality rather than a separate therapy.

He writes: "In the practice of classic psychodrama, most practitioners creatively utilize some facet of almost every other relevant therapeutic system," But perhaps more to the point. The reverse is just as true. In his chapter on 'psychodrama and other therapies', it becomes apparent that psychodramatic techniques havoc been a grabbag for most other approaches. And some of these, notably Gestalt Tlierapy and Transactional Analysis, have acknowledged this debt.

What makes the book useful to both professional and lay readers is its informed discussion of practical and theoretical aspects of the approach. Although psychodrama is seen as a normal and natural process in life, a basic theme of the book is that psychodrama is a happening or a productive experience rather than exclusively a !therapy. Psychodrama sessions, includes scenes. places. role reversal and auxiliary egos can benefit from techniques and experiences described here.

Thus to see notions of "surplus reality," i.e., a situation blown out of proportion, magnified to allow the subject and group a closer *look; to study "philosophical aspects" which go beyond problem resolution to an examination of broader implications; and to be introduced to methods of promoting empathy or rehearsals for situations or playing out roles for which we are imperfect in life.*

This is made explicit later on. Though directed sessions with trained psychodramatists may be "most potent," the techniques can be applied in informal, irnpromptu, spontaneous situations with equally interesting results. I think this relaxed and low-key view of psychodrama, so much at odds with the messianic claims of therapeutic cults and sects, is refreshing. I don't suggest there is anything half-hearted about Yablonsky. but he is too complex and too inquiring a man to be bound to the discipline of movements.

It is obvious that he is open to improvising and that psychodrama offered him latitude for adventure and playing many roles. ("Everyone is an actor ... All people perform In everyday life.") Psychodrama has enabled him to work inside violent gangs and to explore such movements aa Sienna before they became academically respectable.

His own career is the best bona, fides, Through Dr. Moreno, pioneer of psychodrama and group psychotherapy, Yablonsky learned a vocabulary of concepts and went on to make what is his most important contribution to contemporary theory in social psychology, the syndrome of robopathology. The flat, stereotyped. frozen-in-a-role behavior which marks the age of conformity and alienation, Psychodrama, he believes. can overcome this lack of, compassion and courage. Moreno's "first psychodramatlc law: Put yourself into the place of a victim of injustice and share his hurt. Reverse roles with him."

The potential of theater as a metaphor for life is far from exhausted by this book. But it is an important contribution, first as an introduction to Moreno, that neglected seer, then as a journey through Yablonsky's career. and finally as a challenge to others prepared to explore other challenges of drama and life."

When they have another trial on Moreno and psychodrama In heaven--I plan to be present to thank Moreno again for all he did for me and my life.

Chapter 3

Directing a Crime Prevention Program in New York and the Violent Gang (1953-58)

My matriculation at NYU for my Ph.D, along with psychodrama and the various other Projects I worked on in the early 1950s prepared me for acquiring my most important job in 1953 at the age of 30. I was hired as Director of a Crime Prevention Program on the upper West Side.

I made it a condition of my employment that the organization would send me to Chicago for a week to meet with community leaders who were directing crime and gang prevention programs in the Windy City. I did go, and met people in the so-called "Chicago School of Criminology" at the University of Chicago. This included some of the sociologists whose articles and books I had read like Clifford Shaw, Sol Alinsky, and Professor's Jim Short and Henry McKay. All of these well-known men had been doing community organization and gang prevention work in Chicago. .

My work over a 5 year period (1953 to 1958) as Director of a Crime Prevention Program for the Morningside Heights, Inc. community improvement agency was a significant aspect of my personal and professional life. I organized many programs that were funded and supported by fourteen major educational, religious and medical institutions. My work on this project became an important part of my qualifications for my work in my later years as a professor of criminology, legal-consultant and expert witness in the criminal justice system.

The institutions I worked for, as Director of the Crime Prevention Program in New York City, included: Columbia University, Barnard College, Teachers College, St. Lukes Hospital, Julliard, and Riverside Church.

As Director of the program, I coordinated various community crime prevention projects on the upper West Side of Manhattan. I was hired because the institutions were experiencing a variety of criminal activities including burglaries, violent offenses, gang vandalism and violence. I was a consultant on appropriate security prevention methods for their security systems and dealt with over a hundred security guards who were protecting these 14 prominent institutions.

My role involved periodic lectures and advising the security personnel of these institutions on effective crime prevention and security measures for preventing crime in the buildings and surrounding areas. My work included analyzing crime scenes and situations to determine the legal and financial responsibility of the institutions in various criminal, civil cases and law suits brought against the institutions.

This job also involved me in providing consultations to these institutions on how to relate appropriately to the New York City Police Department, and the judicial processes in various court cases.

David Rockefeller was Chairman of the Board of Directors of MH Inc. Rockefeller, of course, had the power to set up a meeting with then Police Commissioner of New York City Francis Adams to further our programs cooperation with the NYPD. As a young criminologist, I was in awe of being with the Police Commissioner and David Rockefeller. Despite my feelings, I was calm in presenting some of my reasonable ideas for dealing with the crime and gang problems in our area--and how we could cooperate with the NYPD.

Because of the Commissioner's clout our program received the full cooperation of the 24th Police Precinct in the administration our Crime Prevention Program.

I apparently appeared to the various captains and police executives I met with to be a "young guy to get such a big job." Some quizzed me on how I got this important job. I recall, a police captain who made the following remark at one of our meetings. "This guy Yablonsky must have a Rabbi with a very long beard." I soon learned that a "Rabbi" in the PD was not a religious leader, he was someone in power who had the clout to reach down and promote you. I was accepted by the NYPD after a time, and they were very cooperative and helpful with my crime prevention program.

In particular the Commissioner had sent out word to Captain Herb Kohler, in charge of the 24th precinct in our area to cooperate with me and our program. The "24th" serviced our area from 110 St south to 145th St north into Harlem. And from the Hudson River east to Morningside Park east.

The thing I remember most about Koehler who was a nice guy, was the differential between our political viewpoints. One day, in Koehler's office we watched the Senator Mccarthy v the U.S. Army Hearings that were at that time dominant on TV. As Koehler and I watched the hearing, he kept cheering on McCarthy to get "those fuckin Reds." I of course was vehemently against McCarthy's 1st amendment violations but kept my mouth shut.

Koehler and I were cooperative on my work on the crime problem. In addition to my role as Director of Crime Prevention which involved educating and utilizing the security guards, for crime prevention I instituted projects for working directly with the many gangs in the area.

The gang project was helpful in my acquiring my Ph.D. since my doctoral dissertation was on gangs. After considerable editing my dissertation later on led to my first published book THE VIOLENT GANG (Macmillan, 1962.)

It was the first time in my life that the media began to take an interest in my work and it was exhilarating. Among other press reports I was interviewed on radio and TV related to my work with gangs. One project I set up for gang prevention that received a lot notice by the press was a baseball league for gang kids in the neighborhood. Many of them often vandalized buildings in the area including one of our sponsors Columbia University. With some of the citizens from the community the help of a Youth Police Officer I organized a baseball league and was able to involve many gang kids in our program to divert them from delinquent behavior.

Lewis Yablonsky Ph.D

The baseball project was reported in the NEW YORK HERALD TRIBUNE 7/19/54

Civic Group SetsUpTeen Ball Teams

A group of teen-age boys converged on Columbia University's Baker Field in upper Manhattan shortly before noon yesterday. They carried such familiar equipment as baseball bats and gloves, and soon the air of Th.& Columbia baseball diamond was filled with dust and baseball talk. But there was more to this activity than baseball- and the boys knew it. They were participating in a program directed by Morningside Heights, Inc., in cooperation with the New York City Police Department and aimed at combating juvenile delinquency in a large mid-Manhattan area.

Morningside Heights, Inc. .. was formed in 1947 to improve the community socially and physically and is comprised of thirteen educational, religious and health institutions of the upper West Side area. These include Columbia University, which consented to the use of Baker Field for the program. This is the first time the Columbia Field has been put at the disposal of an outside group. Aim: Law-Abiding Citizens "Actually, baseball is our least concern," Lewis Yablonsky, public safety director of Morningside Heights. Inc., who directs the program, said yesterday. "What we are trying to do is to conduct a program of character building, teach the yoUngsters to respect property. and, in general, develop law-abiding citizens."

To this end. Mr. Yablonsky has organized six baseball teams of youngsters from the Morningside Heights area. He was aided bY· Police Commissioner Francis W. H. Adams who assigned Capt. Herbert W. Koehler, commanding officer of the 24th Precinct, to work with the Morningside Heights group. Both Mr. Yablonsky and Captain Koehler agreed that the youths' baseball activities, which began only three weeks ago, have alreadY favorably changed the attitude of many of the area's youths toward the police. and society as a whole.

Need for Activities Cited "You must remember that these youngsters, thirteen through eighteen years old, really live in a state of vacuum as far as group life is concerned," Mr. Yablonsky, who is presently completing the requirements for a doctorate in sociology at

New York University, explained. "Their playing baseball with other neighborhood groups and the realization that the community is trying to help them gives them something to do and has already changed the attitude of many people in our neighborhood," he said. Mr. Yablonsky said members of the Police Department often drop in to watch the games and in this way help to dispel some of the basic hostility toward law enforcement officers often found among teen-age groups. One of the participating groups has changed its name significantly-from "The Terrors" to "The Saints," Mr. Yablonsky said.

I worked on the MH Inc. Project for five years meeting with gangsters, police, and community workers. During this period I began, as indicated, teaching criminology and sociology at Columbia University and The City College of New York.

One evening I invited 2 gang kids I was working with to attend my criminology class at Columbia. I gave my lecture and we had coffee after to discuss their impressions. One Puerto Rican gang kid from the barrio put it in a nutshell. He said over coffee, after my lecture, "Is this the bullshit that goes on in classes at Columbia? Shit man, I can do that."

During this time, I enacted 5 roles: completing my graduate work at NYU, college professor, gang researcher, gang treatment worker and I continued my psychodrama work with Moreno at his Institute. I also directed psychodrama at two facilities Rikers Island Prison and the Riverside Hospital for Drug Addicts.

The MHINC project involved me day and night with gangster interviews in my office and on the streets.

I was working in a fascinating crime community The neighborhood surrounding Columbia University and the Morningside Heights Project was comprised of almost a half-million people from every possible ethnic, racial, religious and economic background.

The residents of the neighborhood seemed to understand that we were not simply poking around in their lives for the purpose of some impersonal research project. Rather, they knew our agency was attempting to do something concrete to prevent and control the crime and delinquency of the area through various social, recreational and family projects that we developed. Because they had an awareness of our efforts, many citizens in the area cooperated with our project and we were able to form positive community groups.

In particular, Sam and Fred, two individuals, who lived in the community joined with me in my gang control work. San had family who had been in the holocaust, and Fred had a small record. They were both invaluable in helping to form the sports leagues we ran for the purpose of controlling violent gang behavior.

The overall crime picture included robbery, burglary, homicide, drug addiction and assault. Many, if not most, of these crimes were perpetrated by young gangsters. The lack of substantial knowledge about gangs and gang violence made it difficult to develop effective methods of gang control. It was this lack of understanding and the absence of an adequate prevention program that spurred my intensive gang research at that time. There were a few city programs to deal with gang violence, however, they were not in my opinion very successful.

If I was going to develop an effective program for the prevention and control of gang violence, it was necessary for me to understand the gang's structure, organization and motivation for violence. My Newark background was helpful in understanding who told me B.S. and who knew some things that were helpful in my work.

I, along with a small staff, gathered data through interviews, questionnaires, gang discussions, agency conferences, and talks with the NYPD Youth Gang Squad, police commanders, and other officials.

These interactions were not designed for research purposes alone; they were part of the project's day-to-day activity to control the problems.

I developed a useful database of gang information through our work. I formed and became the Chairman of several community committees devoted to crime and gang prevention. One day, someone asked me how I became the Director of these various committees. My answer was---"I start them."

A Report I wrote on my work was featured in an Editorial in the New York Time on 8/24/54 under the heading "Morningside Heights Rebuilds."

"Visitors to this city are often heard to comment that New York is devoid of such qualities as community spirit or civic pride. It is understandable how visitors might gain this impression of our city, for manifestations of community spirit are not so easy to discern here as they are in smaller municipalities. But a convincing demonstration that this spirit is alive and vital force in this city may be found in the series of projects now under way on Manhattan's Morningside Heights.

Under the coordination and guidance of Morningside Heights, Inc." an association formed in 1947 and representing thirteen educational, religious and service institutions, a multifaceted campaign is being waged to solve pressing community problems. These problems are representative of those faced by other communities, they are even more urgent on Morningside Heights, because of the vast rebuilding program that eventually will provide new housing for 2,900 families.

The current report of Lewis Yablonsky upon completion of his first six months as Morningside's Director of PUblic Safety describes a number of the plans and activities designed to cope with these civic problems. A baseball league has been organized, for example, to occupy teen-age boys during the summer. Educational programs dealing with crime and narcotics have been launched to ease tension and to circulate legitimate information. Working cooperation between the police and the citizenry will be advanced and overall morale improved by a projected series of monthly neighborhood police merit awards. Conferences have been arranged between youthful' first offenders, parents, social workers and members of community groups. And additional citizens from the neighborhood are being recruited to. further the program of community action that is aimed at rebuilding Morningside Heights 'from the sociological as well as the physical standpoint. The rest of the city should follow with great interest the imaginative "pilot project" in community redevelopment that is being undertaken in Morningside Heights.

At that time I also taught a special criminology course to police officers in an arrangement between City College of New York and the NY Police Department. From this experience I learned a great deal about the police perspective on crime and gangs.

One incident stands out related to my communication and perspective on police. That evening I was lecturing on crime prevention, treatment, and punishment to the police class. Outside the second floor of the building some kids were throwing snowballs at the classroom window. I recall a police sergeant in uniform in the class told me "I'll take care of those kids." He went out and on his return around 15 minutes later he said, "I took care of it. I kicked this one kids ass." My lectures apparently did not fully get through to all my police students. Basically, they were in my classes to get points toward their promotions in the Department.

At the time, I lived in the hood at a low-rent apartment owned by Columbia University. The building I lived in was a block away from office which was housed in an apartment building owned by Columbia. At that time Dwight Eisenhower was President of Columbia University and was housed a few blocks down the street on Morningside Drive.

My relationship to the gang youths in the hood was similar to that of an anthropologist engaged in field work. During the time I directed the project since I lived and worked in the area I bonded in friendships with many gangsters. In the basement of my office building I had some barbells, and often worked out with the kids. The workouts led to many useful discussions about their lives and why they joined gangs.

It became natural for them to hang out in my office and, under certain circumstances, to visit my home. Phone calls and contacts at all hours from gang kids with special problems, youths in jail, citizen volunteers with emergency gang-war problems, or the police, became part of my daily routine.

In addition to some of the more formal methods of gathering information (e.g., questionnaires and focus groups), my daily exposure to the people and conditions I was trying to change significantly advanced elements of my overall research into gangs. I learned firsthand what the noted psychologist Dr. Kurt Lewin meant by his assertion that "attempting to produce change in people was an intrinsic element in learning about the overt and underlying dynamics of their behavior."

My relationship with the gang youths in the neighborhood was a two-way street. My concern with their motives and activities led to their concern with mine. Many long, "philosophical" afternoons and evenings were spent with gangsters in my office or on the corner discussing "life."

Much was learned on both sides about "the world." The essence and meaning of gang behavior and its violence were often more clearly revealed in these discussions than in the many formal research methods I used during this five-year period. Among the methods I used for both research and gang prevention was psychodrama. On one occasion of using psychodrama--I believe I prevented a murder.

Preventing a Murder?

When I worked with violent gangs in New York, I was often confronted with emergency problems that required immediate attention. The potential problem often involved potential violence. On several occasions I was able to head off potentially violent consequences with a preventive psychodrama.

In one case, a gang leader that I knew, accompanied by two friends, saw me as I was walking down the street in the hood. We exchanged greetings, and I saw that one of them, a violent gangster know as the "Ape" was angry about something. I asked him, "Whats up." He pulled out a switchblade knife, and announced that he was on his way to kill a member of another gang from a nearby neighborhood on the Upper West Side of Manhattan.

I knew the gangs that were feuding and the leadership patterns of each group. More than that, I had run psychodrama sessions with many gang members, including the youths in my presence. I invited the trio to my office to talk it over.

They agreed to go along with me, and on the way I of course considered the question: Why did he come with me instead of following through to stab his intended victim? I suspected the chances were good that he really did not want to commit this violence and wanted me to help him find a way out.

The "Ape" remained defiant and upset when we went to my office. Ape and the group agreed to have a psychodrama to explore the situation. The Apes opening remark was: "Man, I'm packin';

I got my blade [switchblade knife] right here. I'm going to cut the shit out of those mother-fuckin' Dragons [the rival gang]. I'm goin' up and get one of them now ... once and for all." Briefly, he had his knife and was going to stab any Dragon gang boy he met that day.

In the session I use of one of the other gang boys as an auxiliary ego in the role of the potential Dragon gang victim. A paper ruler replaced the knife (for obvious reasons), and the "killing" was acted-out in my office under controlled psychodramatic conditions.

The psychodrama had all of the elements of a real gang killing. The Ape (as protagonist) cursed, fumed, threatened, and shouted at the victim, who hurled threats and insults in return. Ape worked himself into a frenzy and then stabbed the auxiliary ego victim with the paper knife. The psychodramatic victim fell dead on the floor.

The Ape was then confronted with the consequences of his act in all of its dimensions, including the effect on his family. He began to regret what he had done and was particularly remorseful when (psychodramatically) an auxiliary ego playing the role of a court judge sentenced him "to death in the electric chair." In order to reinforce the meaning of the consequences of his potential act, I had him reverse roles and, from the position of the judge, he sentenced himself to death. This performance had a profound emotional impact on the Ape.

The psychodrama accomplished at least two things for this very potential killer: (1) He seemed less motivated to kill, since he had already completed the act psychodramatically by spewing his anger. (2) He was confronted with the consequences of the violent act he was going to commit. An important aspect of the session was that in general, most violence-prone individuals like the Ape are unable to think ahead in a situation to the outcome.

These factors possibly served as a deterrent to the actual commission of a murder. Of course, this boy required other sessions which sought to deal with his more basic personality problems. Moreover, considerably more work was attempted on the gang networks, so as to minimize their potential for violence. However, the emergency psychodrama, I did appear to deter the possibility of Ape committing a homicide, at least on that particular day.

Gang War Peace Meetings

An important source of data on gangs in my work was derived from about twenty "emergency" gang-war peace conferences I held in my Morningside office. Local gangsters trusted me and were free to use my offices and meeting rooms to discuss their problems. I was allowed to listen to and participate in discussions related to the real and imaginary threats of attack by other gangs.

Some of these peace conferences consisted of harangues about enemy gangs, and discussions about plans for attack, elaborate means of defense, and an accounting of real and imaginary members of their own and other gangs. Emotional heat was always high, and many deep paranoid feelings were freely expressed. These meeting were very important to me in the process of developing my theories on gangs in particular and crime in general.

The media picked up on the hysteria of the gang scene I was working on in New York at that time. This media hysteria and belief of everything they are told about gang organizations that I have found to be an exaggeration continues in 2010 with stories about the modern Crips, Bloods, and Mexican Mafia gangs. In 2010 the TV "History" and "National Geographic" channels report the hysteria, paranoia, and exaggerated stories of a few gangsters as fact about their gangs.

The following front-page story appeared in the New York World-Telegram and Sun on 30 November 1955. The article delineates how reporters, who don't understand the fact that a lot of gang behavior is simply talk and exaggeration. I knew directly that most of report in this article was not true.

Teen Gangs Band for Crime by Wm. Michelfelder

The Police Department has uncovered a brazen plan by a syndicate of seven of Manhattan's toughest juvenile gangs to organize all of the city's hoodlum mobs under the leadership of adult criminals, the World-Telegram and Sun learned today. The toughest and oldest of these gangs, the Dragons, has already absorbed 400 to 600 youngsters from the now defunct Crusaders, Sportsmen, Imperial Knights, Politicians, and truce divisions of the Scorpions, also called

Lewis Yablonsky Ph.D

the Villains. All of these gangs roam the upper West Side from 59th to 165th Sts.

'Charter Signing'

A 27-year-old hoodlum, known only to gang leaders as 'Bobby', recently conducted a syndicate' charter signing' in a Manhattan community center. [My Office] More than 60 gang leaders attended, including gang bosses from Brooklyn and Queens who were ready for a citywide syndicate. For several weeks, this newspaper learned, the Police Department's youth squad and Juvenile Aid Bureau have been watching the syndicate trend. The motive is still unclear to the police. But the best investigators in the department surmise that the youthful gangs are banding together to end fights among themselves and conserve their energy for a concentrated assault on law and order.

Independents Resist

Recent flareups in YMCA buildings and various youth centers in Manhattan and Brooklyn have been touched off by independent gangs resisting efforts by the syndicate to recruit them into the new organization, one police source says.

The clearest picture the police have at the moment is that the Dragon gang has assumed control of the syndicate. The Dragons started out on the East Side, according to police sources, and gained strength and prestige so quickly they moved across Manhattan and over into Brooklyn. One police informant said that adult criminals, some with The Dragons Invade 113 long records, have been seen hanging around Dragon meetings in some community centers.

60 Leaders Meet

On November 9, it was learned, the 'syndicate' met in the basement of a Manhattan recreational center. At least 60 gang leaders were present. Another 100 youngsters remained on the first floor waiting for instructions that would come from the conference.

Leaders of the Dragons held the floor, under the direction of the 27-year-old Bobby, who has a long police record. The syndicate agreed on the following:

That gang territories would remain about the same. But that tenitory leaders would not order 'rumbles' without consulting the syndicate. That all gangs in Manhattan, and later in other boroughs, would be broken up into 'divisions' of the Dragons. The rumours and Japs persisted, along with planning for the' once-and-for-all rumble' that would rock New York

The apparent inability of the leaders, I knew well to produce these exaggerated alliances were the main discussion topics at the meetings held practically every night for the next several weeks in my office At the sessions the boys continued to assess, evaluate, and hash over their frightening positions vis-a.-vis the Dragons. I cooperated fully with holding the meetings because they proved to be excellent opportunities for tape-recording data on gang organization and reaction to the invading hordes.

The article was only one example of how the press jumps on board with gang exaggerations. From my firsthand viewpoint it was par for the course for the kids in the 1950s to bluster and exaggerate their alliances and affiliations to any reporter who would listen.

In 2010 my analysis of gangs like the Crips, the Bloods, the Mexican-Mafiaand MS-13 is that like the Dragons of the 1950s the media tends to believe the hysterical commentary by gangsters of gang organization and power that is nonexistent.

From my viewpoint my near-group theory of gangs has held up to my analysis for 60 years. My near-group theory is bolstered by the 300+ gang cases I have worked on in the past decade. (My theory of the gang as a "near-group" will be expanded on in Chapter 10 based on my work as an expert witness.)

I had considerable trust from many of the gang youths, and because of this I was allowed to tape-record many of these hysterical gang war encounter sessions. One reason for the kids permitting tape recordings was their desire to hear themselves on a playback. Their egos seemed to be nourished by hearing a playback of their voices on the old-fashioned tape recorder I had in my office. Increasingly, they permitted me to influence their emergency meetings and, in some cases, I succeeded in intervening to control their post-meeting violent behavior.

Their recordings were a source of invaluable information, since the boys were very spontaneous and open in these discussions. In the gang-war discussions they appeared to be freer than when other, more formal, research devices were employed. (Many of these audio tapes, and my viewpoint on gangs, were later used in a CBS network broadcast on a violent gang murder in my area. I was a consultant on the program that was narrated by the legendary TV newscaster, Edward R. Murrow. The program became a kind of history of that crime period, and in 2008 I was interview for my perspective on gangs for a radio documentary.)

My gang research in New York City became the basis for my NYU doctoral dissertation, and my thesis was the foundation for my first book on gangs THE VIOLENT GANG (Macmillan, 1962) and the later IUniverse version (2009). I have continued my work since 1990, as a group therapist working with incarcerated gang members in the Amity Therapeutic Community projects in several prisons in California and Texas. This work produced additional data about gangs and how we can resocialize gang members into law-abiding productive citizens.

Based on my overall gang research I have developed the opinion that most gang violence can be attributed to a kind of individual insanity. The gang killer has a cloak of immunity for his senseless violence. A gang-murder is considered more rational to most people than the reality--which is that it is really an act of incredibly senseless violence. The violent act expresses the killers feelings of individualistic rage. In brief, a "gang murder" makes more sense to the average person than my viewpoint of the reality which is: that it is an individual act of insanity.

My opinion was reinforced by one of my psychodrama sessions, later on in a California prison where I utilized a specific role-playing method. In the session I place 2 gangsters in chairs facing each other--one was a self-identified Crip, and the other was a self-identified Blood. Both had murdered an opposing gang "member" and were doing 25 years to life.

In the role-playing situation I had each of them soliloquize why they wanted to kill the other one because he was a Crip or a Blood. I presented the reality that they were both Black men in their 20s who did not know each other. Why were they sworn enemies in the context of the stupidity of Crip/Blood gang hatred? They had no logical answer, and they realized this fact in the process of the session.

The answer is that most of these youths in their feelings of loneliness, hopelessness and alienation "fill-in" cohesive gang structure in order to feel some power and a sense of belonging when they in fact have neither in the stupidity of their gang behavior. They tend to believe that "If the gang is not strong and coherent than I am crazy to have all of these beliefs about my gang. Consequently I want to believe my gang is powerful since it give me a feeling of personal power--and is a reaction-formation to my feeling of being nuts and powerless" The police and prosecution want to believe all of the gang mythology since it makes their cases easier to prove and convict.

When I present the reality to gang groups I have worked with that being in a gang and following its violent dictates is really dumb--their first reaction is "Who the fuck are you to make fun of our life." As the session becomes more intense, a light often goes on in their heads, and they often begin to see the stupidity of gang life that leads to prison and too often death. My message on this issue often resonates with gangsters, and they change their behavior to more sensible endeavors like getting an education and leading a more sensible productive life.

I gathered considerable relevant data from gangsters about their gangs through various methodologies, including regular psychodrama and group therapy sessions in prison, individual interviews, written questionnaires and a special research method I have developed involving "prison gang focus groups."

To elaborate on this method, "prison gang focus groups" involve around two-hour sessions, in which 10 to 15 gangsters in the groups and I discussed why and how they became involved in their gang crimes. The fact that my subjects had already been sentenced, and were already in prison, led many of them who volunteered to be more open about their past gang life. Of course, many still hung tough to what in my opinion was their stupid gang affiliations. My research approach of using "prison gang focus groups" has been of special importance in the process of writing my later gang books: my 2nd book on gangs, GANGSTERS: 50 YEARS OF MADNESS, DRUGS, AND DEATH ON THE STREETS OF AMERICA (New York University Press, 1997); and contributed to my 3d book on gangs, GANGS IN COURT Lawyers & Judges Publishers, 2008)

THE UNIVERSITY OF MASSACHUSSETTS-1958-1960

My work with gangs in New York, and my many other projects wore me down. I decided to become a fulltime college professor out of New York city. I applied for and was hired as an Assistant Professor at the University of Massachussetts-Amherst. The rural University environment of Amherst facilitated the completion of several writing projects, and gave me the opportunity to take a breather, and figure out my future career.

I did, however, commute regularly between Amherst and New York City for my research and contact with my friends and family.

On one trip to the City I encountered a bizarre incident that was somewhat scary. I thought I was going to be arrested by a police officer who had been in one of my classes when I taught in the CCNY-NYPD program.

The incident involved a midterm exam where a ridiculous and apparently stupid cop was cheating like mad. He kept looking at the exams of other cops. He was blatantly cheating. I stared at him and moved him a few times. He had apparently become deranged and couldn't stop cheating. Finally, I almost physically had to place this police officer in the corner of the room facing the wall. I think he wound up with a D for the course.

The bizarre incident occurred when, a few months after the cheating incident I was in NY walking up 2nd Avenue. A police car pulled up and skidded to a halt right next to me. I looked at the driver and it was the cheating cop! I thought for sure, he was going to get revenge for the way I handled him in class. All he did was give me a big "hello Dr. Yablonsky, how are you doing." Apparently my rough treatment of him--didn't at all bother him. After a brief stop and chat with him I walked away fast.

Life in Amherst was a delightful break from the tumult of New York City, and its fast pace. I lived about 10 miles off-campus at an apartment in Leverett. My home was around 50 yards from a wonderful waterfall and I could see cows on adjacent farm from my bedroom.

The students at UMass seemed to appreciate a Professor who had just arrived from the combat zone of NYC. I interlarded my lectures with stories about my gang work. For example, I told the class's about an experience when I felt most threatened in my life with gangs.

This incident took place on a broken down pier on 125th St. and the Hudson River. I was looking for a Dragon gang kid named Lucky. Out on the pier were around 80 gangsters. A potential murder came to my attention.

Two kids were about to throw a 12 year old off the pier into the water. He kept screaming "I can't swim." Everyone was looking at the unfolding potential murder but no one was helping the kid. I went over to the scene and said something like "leave the kid alone." The would be murderers promptly dropped him and the potential victim bounced hard on the pier planks. Then around 10 gangsters encircled me with a "who the fuck are you attitude." Some had knives and possibly guns. Thinking fast, and using my old Newark training I confronted the kid closest to me, and started pushing him in the shoulder. At the same time I kept talking stupid confrontational nonsense like, "What are you motherfuckers going to do--kill me." For whatever reasons the action from my potential assailants slowed down. I then saw an opening and ran faster than I ever have in my life. I obviously got away.

From 1958 to around 1960, I was a fulltime assistant professor at UMass, and in the 2 year period was promoted to Associate Professor. Out of the blue I received an invitation to teach a criminology class in the Department of Social Relations at Harvard. I hesitate to state "it was an offer, I couldn't refuse." I traveled twice a week from Amherst to Cambridge to teach the course. The Harvard students were amazing. One day, I gave my best lecture on gangs. The students rose and applauded. On another day, I was tired and not lecturing too well--they booed me!

All in all it was a great time. I met and became friends with a Harvard law student--David Steinberg. He was a friend of Margo

Lederer who was the daughter of the famous advice columnist Ann Landers. She was a student at Brandies University.

Margo and I hit it off, and had a great relationship. After a few dates, she invited me to visit with her mom and dad in Chicago during one of the holidays. Her mom Ann Landers and I became friends and communicated about various social issues. She used some of my material from my later book JUVENILE DELINQUENCY in one of her books.

Margo's father was rather wealthy and was the owner of a Rent-A-Car business. He didn't like me. I recall his sarcastic comment that said it all, "Yeah, I would like a son-in-law older than me." Margo and I drifted apart after that Chicago trip. We did meet again, years later when I had an appointment in Chicago with Playboy books who were going to publish a book I wrote called THE EXTRA-SEX FACTOR. (It was later published by New York Times Books and additional version was published by IUniverse Press in 2009)

After Margo and I ended our brief relationship I began dating a very beautiful 18 year old Smith student named Marta Foster. We went on trips to Vermont and New York, and stayed a few times at a friend of mine's Hotel in Stockbridge, Mass. We were in love and almost married. Life was good at UMass, and I would have continued my career there--except for a professorial offer that brought me back to California.

Chapter 4

Ucla, Synanon, Donna and Mitch (1960 to 1965)

I enjoyed my experience teaching at UMass and at Harvard. During that period I also taught some classes at near by Smith College in Northhampton, Mass. It was the first protracted time I had lived in a small town.

In addition to finishing THE VIOLENT GANG while at UMass I had written a paper on gangs published in an Interpol Journal. The article caught the attention of the planners of the 1960 United Nations Crime and Delinquency Conference in London and I was invited to deliver a paper at the Congress.

This was my first trip to Europe, and it significantly changed my life. My experience in London at the Conference was instrumental in causing me to later move to California where I met my beautiful wife Donna and we had my beloved son Mitch.

My presentation at the U.N. Conference was was well received and written up in.THE LONDON TIMES 8/14/60 BY TREVOR PHILPOTT

"NO FRONTIER FOR DELINQUENCY"

One of the research workers from New York, Dr. Lewis Yablonsky, who has spent five years studying gangs in New York City, tried to explain to me why boys join these gangs. "We live in a success-motivated society, We say that anybody can be president .. We say every. body is entitled to cars and other luxuries they see and hear about. These 'kids are failures at school and see no hope in their future. I don't believe they join gangs for security, they join for prestige, for what they call 'rep.' One boy in a gang called the 'Egyptian Kings,' the gang that stabbed a polio victim to death, put it like this; 'I have my mind made up I'm not going to be in no gang. Then they come up to me and they talk to me about what they are going to do, like, "Man we'll go out here and kill this guy," so I say he isn't. going to take over my rep. I ain't going to let him be ,known more then me. I go 'ahead just for selfishness."

Dr. Yablonsky pointed out that the modern American gang was not a tightly·knit loyal community, .. Asking a boy whether he belongs to the Dragons or the Kings is like asking him how he feels today. There are a few hardened troublemakers who spend practically all their waking time in recruiting new members, making alliances and having 'war councils.' Butl most boys just go along when they need to feel important, or have some power. Sometimes after they have some trouble at home" These boys, Dr. Yablonsky feels, are best approached, not by police but by reviving their community, getting ordinary adults people who live in the neighbourhood, like the store keeper or the bartender, to take an interest in them. Usually the parents have no interest in the boys. Our adult youth association organised a parent day once for 200 gang kids,one parent showed up..."

In London, when not attending lectures at the CongressI hung out at a kind of den-bar called The Nucleus. In London, given my early background I found myself at home with criminals.The Nucleus was infested with pimps, hookers, and various other criminal types. I thoroughly enjoyed the evenings I spent at the Nucleus, made many friends, and learned a great deal about crime and addiction, so to speak, from the source in London. One time I recall sitting at a table with a bunch of "spivs" and someone whispered in the ear of another guy at our table. He announced to the group, "one my girls just got locked up and I have to go bail her out."

I decided to share my experiences at the Nucleus with several of the American criminologist friends of mine, who were attending the Congress. I invited several of them to join me at the Nucleus. They enjoyed an interesting evening with the Nucleus characters.

I especially enjoyed meeting and became friends with Professor Donald Cressey who came to the event at the Nucleus. Don was then Chairman of the Sociology Department at UCLA. He was a very nice and cordial person--and I knew of his work with one of legends of criminology Donald Sutherland.

I recall walking along with Cressey, after a drinking evening at the nucleus, down the middle of a Soho around 3AM. He ran a rap on a new approach to treating drug addiction called Synanon. I did not know, at that time, that this meeting with Cressey would lead to my writing the first book on Synanon, and also meeting the woman who was to become my wife in California.

I found Cressey's remarks about Synanon exciting-but not fully believable. Not that I didn't trust Cressey's opinion, however In more than ten years of work with the crime problem on the East Coast, I did not know one so-called heroine addict who had totally quit using drugs. If there were more than 50 former addicts and criminals staying "clean" in Synanon as Cressey informed me, this was a major breakthrough in treating the problem.

According to Cressey, this small band of former addicts lived together in an old beach house in Santa Monica. They regularly participated in seminar discussions and a new form of encounter group psychotherapy devised by Synanon's founder, an ex-alcoholic, Chuck Dederich.

Cressey sketched a vivid picture of the sessions where a group of 10 to 15 people loudly arguing philosophical concepts and amateur psychology into all hours of the night while a hi-fi blared out jazz music in the background. I especially remember his description of an addict going through drug withdrawal pains on a living-room couch in the center of this bizarre scene.

The Synanon organization, described by Cressey seemed strange. But it did make some sense to me that it would probably take a radical set of circumstances to get criminal/addicts off drugs. All other methods that I knew of had failed. If this one worked, I wanted to see this sociological freak of nature first hand.

Around 8 months later, I received what I would call a Hollywood phone call at UMass from Cressey at UCLA. He asked me if I would be interested in becoming a Visiting Professor at UCLA during the 2 years he was going to be teaching at Cambridge University in England on sabbatical. I, of course jumped at the chance to get back for a time to sunny California. Going to California would also provide the opportunity for me to see Synanon at firsthand. I accepted the appointment to UCLA.

When I arrived in Los Angeles in September,1960 I I moved into a great apartment right on the beach in Malibu and began teaching my courses at UCLA. The rent at that time in 1961 was $160 per month! I rented from a man named Peter Baldwin who was one of the directors of the Sanford and Son Red Foxx TV show. The actor who played in the series Paladin lived next door.

I quickly learned of Synanon's zoning battle with the City of Santa Monica. They were in a building right on the beach in the middle of million dollar homes. Nearby were the hiomes of such celebrities as King Cole, Mae West, and Darryl Zanuck.

Stories were in the local press almost daily, and several colleagues gave me additional background information. Apparently, the city officials, prodded by many irate neighbors, wanted to run Synanon out of town. They understandably did not want a group of criminals and drug addicts living nearby.

There were some citizens groups that supported Synanon's right to exist. A member of a pro-Synanon. citizens' group invited me, no doubt because of my role as a UCLA professor to testify on Synanon's behalf at a City Council meeting. This gave me the opportunity I wanted --to see Synanon at firsthand and learn something directly about the organization.

I read several articles about Synanon. and made an appointment to visit and meet with a "Synanon director," Charlie Hamer and Chuck Dederich the founder. My first look at Synanon surprised me. The immense five-story red-brick armory was nothing like the beatnik beach-house pad I was led to expect. The large, respectable black-and-yellow SYNANON HOUSE sign on the front of the building on the ocean front in Santa Monica was also a surprise. Somehow I had expected Synanon to have a more clandestine face to the world.

The large front door to the building opened into an impressive waiting room. On a bulletin board right inside the door, I noticed pictures of many celebrities with Synanon members including Steve Allen, Ben Gazzara, Leonard Nimoy, Rod Serling, and Ray Bradbury. Obviously they had all visited the place. One picture showed Chuck Dederich and several Synanon members. Also in the foyer was a counter with a variety of· Synanon literature. There were reprints of articles, on Synanon from Time, Down Beat, The Nation, and other publications.

Several feet from the entrance, a young man, the gatekeeper greeted me in a husinesslike manner . He asked me to. state my business and then sign a guest register. I noticed that he had the healed scars of an ex-addict on the inside crook of his arm. This "administrative approach," coming from a former addict, was an unusual experience for me. I had met and worked with many junkies during the time I had directed various projects in my group therapy work at, among other prisons--Rikers Island and Riverside Hospital in New York and had a different image of drug addicts..

I told the receptionist about my appointment with Hamer and Dederich. He called my name into an intercom that connected with the "coordinator's office." I· was now apparently properly checked into the . building. ·and ·the squawk box answered back, "Send him on up."

It became increasingly difficult for me to believe that the place was mainly managed hy criminal ex-addicts. Everywhere I looked I saw signs of efficient organization. On my way to the second floor, I passed a sign stating "Business Office." The large room had rows of typewriters, files, and ·the other accouterments. of an office. A small theater marked "Stage One" was at the foot of the stairs. The hall was Carpeted. with various colored rugs, which were well-worn but neat and clean. It didn't look like other rehab places I had seen.

On the second floor, I saw men and women bustling around in different directions. They all seemed to be on important errands, With the exception of the sight of several jail-scarred faces and a young man going through drug-withdrawal pains on a couch in the center of the Iivingroom, I found it difficult to believe this was a "drug-addict. rehabilitation center." It. seemed to be more of a poorman's version of a co-ed college fraternity house.

Charlie Hamer. introduced. himself, welcomed me, and introduced me to another "member of Synanon," Jack Hurst. After a brief exchange of handshakes and pleasantries,l was informed that"any friend of Don Cressey's is a friend of ours." (Cressey had published a paper that had helped Synanon.) They then told me that they really expected a bearded older man and l didn't look like a professor." (I thought to myself, "You guys don't look like junkies·· I have· known either.")

Hurst was a thin young man, about thirty-two years old. I later found out that. he had been a Hells Angel biker heroine addict for nine Years prior to coming to Synanon. Hamer was about sixty. He was ruddyfaced . and very talky, with a Southwestern twang in his voice.

Hamer's opening remarks lauding Synanon were very much in the style. of many intelligent old "cons" I had met in my past prison work. Most of these old-timers had their theories on· treatment. There was one major difference . between Hamer's dialogue and stories I had heard in the past. He wasn't giving me the usual story of. the locked-up.prisoner and failure . who now saw the. "light." He was talking from the unusual position of a living embodiment of his preachments.

This encouraged me to listen more attentively to his story. I later found out. that Hamer was probably one of the oldest living addicts in the country. The first drug he used was opium. This was given to him by a Chinese family in Oklahoma in 1922. This had. launched him into forty years of leading a life of crime, prison and addiction. There were many former hardcore ex-criminal-addicts like Hamer in Synanon.

When I met the founder of Synanon Chuck we hit it off immediately. We spent many hours discussing the synanon process. During my first semester at UCLA I was down at Synanon around 4 days a week. The residents were totally open with me about their past and the group recesses they were going through . They all seemed hopeful about leaving their criminal drug addiction past life, and were optimistic about their future.

Chuck and I had many meetings discussing the formation of Synanon. His personal story was interesting. He was an executive in a major oil company and had become an alcoholic. He cleaned up through the AA program and had been an avid AA member. He had rented a small apartment down at the beach in Venice on his unemployment checks.

At first he held regular evening group sessions with alcoholics he knew. He told me: "some junkies off the beach stumbled into our sessions and I began to notice as a result of our encounter groups they started to stay clean. I knew I had found something that worked ex-alcoholics and ex-addicts could help each other stop using. The next step was to pool our money and rent the place you are now in."

Chuck and I began to get together several times a week to discuss Synanon and the group methods. Of course, I shared my expertise and experiences as a group therapist and psychodramatist. The fact that I was a UCLA professor, and an experienced group therapist was of interest to Chuck, and gave me entree to studying Synanon.

Around that time Synanon was receiving attention in the national press. On April 7, 1962 the following article appeared in Time Magazine

Medicine: S.S. Hang Tough

Early in August 1959, homeowners along the stylish Pacific Ocean beaches in Santa Monica, Calif., were dismayed to get a new set of neighbors: a bedraggled platoon of half a hundred men and women, who moved into a rundown, three-story, red brick building that once was a National Guard armory. White and black, young and middleaged, criminals and innocents, artists and loafers, the unlikely assortment shared one trait: they were narcotics addicts determined to kick their habit for good.

Scrounging lumber, paint and old furniture, the troupe converted the top floor of the armory into a barracks-style men's dormitory. They turned the second floor into offices, kitchen, dining hall and living room, and the main floor into women's sleeping quarters. Over the doors in the living room they hung their emblem: a life preserver with the words "S.S. Hang Tough," slang for "don't give up."

"Look at Me." Such was the formal dedication of Synanon House a self-run, haphazardly financed experiment in human reclamation whose success has been hailed by Dr. Donald Cressey, University of California at Los Angeles sociologist, as "the most significant attempt to keep addicts off drugs that has ever been made."

Thus far, in 2? years, of 150 addicts who voluntarily enrolled as roommates in Synanon House for at least one month, only half went back to drugs, and of 90 who stayed longer than three months, only 15 fell back. "Look at me," said one proud graduate, a recent father who works steadily in an electronics plant, "a real square." Such success is hardly even fractional compared with the overall U.S.

narcotics problem, which claims from 45,000 to 100,000 addicts. But Synanon* offers more than a few cures: it offers a workable formula of rehabilitation—something that most local authorities, who confine themselves to jailing addicts after they steal to get dope, do not tackle.

"Something That Works." The technique was patterned roughly after the group-therapy methods of Alcoholics Anonymous. The Synanon system cannot work until the addict really decides that he wants to kick the habit; but after that, it promises critical discipline and confinement through the first bad days of withdrawal, followed by a psychological treatment that usually kills the desire. Dr. Cressey describes the psychology: "A group in which Criminal A joins with some noncriminals to change Criminal B is probably most effective in changing Criminal A."

In the often brutally frank personal exchanges", the addicts slowly reveal to themselves the anxieties that led them to the needle, and through daily contact with similarly beset persons are reinforced in their determination to quit narcotics permanently. Says the founder of Synanon House, 48-year-old Charles E. Dederich, a potbellied Irishman who was once an alcoholic but never a drug addict: "It is something that works."

"They're like Children." The Synanon curriculum is divided into three stages. During the first phase, the emotionally shaken, physically weak addict gradually adjusts to his new surroundings. Says Dederich: "Addicts are babies who look like men and women. They have to grow up emotionally. After they've kicked, they're like children, and they have to be told to turn off the lights, flush the toilet, keep their fingers out of lamp sockets." Such, for example, is Synanon's youngest member, a plump girl of 19 who was trapped by narcotics at 13. After eight months at Synanon, she finally had the courage to raise a shaky voice to sing with a four-man musical combo that is a feature of Saturday night socials. Her emotional triumph won a thunderous ovation from the crowd.

During the second stage, the ex-addict works at a regular job on the outside, contributes part of his wages to the group, continues to live at the house. One such is a middle-class college graduate who is now a salesgirl in a Santa Monica department store, after a flight *that took her through prostitution and prison. Despite the new start, she still feels unable to live on her own in the world.*

In its final stage, Synanon sends its member out into society, but not until he has saved a few hundred dollars, owns a car, and has a place to live away from the haunts of addicts. Said the electronics worker: "There's much I want and nothing I need. I get home tired, and I look in that crib and I say everything's O.K."

Local Hostility. Synanon's record in curing narcotics addicts is a matter of indifference to many of its respectable neighbors along the Santa Monica beachfront. Although the institution has won many friends in the community by dispatching its members to address local service-club meetings and high school assemblies, within days after it moved into the deserted armory a petition signed by 31 of Synanon's neighbors protested the invasion. Six months later, a municipal judge found Synanon guilty of violating the local zoning ordnance. A final appeal to the U.S. Supreme Court failed last February when the court refused to hear the case, and Synanon House may now have to find a new location.

There is little gloom on the premises, however. In the course of legal battles, Synanon House was designated by the Internal Revenue Bureau as a tax-deductible foundation. And it managed to support an average of 50 residents all last year for just $26,000. For Synanon's essential needs are simple: a roomy house with a place to hang the life preserver. (The word Synanon was derive from one addict's mispronunciation of seminar, which is part of Synanon's program for rehabilitation.)

In our many sessions during my research for a book I decided to write on Synanon Chuck played many audio tapes of Synanon group sessions for me. One day when Chuck was playing a tape--I interrupted and said that one of the voices on the tape was very familiar. He told me it was the voice of a New York gangster named Frankie Lago.

I made a connection with the voice because around 5 years before during my work in New York. I had interviewed Frankies brother Ralph Lago who had participated in the infamous Egyptian King gang murder that was in part the basis for my book THE VIOLENT GANG. I clearly determined that he familiar voice I remembered was Ralph Lago who was one of the Egyptian King gang that killed Michael Farmer.

Ralph's commentary was part of the Edward R. Murrow program I had worked on as a consultant. Small criminal world. (In 2008 National Public Radio did a followup on the 1957 murder of Farmer entitled "West Side Story", and I was able to contact Ralph Lago. He had gone straight, after a prison term, and was doing well. He didn't want to appear on the NPR program and wanted to forget the incident. Despite this we did enjoy reminiscing on the old days in New York on the upper West Side.)

When we determined that Frankie Lago, who was now in Synanon, was Ralph's older brother Chuck called him up to the office. Frankie and I met and later on became good friends. I brought him to my classes at UCLA and he told his NY gang drug addict story to a few of my criminology classes.

Frankie's story, in many ways, was prototypical of many residents of Synanon. Frankie's early case history and violent-gang life pattern paralleled his younger brother Ralph who, as mentioned, I wrote about in THE VIOLENT GANG. This meshing of people I knew from New York gangs and the Lagos enhanced my interest in Synanon and the organization's potential for effectively treating criminal/addict gangsters.

The following case study of Frankie is derived from my t book SYNANON: THE TUNNEL BACK. After his violent-gang period of his life, Frank turned to a criminal career of using and selling drugs. This life resulted in his "doing time" in a federal prison (Danbury), New York City's Riker's Island Penitentiary (five times), Bellevue Hospital in New York City, and the federal hospital in Lexington, Kentucky. Frankie was probably in Rikers when I directed my psychodrama sessions in the prison back in the 1950s.

In addition to a pattern of drug addiction, pimping, and theft, Frank had a violent streak. His wife Carmen who was also in Synanon at the time of my interviews with Frankie told me, "Frankie would never use a knife, unless he had to. Mostly with his fists he would beat a guy down and try to kill him right there. They pulled him off this big guy one time-he wouldn't stop punching him in the face." This was the casual observation made by Frankie's ex-crime partner, Carmen with whom he had lived for five years in New York and who was now living in Synanon.

Frank went to California at the insistence of his parents "to try a new way of life." "The family chipped in, gave me a plane ticket, and told me to straighten out or drop dead." He accepted the plane ticket they bought and left under the assumption of continuing his old way of life. In Los Angeles, he had trouble getting a good drug connection and stealing enough money to supply his habit. He heard about Synanon and decided to try it. His initial motives were not pure. His thought was "to get cleaned up a little" and either get organized for a new onslaught on Los Angeles or steal enough to return to New York and his old criminal pattern. Something happened at Synanon to make Frankie stay "clean."

Frankie's first reaction to Synanon was confusion: "The first thing they hit me with flipped me. This tough-looking cat says to me, 'There are two things you can't do here, shoot drugs or fight.'" Frankie said, scratching his head, "I was all mixed up these were the only two things I knew how to do." One day Frankie mad a simple comment to me that I always remembered "In New York no one besides my parents ever told me not to use drugs."

Frankie found the Synanon environment interesting and exciting. There were, in the addict's jargon, "lots of hip people." This included Jimmy the Greek, who at forty-eight had been an addict, a criminal, and a con man for more than thirty years and was now a "therapist" in Synanon.

Frankie got his first job in Synanon, scouring pots and pans and mopping floors. According to Frankie, his boss in the kitchen Jimmy Middleton could not be "conned" or manipulated out of position like the guards and therapists that Frankie had encountered at Riker's Island or other places where he had done time.

Jimmy, of course, knew the score. He had done around 20 years in prison for violence To him Frankie, with all his exploits, was a "young punk," who could give him no trouble. "I've met kids like this all my life-in and out of the joint," he said.

(After I had been around Synanon for about a year Chuck had me direct a number of psychodramas around once a week with the residents. In one session Jimmy became the subject and revealed an experience in Detroit. The session revolved around his confession that "I killed a 'fag' in a hotel room for his money." I was often confronted in therapeutic sessions I ran where confessions of serious crimes were made, and I took no action. Murder, obviously, has no statute of limitations.")

Frankie's feeling about being pushed around by his "boss" Jimmy were homicidal. "1 hated this bastard Jimmie. I used to sometimes sit and plan ways to kill him." When Frankie wanted to fight Jimmy over a disagreement about work, Jimmy laughed and told him that if he got into a fight, he would be thrown out of Synanon. In a standard prison the feud between Jimmy and Frankie would have resulted in a homicide. However in Synanon these possible violent conflicts were handled in the encounter groups on a verbal level.

The usual prison situation was reversed, and this confused Frankie. In the "joint" (prison), if Frankie got in trouble, confinement became increasingly severe, with the "hole" (solitary confinement) as an end point. In the Bellevue Hospital psychiatric ward, where Frankie had also "done time," it was a straitjacket. In Synanon the punishment was getting kicked out. This new situation baffled Frankie, and as a rebel he was going to stay in Synanon.

What interested me as a criminologist was what made Frankie behave in order to stay at Synanon, with its open door? Geography was a factor. The fact that Frankie was exported from New York to Los Angeles was a significant initial force in keeping him in Synanon. As he commented: "At times I felt like splitting, then I thought it would be hard to make it back to New York. I didn't know Los Angeles and was afraid to make it out there, because I didn't know the people. Synanon was better than anything else I could do- at the time."

Other factors that kept Frankie and others in Synanon was the beautiful beach, and the meals were good. In the evening, many ex-addict top musicians played cool jazz." Also, there were, according to Frankie, "broads to dance with and get to know." But highly important in this anticriminal society, there were others who understood him, had made the same "scenes," intuitively knew his problems and how to handle him. He respected people he could not "con." He belonged and was now part of a "family" he could accept.

Frankie found that "rep" was acquired in this new social system (unlike the prisons he had known) by truth, honesty, and industry. The values of his other life required the reverse If he was to gain a "rep" at Synanon. These values were not goals per se that someone moralized about in a meaningless vacuum; they were means to the end of acquiring prestige in this tough social system with which he and other residents increasingly identified with and enjoyed their new life.

In "synanons", the Synanon form of encounter group therapy truth was viciously demanded. Any foolish rationalizations or BS stories about past or current experiences were brutally demolished by the group. There was an intensive search for true self-identity.

Residents like Frankie found that, in the process, he learned something of what went on beneath the surface of his thoughts. Frankie admitted that for the first time in his life he had found other people who had some idea of his underlying thoughts. He had had individual and group therapy in prison, but there he could "con" the therapist and most important, "I said what I thought they wanted to hear so I could get out sooner."

Frankie at first followed his usual pattern of self-centered manipulation of others. However, a new element was introduced into the situation. He began to care about what happened to others at Synanon. This was, at first, selfish. Synanon was for him a good, interesting way of life. He identified with the organization and learned at "gut level" that if any Synanon member failed, in some measure he too had failed.

I personally participated in the group therapy and became close to the residents. I related easily to Frankie and other Synanon residents, because of my early socialization with my Newark buddies. My friends in Synanon were not my criminal cohorts. They were individuals attempting to quit their past lives as junkies and criminals.

They included people like Jimmie the Greek, Candy Latson, and Charlie Hamer all ex self-named "dope fiends" were fighting for their lives and I was their friend. I, course was also researching my book which was published by Macmillan in 1965.

Following is one of the positive reviews of THE TUNNEL BACK: SYNANON (Macmillan, 1965) I received. Entitled, "THE

Lewis Yablonsky Ph.D

LIFE OF THE JUNKIE" my book was reviewed by Nat Hentoff for the New York Times Book Review, February 18, 1965

"The Tunnel Back: Syna.non" is an unabashedly partisan but convincing analysis by sociologist Lewis Yablonsky of the most successful way so far by which a growing number of American addicts ,have helped themselves. Since 1958, some 500 former junkies have stayed clean through voluntarily undergoing the Synanon life experience. This route back to society is based. to begin with, on total abstinence from drugs or chemicals of any kind. Alcohol is also forbidden. Tlle setting is one of several Synanon houses in which the addict lives as part of an extended family of former junkies who are both "patients" and therapists,

He may leave at any time, but so long as he stays, he must remain off drugs and 'behave responsibly by participating in the work of Synanon - from kitchen detail at the start to gradually more important staff assignments as he gains in self-assurance. Synanon opens his treatment by reversing the usual assumption in professional I therapy that, as Yablonsky notes, "if a person's inner problems are somehow adjusted, he will stop 'acting out' his bad behavior. Synanon starts with I an attack on the reality of overt bad behavior."

'As an apprentice starts acting as a productive member of the Synanon community, he simultaneously begins getting at his inner problems through participation in regular synanon group encounter. (The word "synanon" in lower case describes the group therapy session, a fundamental element in the long process of self-realization at a Synanon house.)

In large part, the synanons consist of relentless, probing attacks by the members on e~h other's self-evasions, rationalizations and manifestations of plain dishonesty. There is no "we-they" caste system in these sessions because the Synanist (moderator) is himself a former addict and often brings his own problems into the exchange. If he stays, the ex-addict not only achieves an increasingly secure knowledge of himself but he also acquires-often for the first time in his life-the fulfilling sense of belonging to a primary group which grows in strength as he grows. The Synanon approach, ircidentally, has also shown positive results when applied in the Nevada State Prison at Reno to a variety of hard-core criminals as well as to former addicts; and, in passing, Yablonsky points out the intriguing possibilities of adapting this kind, of group "attack therapy" to'such other areas of conflict as marriages, parent-children relationships and businesses and industries. (1 would add teaching faculties, both in lower schools and colleges).

The method seems to have worked so far for certain kinds of addicts, and Yablonsky, through this exhaustive exploration of the history and methods of. Synanon, has made a formidable case for its extension throughout the country... He has certainly served Synanon well in this book...

Meeting Donna in Synanon- Fall 1961

The best friend I had in Synanon was Donna King. She was the most exciting romance of my life and was the woman who became my wife, and my son Mitch's mother.

The day I met her was at Synanon in Santa Monica. The sun was setting at dusk on the second floor balcony that overlooked the Ocean. She was standing in the sunlight and was one of the most beautiful woman I had ever seen in my life. Donna was standing on the balcony looking out at the Sea. When I saw her that first time it was a peak experience in my life

I walked over and we began to talk. I assumed she was, like me, a "square" visiting Synanon. I soon found out her story, and that she was a resident of the drug rehab center. At that time she 22. Following is her background as I pieced it together and later wrote about her story in THE TUNNEL BACK.

Frankie was a prototypical male in Synanon. Donna's background and experiences reveals some of the prototypical problems that Synanon women experienced before getting into Synanon's therapeutic methodology:

Donna had a problem family: a mother and father who were alcoholics. They were always fighting and separating. Their destructive parental approach drove Donna out of the house into a search for the thrills and kicks that she mistakenly believed could assuage her emotional problems. Following is her story in her own words as I taped them back in 1962:

"They were never there when I needed them. They would just go away and leave me. I remember being alone most of the time, as a child. They would always lie, on top of it, and this made it worse. They said they would be right back, and then they would go away, sometimes for a day or more.

"I was bad and rebellious from the first grade on. I wouldn't behave, and my parents were always being called to school. They seldom carne, because they were always out either working or drinking. I don't blame them now; they were like children themselves, always arguing and fighting with each other. In spite of this I always remember that they were basically kind.

" I didn't have a stable home, since we were always moving around. I changed schools several times a year, and I never really got going in any school. It seemed that just when I would begin to get interested in a school, we would move. I began to play hooky most of the time.

"At fourteen, everything seemed to happen to me at once. It was really a weird year in my life. I began dating older men; going to bars, nightclubs, and jazz joints. That year, I began drinking, smoking pot, and taking pills. I had my hair dyed red, black, and finally silver-blond. I had few problems in getting almost any man I wanted. But I still felt all alone.

"The year I was fourteen, I also got involved in another ridiculous scene. I ran away [from Los Angeles] to San Francisco. I had taken tap- and toe-dancing lessons on and off since I was five, and thought I could easily get a job dancing. After finding a room, I put my tap- and toe-dancing shoes in a bag and set out to find a nightclub.

"Never having been to San Francisco, I asked someone where I could find a nice nightclub. I was directed to the International Settlement, to a club called the Barbary Coast unbeknownst to me, a strip joint. I saw the manager and asked him if he could use a good toe or tap dancer. He replied, 'No kid, but can ya take it off?'

"He nodded toward a girl on stage who was almost nude doing the bumps and grinds. I had never tried this kind of dancing before, but I was running low on money, so I told him, 'Sure.' 'Okay,' he said, 'you start tomorrow night. I couldn't bring myself to remove every article of stripper's costume.

It was in San Francisco that I took my first fix and start using heroine. One time, I decided to go to Lexington and try to kick my habit. After a few weeks there, I decided it wasn't for me and split. Actually I was thrown out for not following the rules. [In essence Donna was kicked out of a Federal Prison.]

On my way back to L.A., I got involved with some dopefiends in Chicago who had taken over the 2nd floor of an abandoned building. I don't remember the incident clearly. All I know is that I almost died several times in Chicago. I scored with these people and got an overdose of drugs.

I don't remember it all, except I fixed and passed out. I learned later on I was in a coma. The next thing I remember was waking up in this Chicago hospital with a tube down my throat. I was being fed intravenously with wires and oxygen tanks and things. They had to open my throat to restore breathing with a tracheotomy.

As if this wasn't enough, a tube in my throat and all, being the addict that I was, I ran away from the hospital for a day and scored some dope. I fixed and went back to the hospital. The doctor told me by all rights I should be dead. They strapped me to the bed to prevent my running away again."

I returned to LA and hit the streets again. I was arrested and sent to prison for a year and a half. I was miserable in prison. That's where I received my basic training. There I was told about heroin, sex, and things I had never heard of, and all in a very glamorous light. After I was released I continued going around with the same crowd.

"I always had the idea I wanted to lead a glamorous life. Maybe become a movie star. I thought I was on the right path. Inside I always felt twisted and unsure, but outside I always managed to look good. I always played a role and kept an image. I became known as 'Countess' when I was locked up at The Ventura School for Girls. In the reformatory, I learned about everything I hadn't learned about on the streets. My 'Countess' handle stuck with me. I ran with the hippest and the toughest girls in the place."

When I was out I sometimes just walked the streets for hours all alone at night. I got busted a few times and did some small jail bits. They never really pinned me. Finally I was sent to the Terminal

Island Prison for a year. • When I got out of there, I naturally went back to the streets and drugs.

It was the only life I knew. I was desperately trying to quit. One day I heard about Synanon from a connection. Somehow I got down there, and that was it. I've been clean since 1959 because of Synanon. The main thing I was given there was a new direction.

"Down deep somewhere, I guess I always wanted to do something better for myself. I'm now tremendously happy. I'm married to a wonderful man \who knows all about my past and understands me. I have a lovely child, a real home for the first time, and my life is strangely beautiful."

I never forgot Donna telling me about the Chicago near-death episode in her life. She pieced the story together for me one night over dinner. In Chicago she had been in a "shooting gallery" abandoned building. She found out later from a person who was at the scene that she had overdosed and was in a coma.

Her dopefiend "friends" thought she was dead. An argument raged in the group. One faction just wanted to throw her out of the window to protect their drug-safe "home." Others apparently thought she should be taken to a hospital.

Finally one generous soul carried her out of the building, drove her, and dumped her body in front of a Chicago hospital. A doctor going to work in the early morning saw her body and rushed her into emergency where she received a tracheotomy that saved her life. As she told me the story didn't end there. Donna managed to leave the hospital bed, score some dope, and fixed. She was gone one day, and returned to the hospital.

Donna's fateful story was always with me during our relationship. It was no wonder, based on her harsh background that my UCLA friends and others were surprised at how close Donna and I became. They perceived me as a UCLA professor who was running around dating a junkie albeit an ex-junkie in Synanon. But very few of them knew about my socialization process in growing up in Newark. Synanon was for me reliving my earlier years with people I easily related to in a new constructive way. The Synanon family was at that time more important to me than the intellectual friends I made at UCLA. And Donna and I fell "madly" in love.

Despite my intense feelings for Donna I was appropriately ambivalent. If Synanon worked--we worked. If it was like all the other methodologies I knew--marrying Donna was a major mistake in my life. A good friend of mine at that time psychologist George Bach encouraged my relationship with Donna. I had never been love in my life as intensely as I did at that time so I, of course, went with my emotions.

Donna and I were like 2 teenagers dating. I owned an old 1958 Blue and White convertible Oldsmobile. We drove up and down the Coast, and into Hollywood many times. Donna went with me to various lectures I gave at that time. She was the singer for the highly touted Synanon band which included the famous guitarist Joe Pass (who had traveled with Ella Fitzgerald) and pianist Arnold Ross who had accompanied many famous singers and was the piano player for Jane Russell when she sang in a club. Donna and I were no doubt "madly" in love. We kissed so much and often that our lips were sore.

During this period, the early 1960s, I was in heaven. Here I found love with a soulmate, and was also documenting a new approach to the treatment of addiction. Synanon members, Chuck and I appeared before Senator Christopher Dodds U.S. Senate Subcommittee on Drug Addiction. Senator Dodd (Senior) described Synanon in his Senate Report as "the miracle on the beach."

I had many interesting personal and professional experience during the process of writing the Synanon book One was an invitation to attend the 1962 White House Conference on drug addiction. At the Conference, among many other experiences during that week in Washington at one point I was excited to be in the same room with President Kennedy and his then Attorney-General Bobby Kennedy. The assassinations of these 2 great men of the 20th century left me with indelible grief.

Around this time, a movie director Richard Quine became interested in Synanon. A script was written, and filming began. Edmond OBrian played Chuck, Eartha Kitt played Chuck's wife Betty, and there were several other stars of that time period in the film. It was filmed at Synanon, and Donna had a bit part as did the other residents.

Life was exciting. After a year long courtship Donna and I were married in Reno Nevada--at the same time Synanon was opening up a new Synanon House in Reno and an innovative project in the Nevada State Prison.

Some of Synanon's ex-addicts showed a talent as therapists. I later called them "experience therapists" in my Synanon book. They were invited to set up Synanon projects in prison. The first one was started in the Federal Prison at Terminal Island.

Synanon Prison Projects

The first significant TC prison project utilizing the Synanon Method was at the Nevada State Prison in Reno. A cellblock was set aside for the some 50 prisoners who participated in the Project.

The following article was written about the project in the "Reno Evening Gazette" (7/29/63):with a picture of Chuck, Bill Crawford (a Synanon resident) and me. Our visit, and my marriage took place at that time.The article was entitled:

"SYNANON A BREAKTHROUGH IN CORRECTION"

"The formation of Synanon at the Nevada State Prison was called a "major breakthrough" in penal rehabilitation today by a nationally known criminologist. Dr. Lewis Yablonsky, research director of Synanon and a professor of sociology at San Fernando State College in California said Synanon was "one of the most significant developments in '50 years of penology.'

Dr. Yablonsky toured lhe Nevada State prison will members; of Synanon, Its founder, Chuck Dederich, and prison officials. He planned to stay overnight at the prison in the Synanon quarters.

Dr. Yablonsky said he was, spending two days at the prison and at the Synanon House in Reno to write a section of his forthcoming book, "Synanon, an Anticriminal Society." He is writing the book with Dederich. A large' section of the book will be devoted to the Synanon work at the prison. Dr. Yablonsky said the idea of Synanon will change the whole field of criminal correction.

"Chuck (Dederich) has succeeded in unleashing the therapeutic energy that exists in all people," Dr. Yablonsky said. With the

cooperation of the Stale of Nevada and Warden Jack Fogliani, he has been able to organize Synanon so that the men in prison are now moving in a constructive direction.

Synanon was founded in Santa I Monica about five years ago by Dederich as a drug addict rehabilitation organization and has since enlarged its scope to work toward the rehabilitation of general criminals.

Dr. Yablonsky said Synanon is "building' a bridge between the prisoners and society." He said that in talking to prison members of Synanon, one of the major reactions is that "for the first time they see some hope for the future." Dr. Yablonsky said the prisoners have to grow emotionally to take their place in society and Synanon has succeeded in inspiring the prisoners to work toward their own rehabilitation."

I am probably the only non-convict or possibly the only groom who ever spent his wedding night in a cell in the Nevada State Prison. I was the cellmate of an ex-murderer who was in the Synanon Project cell block. I did this because at the time I was researching the chapter "Synanon in Prison" for my book contracted with Macmillan THE TUNNEL BACK--and Donna and I were leaving Reno for LA the next day.

I vividly remember that night in the Nevada State Prison because my cellmate Luke appeared to be as we use to say in Synanon "recklessly eyeballing me." I slept in the top bunk and Luke was in the bottom bunk. I always needed to sleep in pajamas, and I had brought them to the prison. I slept with one eye open. The next morning I said to Luke kind of joking on the square: "What's going on here Luke--I don't like the way you look at me?" Luke responded: "Those are sure beautiful pajamas." I whipped them off and gave my PJs to Luke as a present. However, I did feel slightly personally rejected.

In 1963 there was another interesting article appeared in Time Magazine that summarized Synanon's breakthrough work in prison. Friday, Mar. 01, 1963

"Psychiatry: Mutual Aid in Prison"

Since Synanon House set itself up in Santa Monica four and a half years ago as a mutual self-help cure station for drug addicts, it has seen its fame spread across the country. And for good reason. Addicts given intensive treatment at special federal hospitals have a relapse rate as high as 90%; Synanon, which models itself on Alcoholics Anonymous and uses ex-addicts to give junkies the support and understanding they need to kick the habit and stay clean, has cut the relapse rate to as low as 20%...

The Unconnables. At the prison, Warden Jack Fogliani has set aside a whole tier of cells for Synanon. Occupying it are men who normally would be under maximum security. Yet this tier is the only one in which the cells are left unlocked at night. Each 4-ft. by 8-ft. cubicle is spick-and-span. On the walls, instead of calendar nudes, are reproductions of Van Gogh and art work done by the inmates. Neither Fogliani nor the prison guard captain visits the Synanon tier unless invited.

"Punishment is not the answer, nor keeping a man locked up," says Warden Fogliani. "These Synanon people can approach the convicts in a way that we can't. They've been at the bottom of the barrel, too, so other convicts listen to them. It's the voice of experience." Bill Crawford, one of the Synanon leaders who moved to Reno, and an ex-addict himself, goes further: "The prisoners suddenly found they were with guys who, like themselves, have conned people—and therefore can't be conned by the prisoners."

Socrates in the Cells. Synanon depends heavily on group therapy, and it insists on a tough regime. Since both addict and nonaddict cons have made lying a way of life, absolute truthfulness is demanded. Any hedging, any attempt to shift the blame for their plight to others, is ruthlessly torn apart within the group. Even foul language is banned, because it might snowball into a rumble. And the ultimate punishment is expulsion from the program. But in return, Synanon gives the addict, often for the first time, a sense of belonging to a group. Instead of a "fix," it offers, by the example of the ex-addict leaders, hope that a cure is possible. And because the group governs and disciplines itself, it gives the addicts and other convicts a jolt of self-respect.

Often the starting point for hope is a timeworn epigram that is chalked on a slate, such as Socrates' "All I know is that I know nothing," or Emerson's "Discontent is the want of self-reliance." From there the prisoners take it on their own, analyzing themselves

CONFESSIONS OF A CRIMINOLOGIST

and one another. But the strongest prompting toward cure is the living example of the ex-junkies themselves.

Such a one is Candy Latson, 26, a Houston-born Negro who started using dope when he was 15. He has twice done time in Los Angeles County jail. "I got to the honor camp once there. I went in clean, but I came out hooked again," he says. Through Synanon, Candy learned insight: "I kept telling myself I had four strikes against me: I had only a seventh-grade education, I was black. I was a dope addict, and I had a record. I was using my misfortunes for an excuse to keep using dope." Last week Candy Latson was in Nevada State Prison—not as a prisoner but as an honored guest and Synanon counselor. He has been clean now for three years, and is working fulltime for nothing more than his keep and $2 a week spending money, to help others kick the habit and stay clean."

In the process of my work in Synanon, in addition to my association with Frankie Lago, I met many residents who had been involved in gangs prior to becoming criminal/addicts. Interviews with them enhanced my understanding of violent gang behavior.

Candy Latson (based on the article was now known as "Socrates in Prison") in his earlier years in Texas had been involved in gangs.

Candy was a character, and I especially recall an interesting remark of his. It came after a group of us including Candy had a lengthy Synanon discussion one evening about mental health-- what is it? A Harvard psychologist who was visiting Synanon and I along with Candy and several Synanon residents spent around 2 hours discussing the meaning of "mental health." At the end of our pretentious intellectual discussion I remember Candy ending the evening by thoughtfully musing, "Mental health, if I ever get any of that shit--I'm out of here."

Based on our mutual interests, Candy and I became good friends. We connected again when he left Synanon a few years after his work at the prison to direct a gang prevention program in Venice California. His background and experience at Synanon equipped Candy to direct the program and to work with gangs. This was one of the spinoffs from Synanon. Other programs were developed by people who went through the Synanon process of treatment.

Candy, once invited me to speak to the group of gangsters with whom he was working. When I began my discussion with group, some of the gangsters in the group began to show me bullet wounds and how different gang "sets" in Venice were killing each other. Some gangsters proudly showed me their wounds. They, at first seemed to viewed me as a "bleeding-heart" sociologist, and were startled by my sarcastic comment that opened my lecture to the group: "You guys are out of your fucking minds. Why are you killing each other? Why don't you do something sensible like go to Beverley Hills and rob a Gucci store. It would make more sense than what you are doing to each other."

What I was trying to point out to the group was that their gang violence was not a sign of valor but an act of stupidity. Harming and killing each other in the context of a gang made makes no sense to me. Black on Black and Hispanic on Hispanic gang enemy murders is a form of insanity.

During my research in Synanon for THE TUNNEL BACK, my association with Candy and others in the project provided me with many more insights into gang and crime causation. I found it very useful to bring Synanon residents like Candy, Frankie, Jimmy and others to run their stories in my UCLA classes. This livened up the classroom, and made my lectures more exciting than the usual classes that were presented by "Ivey Tower" lecturers.

During my Synanon years, in my lectures at UCLA, I met a student who because of our backgrounds and interest in criminology became friends and later colleagues. I spotted John Irwin who was in my criminology class as someone with a criminal past based on his comments in class. One day we had coffee together and he related his story. He had recently been released from prison for committing robbery. In fact, when banks had drive-through banking he took advantage of the situation.

John moved up from undergraduate work at UCLA to get a masters degree in sociology. We became close friend when he was a student in one of my graduate seminars. I learned as much from him and his past criminal life-style as he might have learned from me. John had an amazing life story. From UCLA he went on to get a Ph.D. at U.C. Berkley. He became a professor and then chairman of the sociology department at San Francisco State University. One of the several books he wrote, THE FELON based, in part, on his own prison time at the Soledad Prison in California became a criminology classic. He did some interviews for his Ph.D. and book with some old friends of his who were still in prison doing life.

He died 2 days ago, and I am writing this into my autobiography because John was a great friend and criminologist who had an important impact on my life. We spent many hours together at Synanon observing the process. He assisted me enormously in writing several of my books, including this one.

Chapter 5

The Hippie Trip Period (1965-1970)

After I had published THE TUNNEL BACK in 1965, with considerable emphasis on the prison treatment approach, I spent less time at Synanon, and more time on my job as a professor and chairman of the Department at California State University-Northridge.

Despite some distance, after the book was published I kept in touch with Chuck. And as Chairman of the Sociology Department at CSUN I set up a course on Synanon that Chuck taught. My students were fascinated by the course-since Chuck would always bring a Synanon former criminal/addict resident who would tell their story.

Around 1966 I received a call from a publisher who had read my early books and wanted to know if I was interested in doing a book on the burgeoning hippie movement. I told him I would explore the idea to see if I found the subject interesting to me. The so-called hippie movement was catching fire in the media, and the participants were not criminals, however, my early encounters with hippies led me to believe that the individuals who became involved were mostly alienated youths who wanted to live their lives in a different way. I saw a possible 3d interesting book possibility on the horizon.

My journey into the hippie world began with my first really personal encounter with a group of so-called hippies. It happened in the unusual setting of a Jewish restaurant in Santa Monica called Zucky's. While encircling a plate of salami and eggs, I observed the arrival at the next group of tables of Jesus Christ, several apostles, and three Mary Magdelenes. Jesus was like all of the pictures I had seen of him. He was tall, had a reddish-blond beard, and sky-blue eyes. This version of the Savior had bells on his leather boots and looked most beatific.

Along with other patrons in the restaurant, I was somewhat amused by the group's orders of such foods as "bagels and lox," "lean corn beef," and "Matzo ball soup." Some patrons were hostile to the band of people they considered to be weirdos. Sounds like "disgusting" and "go to work" were muffled in pastrami sandwiches. The hostility was met by the beatific group with comments like "Nice to see you, partner" and broad sincere smiles.

I was somewhat surprised when the leader JC himself approached my table with a pleasant smile and greeted me by name. "My name is Gridley Wright. Don't you remember, we met when you gave a talk to a group of probation officers? I use to be a probation officer." I wasn't sure at that moment that I had met Gridley before; however, in his other life, I might have known him. Intrigued by the incongruity of a probation officer turned hippie, I invited him to sit down and we began to discuss his new scene. In short order, I became aware of my past associations with Gridley and expressed my great surprise at his new appearance.

He told me about the new movement he had become a part of over the past year and his "tribe" at Strawberry Fields in the Topanga canyon. He invited me out to visit him and all of his "brothers and sisters."

At that particular time I thought of visiting Gridley's "new community" but I wasn't motivated to actually make the trip-until I began to work on this book. At that point I felt it was most important for me to visit his commune since I had accepted the publisher's offer which included a nice advance.

The directions to Strawberry Fields Gridley had given me at the restaurant carried me through many desolate twisted roads in Malibu Canyon. Finally, at the local fire station in Malibu, I picked up his trail from a hostile fire chief. The chief informed me how the residents of Strawberry Fields had fires at the commune. He had a negative position on Gridley and Strawberry Fields. "Why do you want to find those bastards who burned themselves up? You don't look like one of them. They're all crazy, running around those hills nude. Naturally they finally burned the filthy dump down. They say it was by accident-an overturned candle--but I'm· not sure that they didn't do it on purpose. There's still two of them living there now-a crazy fifteen year-old girl who calls herself Moonglow. She's living in a tree with some young boy. They're both crazy on dope. Just sit around and stare out in space."

After some further discussion on his negative views, the chief gave me directions to where Gridley was now located. He was living with part of his tribe in a house in the hills overlooking Malibu. After much circling and directions from a sheriff's man who ran a prison work camp and delivered another negative diatribe on the commune I found it.

There were around 30 people, young men and women, living there with the Gridley. The details of the commune and the free sex life and drug use in the place are detailed in the book I later wrote THE HIPPIE TRIP (Pegasus, 1968, Penguin Books, 1970, and IUniverse Publication, 2000.

Gridley was important in the process of researching and my writing the book. We became good friends and he sometimes stayed on my then house on Rose Avenue in Venice. He helped me enormously with the book.

My later experiences on the hippie scene further validated that Gridley was a self-styled philosophical leader who became nationally known in the overall movement. (As recently as 2010 there is a web site in his name with all kinds of postings, including my book.)

The following collage of his positions on many issues (prior to his trial and conviction) are essentially taken from an interview with him in the August, 1967, Southern California Oracle and from tapes I made with him myself. The dialogue portrays Gridley's trip and provides, I believe, an excellent introduction into the land of psychedelia from the viewpoint of one of the movement's high priests.

GRIDLEY'S "RAP "I was pretty much living by myself when I completely dropped out. I was a probation officer, which is a pretty dropped-out kind of a job to begin with. I worked in a camp where you work three days and then have four days off.

Well, you can drop a lot further out on those four days than you can on a weekend, if you're working a five-day-a-week job. I had started taking acid about eight months before I quit work and it just occurred to me that it would be interesting to see what would happen if I just did what I felt like doing all the time. You know, get up when I feel like it, wear what I feel like wearing, go to sleep, think, say, do whatever the fuck I felt like. And you can't do that if you're working for somebody else. So I did! I was thirty-three years old, and it was the first time in my life that I ever did really feel free.

I quit my Probation Department job and was on unemployment for about ten months once. I couldn't really enjoy that because I had a certain amount of guilt. You shouldn't be drawing unemployment. But I was able to accept the freedom, and I seem to be able to accept it more and more all the time and this led to my dropping out of society and founding the commune we called Strawberry Field in Topanga Canyon."

LY ON LSD

Gridley and I went on several trips to various communes in California. One trip to a commune in Northern California was especially fascinating to me. There were about 100 people in the commune. That weekend a good supply of LSD was available and almost everyone was nude--except this uptight professor.

The beautiful bodies of several young women did get through to me. Although, I refrained from the drugs at that time, I did participate in and enjoy some sexual experiences with a few women who were very turned on and available. It was one of the few times I "cheated" on my wife--at that time.

Gridley accompanied me on my research trips to many communes in California. I also researched city communes in NYC. In my research which involved several hundred interviews and staying overnight in various communes it was obvious that hippies used lots of drugs especially LSD. I never could smoke pot because I, like Clinton, truly was unable to inhale. However I felt obligated to take LSD in order to enhance my understanding of the experience.

Almost everyone I met during 2 years of research into the hippie phenomenon told me about the wonders of and powerful impact of LSD. The most positive endorsement of the drug came to directly from the top guru of the movement Tim Leary. As chairman of the sociology department, I had invited him to speak to the student body of CSUN. He was eloquent in among other items praising the virtues of LSD to the large audience of over 500 students in our biggest auditorium.

The next day I had breakfast with Leary again he encouraged me to take a trip. Presenting my ambivalence toward LSD--I told Leary in a condescending way "I would have no problem giving acid to all of the convicts on death row at San Quentin." I never forgot his response, "We're all on death row baby!"

At that time in 1966 LSD was still legal. I acquired enough for a good trip for my wife and me from my friend Dr. Dave Smith who founded and directed the Haight-Ashbury Free Clinic. I wanted to make sure I wasn't going to take some phony stuff which was being sold on the streets. I had a weird and great trip on LSD which I acquired from Dave. Following is a partial description of my experience derived from THE HIPPIE TRIP:

"On a Sunday morning at 12:45 a.m., my wife Donna and I very nervously ingested 500 micrograms of LSD each in a special cup of tea brewed for the occasion. I had heard that the drug might put us in a different place in our marriage--so we agreed that she should join me in the experience.

We had prepared for this episode in my research rather assiduously. In addition to a broad examination of the voluminous literature in the LSD field, we both read the "Bible" of the movement, The Psychedelic Experience. We were reasonably aware of the potential agony or ecstasy of the trip and had a great anticipation about new vistas of thought and communication that might open up for us.

We chose our guides based on the directive in the book to "select good friends-who would not play any ego games." We had known Arnie Stonehill and his wife L yn for over a year. During this time we had become very close friends through their participation in a' weekly psychodrama group I ran and through many long evenings of very personal and intimate discussion. Both Arnie and Lyn, prior to our friendship, had had several LSD experiences.

Ann, 18, had been living with us for over a year as our foster daughter. Our close friendship had become a loving family relationship. These three people were the guides we had chosen to be present during our trip.

Twenty minutes after ingesting the bluish-purple "high quality" LSD, we were sitting casually talking with our group in the living room of our home when the acid hit. My first sensation was that a finely wound super watch spring of enormous tensile strength was in my gut, had burst loose, and had begun to unwind.

The next set of flashes involved a feeling of sharp crystals bursting in my brain. Everything began to look like sharpedged crystal snowflakes breaking into arrows. I was filled with awe and became panicky with fright. "Arnie, what have I done? This isn't for me."

I tried to maintain self-control by saying my name to myself, and I tried to stay in the room. For about ten minutes that seemed like a lifetime I fought the power of the LSD. (It was now about 1:15 a.m.) My attempts to maintain control were met with a clear feeling of melting into the floor. I literally felt my backbone, my arms and legs melting like hot lava into the floor. I clutched at my head with my now flickering hands. My head literally felt caved-in! I continued to dissolve into the floor. Waves of nausea and panic engulfed me.

On wobbly legs, with Arnie's help, I staggered into our bedroom, off the living room, and fell onto my bed. I was then alone with Arnie. I began to thrash on the bed, moaning and mumbling. "This is a place I never want to be. What's it all about? I want to be Lew Yablonsky. What's happening to Donna?"

Arnie told me that I must go with it wherever it was trying to take me. I fought a desperate and losing battle. Finally, I let go of Donna, Lew Yablonsky, and a conscious image of the room. This happened partially from the magic phrases that Arnie read to me from Leary and Alpert's book THE PSYCHEDELIC EXPERIENCE. 'That which is called ego death is coming to you. Remember: This is now the hour of death and rebirth. Take advantage of this temporary death to obtain the perfect state enlightenment. Concentrate on the unity of all living beings Hold onto the clear Light Use it to attain understanding and love. I distinctly remember Arnie's reading and my facetious comment: "You're the first Hindu I ever heard with a Brooklyn accent."

Two swirls appeared to be available to me. One was an absolutely magnificent, brightly colored red, white, and blue swirl. I saw it somehow as the masculine swirl. The other one was darker and I was convinced it was feminine. I made the decision to go with the Red, White, and Blue, and it encompassed my conscious mind as I melted into it, in a kind of free fall.

At the core of the incredibly vivid and beautifully colored red, white, and blue swirl, I could see the flicker of a shining white light. I wanted to go there because I knew that there was the center of the Universe-My Universe. I traveled through ages and eons of further swirls. The word Excalibur (a word I had never consciously thought of in my life) seared my thoughts. Excalibur became my theme.

I decided to ride on an available silver space ship. (Arnie later told me I distinctly said, "I'm in a silver space ship. Now I can walk among the stars." He also told me I spoke in the Universal Tongues of glossolalia.) Now in space, I floated with great velocity toward the light. My space ship had a brilliant red, white, and blue flag emblazoned on the front. My voyage was consummated when I arrived at the white light. Its brilliance was astonishing-but I could look directly at it. It flickered between being a shining diamond and a light. The two finally melted together into an almost overpowering bright light. But I felt it was one that I now had in my control. I felt omniscient and omnipotent!

I rose from the bed and informed Arnie that I was one of the greatest patriots of all time. I had Excalibur. I loved America. I loved my friends. I loved Synanon. And I would fight the enemies of my country-those committed to war, false super-patriotism, bigotry, and discrimination.

I kept repeating the word I had never consciously used before in my life-Excalibur! I realized that I had let my wife go into her spiritual feminine trip and I had been to the peak of my red, white, and blue masculine swirl. I was now ready to join her in the living room. (About 2:15 a.m.)

Our living room, which is a large 25' x 25' room, contains a Persian rug and a large fireplace. The room looked remarkable. All of the colors in the room were marvelously brilliant and alive.

My wife was more beautiful than I had evet seen her in my life. Her hair was jet black and flickered in the firelight. Her eyes were very oriental. Her eyes and face were framed with startlingly beautiful diamonds and emeralds. Her body and face swayed with a magnificent smile. I could only try to tell her how much I loved her. I chanted what seemed like a thousand times, "You are the most beautiful woman I have ever known in all the worlds I have ever experienced in all my lifetimes."

We sat on the floor together staring into each other's eyes and I repeated that phrase a hundred different ways. She found me younger and more handsome than she had ever seen me. The room became the inside of a Turkish-oriental mosque.

There were no sharp corners. Everything flowed together like oriental architecture. Everything swayed with the rhythm of the Ravi Shankar sitar music that was (actually) playing. We devoured each other with enormous electric sensations of touch and sight. If our friends hadn't> been present at the moment, we would have made love. These feelings went on for about an hour. (3:15 a.m.)

Suddenly I stood up and declared that I had seen a flash of dawn break through our windows. I pointed out to the rooftops of Paris that shone from our window. It was a very rich and beautiful sight.

Then, for no reason, I shifted to the 1930's. I declared, "Let's all go back to the '30's." I flashed on to thoughts I had had during the opening of my trip. Thoughts about Jack Oakie, Ronnie Reagan, George Murphy, Dick Powell, and Ruby Keeler appeared visually to me. In my mind I saw the movie

Vitaphone production, "42nd Street," the swirling girlie movie scenes of the '30's, and especially the college pictures. I wanted some college cheerleaders. It was all gay and magnificent. I was part of the '30's. I was a writer in the '30's.

I began to talk excitedly: "1 see all those fantastic college 9 movies with Dick Powell, Patsy Kelly, and Ronald Reagan. [At that time Reagan was governor of California.] Then, of course, Ronnie was really a 'mensch'-he was Reagan at his best, a laughing college boy with a big letter on his sweater. How did he get cast in this new role of governor? He belongs back there singing with Dick Powell in front of the girls dorm the night before the big game." We were all happy and laughing about these thoughts.

Everyone and everything in the room looked fantastic. The colors were deep and pulsating. Donna looked unbelievably beautiful and we decided to return to our Turkish mosque. This move happened several more times. (About 4:00 a.m.)

Nothing in the room had any sharp corners. Everything was curved, carved, rich, and ecstatically beautiful. The fire in the fireplace was brilliant. All of the people were shining images. Despite this enormous high feeling, several times during the night I panicked about being out of control. Part of me resisted being high on a drug.

Donna and I began to talk very rapidly about our love for each other, our child Mitch, and our friends. At certain moments we conflicted. When this happened her face began to sharpen like a witch's. I would bring her back to her beauty by changing the subject. Apparently there were areas of conflict I didn't want to pursue.

Arnie and Lyn left about this time (about 4:15 a.m.), "now that they knew we were OK." Ann, Donna, and I began to talk about the love we had for each other. Although I had known of my affection for Ann, I realized enormous waves of love for her as the daughter I had never had. At one point the three of us were hugging each other, crying and talking about the home we had all found with each other. It was sad, yet enormously beautiful.

All of our feelings were tremendously sharpened. It seemed rather amazing that Ann, who had taken no drug at all, could stay with all of our feelings and emotions. She wasn't patronizing or removed from our condition. With the exception of the hallucinatory effect of pulsating images, she was emotionally tuned-in. She apparently had what was called, in the LSD world, "a contact high."

We looked at a picture of our 3 1/!-year-old Mitchell, and it began to pulsate with life. He was exquisite. For that evening Mitch was sent to be with his grandmother]

We went back to our bedroom, where I previously had had my spiritual trip. Donna, Ann, and I began to discuss it. We all agreed I was "true blue Lew-a sincere American patriot." Donna looked at me and said seriously, but with joy, "1 really can see it. You love this country." I told her it was true. I was a patriot of the old school. Not a Bircher or bigot, or necessarily an admirer of Johnson's Great Society. I was a patriot in the Tom Payne sense. I wanted to help right the wrongs that existed in the country I loved.

We looked at flowers and oranges that pulsated with life. Donna and I focused on an orange and mutually saw molecules, fetuses, and electrical live pulses.

I flashed on a scene in my childhood back in Newark, N.J., where I would wait for my mother to throw a dime \vrapped in a newspaper to me from a third-story tenement window. The dime was my key to the beautiful movies of "42nd Street" and noble Dick Powell standing patriotically on the deck of a United States Navy ship wrapped in red, white, and blue, singing the corny, but beautiful song "Shipmates Stand Together, Don't Give Up the Ship."

Everything seemed corny and magnificent. We looked out from our balcony as the dawn seemed to break, about 5 :30 a.m. I literally felt myself in the center of a fantastic Swiss chalet looking over the roofs of a magnificent green countryside. The view was the actual one from Qur balcony, but it was enhanced a thousandfold.

At dawn I could begin to feel the drug in the pit of my stomach churning as the sharp coil continued to unwind. I felt control of it. We were now about six hours into the trip and I began to feel that I could turn the acid on in order to focus on an idea or a thing at will. I felt that I knew how much was left and that now the amount was finite. I thought about the book I was writing. And I had a distinct feeling that the carnival, newspaper, flower-child nature of the hippie scene was ludicrous and irrelevant within the framework of the enormous power and potential use of LSD.

I felt that acid was wasted on that scene and that it should be in the hands of more responsible people than the kids in the movement. I felt that some of the flower children were destroying themselves with this powerful drug. It was unfortunate because under proper conditions it could be an enormously valuable instrument.

This tripping out on that subject was interrupted by Donna entering and telling me about the resolution of her lifedeath conflict. She and Ann had discussed Donna's great fear of people dying. Donna talked intensely and eloquently about not living and loving fully because of a great sadness with the fact that "all this love and devotion disappeared with death." She had flashed on a new thought or insight that "all love goes on into the mainstream of life and that it is never lost." She saw the unity of all things and her connection to the cosmos.

We discussed the male-female delineation and agreed that men and women have a different total, life trip. Nomen have the power of creating life, and this is an area that men will never understand. We agreed that men were more superficially creative than women. Even men intellectually endowed involved in writing books and philosophy were insignificant compared to the power a woman has of giving life through childbirth. She copped out that, as a woman, she didn't fully understand and probably never would how men could focus for long periods of time on intellectual matters.

We happily agreed to let each other do our "own things." We agreed to help rather than to hassle each other. We were now a grand and harmonious duet. (About 6:00 a.m.)

Ann went downstairs to sleep. Donna and I returned to Turkistan and made love to the exotic sounds of Ravi Shankar, the LSD, and our hearts. About an hour later we took a bath together, ate lightly, and~ high as kites, drove the five minutes from our house to the Pacific Ocean.

My car (actually a silver gray 1967 Chrysler sedan) became a silver space ship zooming over the earth's surcracked up laughing when I truly noticed for the that my car's hood emblem was a red, white, and blue. I simply said, "Excalibur I"

We went for coffee at a small all-night coffee shop near the ocean. The scene was unbelievable. A motorcycle "wino" young men appeared to be more evil than any violent delinquent I had ever seen Despite the fact that I felt they eyed my wallet, I had no fear of them. A woman at the counter looked like a sparrow talking to an old man two seats away. I could actually see the rising through the veins on her gnarled hands!

We went to the beach. Here I found one of the most astonishing sights of the total experience. I saw the sand as a tan and gold rainbow-colored . the finest oriental rug in existence. The ocean blended with the sky and had every color in the rainbow. The air was clearer than I had ever known it

We went home about 10 :00 a.m. and sat in our back yard. An enormous, bright, very blue bluebird perched on the oleander tree in our yard. We both felt he was chirping a message to us and we tried hard to understand it. Donna talked to it. It was friendly and flew around the yard for an indeterminate time. We went back to our bedroom to rest and couldn't sleep. Our minds were too alive and active. For literally hours we discussed many old and new facets of all relationship and our marriage. We talked into the afternoon, as our high and hallucinatory visions faded out of existence.

In the early evening we knew that we had returned to a non-drug reality. We had dinner and then went to sleep around 9:00 p.m. I had not slept as deeply as I did that night for many years. We woke up the next morning at 7 AM. to what we both felt was a new and better world."

This account of my LSD experience was written about a week after it happened--in a first draft without any editing. I have left the report of the event in the original form in which it was written in order to convey some of the flavor of my emotions at that time.

The experience was enormously important to me in a way that I find difficult to communicate. It did produce some insights, essentially related to the strong love my wife and I felt for each other.

Another issue that I had never consciously pondered in depth was my red, white, and blue patriotism. Somehow my role as a sociologist was clarified. I could better understand how I found it absolutely vital to merge my personal self with my work.

In 2009, as I reread what I wrote about my trip--I found it both corny and amazing. I have never been a so-called spiritual person who believed in crazy stuff that happened to me during my trip. Yet that's the way it happened.

Another "happening" emanated from my research and work on THE HIPPIE TRIP at that time. It was an encounter I had with Gridley and testimony in a Los Angeles Superior Court.

Gridley used lots of drugs and marijuana daily. As a so called high priest in the movement he was on various radio talk shows discussing the wonderful things about drugs especially marijuana. On the air he mentioned that he was lighting up right then. When he got back to his car the police were waiting and arrested him. I didn't want to testify at his trial however he supoened me. In reality I never saw a day when I was with Gridley when he wasn't smoking pot.

However during my testimony at his trial I remembered that being in the presence, at that time, of someone using drugs was a legal violation. So like members of a mobster I took the 5th.

An LA Times reporter wrote my testimony up in the LA Times on ' October 11, 1967 as follows:

"A College professor took the Fifth Amendment nine times Tuesday when asked by a judge if he based his observations about marijuana on its being smoked in his presence. "I refuse to answer on the grounds that it might tend to incriminate me," Lewis Yablonsky replied to the questions put to him by Superior Judge Mark Brandler .... Yablonsky testified that Wright had helped him research a book he is writing, "The New Community The Hippie Scene." In the process, he said Wright, 33, had traveled with him to several hippie communities in California. He also testified that the "subculture" of hippiedom is "characterized by the prevalent use of psychedelic drugs."

Wright, who is acting as his own attorney, sought during his examination of the sociologist to establish that Wright used marijuana because he considers it a religious sacrament and that his use of the drug is neither injurious to society or himself. Yablonsky testified that he had found Wright docile during their travels and had heard the defendant discuss marijuana in a religious context on visits to hippie communities.

Most of the questions at which the professor balked resulted from Judge Brandler's asking if Wright had smoked marijuana during these discussions and travels."

I invoked the Fifth Amendment against self-incrimination for several reasons: (1) I did not want to drive another legal nail into Gridley's conviction; (2) according to a California statute, it is a misdemeanor to be in the presence of someone using illegal drugs; and (3) I have a firm belief in the rights and privileges of a research sociologist to be on any scene (even an illegal one) in the legitimate pursuit of acquiring social science research data. *

Gridley was not particularly disturbed by my testimony and in later discussions he told me he believed it helped his cause. In any event my testimony did not negatively affect our continuing research association.

At the conclusion of the two-week trial, the Judge called Gridley a "false prophet" and convicted him for the possession of marijuana. He appealed the case, but the conviction was upheld. Gridley was sentenced to five years on probation and was fined $300.00. A stipulation of his probation was that he would cease and desist from using and advocating the use of drugs. Of course he never stopped talking about the power of drugs, and ironically his probation was later revoked and he was Imprisoned.

What is ludicrous about my court experience with Gridley on that day 10/11/67 and the LA Times front page Report on the incident was that on that same day at CSUN there was a lunch in my honor for being awarded the all California State University Distinguished Professor Award. The court incident was on the front page and inside the LA Times was the announcement of my Distinguished Professor Award.

Gridley's militant philosophical position on drugs at his trial enhanced his status in the hippie world. His status in the "psychedelic revolution," however, had already been firmly established by his past almost legendary role as a founder and leader of a hip community known throughout the hippie world as "Strawberry Fields." The community lasted about six months and ended when an overturned candle set fire to the main building and reduced the place to ashes.

Of course, I was in Gridley's presence on many occasions when he was smoking pot. I chose not to admit to this situation at that time because the role of witness in a trial is an inflexible one that would not provide me with the necessary and proper opportunity to present all of the scientific reasons for the validity and necessary privilege of live-research. In brief, I am adamant about the rights of a social researcher to investigate live situations as they are happening.

The Gridley court incident no doubt influenced my being interviewed for the following Time Magazine article on the "risks" of deviant research":

TIME MAGAZINE Friday, Dec. 22, 1967
Universities: Risks of Research

The force of law in most cases protects the confidential nature of communications between lawyer and client, psychiatrist and patient, pastor and penitent (see RELIGION). Yet scientists studying antisocial or abnormal human behavior have no such protection, and are wide open to arrest for participating in illegal activities or concealing information about them. The result, many of them claim, is that little meaningful research is being done in the field of what sociologists call "deviant behavior."

The perils of this work were recently exemplified by the dilemma that faced California Sociologist Lewis Yablonsky, whose books on teen-age gang life in New York (The Violent Gang) and the Synanon cure for drug addiction (Synanon: The Tunnel Back) have been widely praised for telling it like it is. Yablonsky could tell it, because he lived with the people he studied—and his classroom presentation at San Fernando Valley State College this month earned him an "outstanding teacher" award over 9,000 of his colleagues in the California state colleges.

Shortly before he won the award, however, Yablonsky—who is now studying the hippie movement—was subpoenaed to testify at the marijuana trial of a friendly flower child. On the stand, Yablonsky pleaded possible self-incrimination and refused to answer nine questions aimed at discovering whether he had observed anyone smoking pot. "Of course I had," Yablonsky conceded out of court. "But I took the Fifth because I didn't want to go to jail. I feel very strongly that a sociologist should be able to study a social problem without fear of being guilty of illegal behavior." In his book on tne hippies, to be published in March, Yablonsky not only admits that he observed drug use and sales, but describes his own experiment with marijuana and a harrowing LSD trip he and his wife took together—all illegal activities.

The trip, Yablonsky contends, gave him "invaluable perspective" on the drug. Throughout his research, Yablonsky says, he found the possibility of arrest or being forced to reveal sources a "constant source of concern, anxiety and fear." It caused him to turn down an offer to meet "the biggest pusher in California." While such an interview might have aided his sociological insights, he figured that the need to keep the man's identity secret presented an insuperable scholarly dilemma. In the past, he has been bothered by revelations of unpunished crimes turned up in group-therapy work among *prison inmates and addicts, finally decided not to report them...To free the social scientist,*

Yablonsky argues, states should either pass laws granting immunity against prosecution to qualified researchers or allow attorney generals to grant immunity for specific projects. He vows never to take LSD again, opposes hallucinogenic drugs on medical, mental and legal grounds: "I find reality stimulating and interesting—I am against any artificial stimulants that foul up the emotions."

In 1968 when THE HIPPIE TRIP was published I was invited to lecture at numerous colleges, and among many other TV interviews I was invited to be on a talkshow with William F. Buckley. The program was of course Buckley's "Firing Line."

In 2006 a group of actors wrote and put on a play about the Buckley interview with Jack Kerouac and me. The off-Broadway play was favorably reviewed in the New York Times. The play was based on Buckley's interview with Kerouac, Ed Sanders and me with Allen Ginsberg chanting OM in the audience.

After I read the very positive New York Times Review I wrote up my experience on the program and sent the following commentary in 2/06 to the New York Times; and the letter that follows to the actor Vin Knight who played "Dr. Lewis Yablonsky" in the play. The commentary I sent to the "commentary" section of the Times was reprinted as follows:

"I am the "academic" Dr. Lewis Yablonsky referred to in Jason Zinoman's review of "No Great Society" in the NY Times. Around that time my book "The Hippie Trip" was published, and I went on a number of TV shows promoting the book. The Wm. F. Buckley Show with Kerouac and Sanders was part of my book tour. My memory of the actual evening of that TV show in 1968 may be of interest to the play's Director John Collins, Vin Knight who plays me as the Times review calls me a "nasal sounding Professor," and people who might see the play. This is my brief "memoir" (if you will pardon the expression) of the event.

It was a totally bizarre evening. When I arrived at Buckley's TV studio, which at that time was on top of a then porno movie theater on the corner of Broadway and 42nd Street, I was introduced by

Warren Steibel the producer to Kerouac in the Green Room prior to the Show. Kerouac was roaring drunk, and responded to my introduction, which he apparently didn't hear, by asking me, "Did you get the whiskey?" He mistook me for a go-fer he had sent out for another bottle.

During the hour show, I recall Kerouac being very drunk and nuts. To add to the weirdness of the evening, Allen Ginsberg was in the audience chanting OM for our good luck. During the taping breaks, off the air I recall Kerouac referring to Ginsberg as "that adorable fag."

While on the air Kerouac kept sliding off his chair, and Buckley kept smiling and benevolently propping him up. In a peculiar way Kerouac (alleged to be an anti-semite), when referring to me, kept insulting me. Spewing an anti-semitic undertone he kept slurring my name by sarcastically calling me "Skukinsky" and "Pupinsky." Finally, on national TV, I turned to Kerouac and said something like, "you know Kerouac I'm really tired of your anti-semitic bullshit." Buckley calmed us both down and the program continued. It was for me a memorable, crazy and fun night that shed no light on the purported theme of comparisons between the "hippies" and the "beat generation."

I emailed the commentary to Vin Knight who enacted the role of "Professor Lewis Yablonsky" in the play. He wrote back to me on 2/16/06 as follows:

To: expertwitness@lewyablonsky.com

Subject: Kerouac play

Dr. Yablonsky,

Thank you so much for your message. This is the first time I have ever had any contact with a person I play as a character, and I very much appreciate your sharing your memories of the Firing Line taping. It definitely appears from the videotape to have been a wildly unpredictable evening. We certainly try to recreate that feeling onstage. You seem to have been understandably and alternately bemused and irritated by Kerouac, and I hope I've been able to capture some of that. As for sounding nasal, I think that comment in the review is merely a reflection of a slight theatrical exaggeration in my characterization which I hope would entertain and not offend you. Working on this piece has been a completely enjoyable experience for me as I believe it has also been for our audiences. Speaking of which, Mr. Buckley was in attendance last night. He didn't stay afterwards to meet the cast, but he did speak to John [the director] and seemed to have had a good time.

(The legendary William F. Buckley died in 2009 after a remarkable career as a writer and TV interviewer. "The Firing Line" series of tapes are available from the Yale University Archives.)

From my viewpoint around 1969 the hippie "peace and love" movement took a turn to violence. I was interviewed around that time, and some of my viewpoints on the demise of the hippie phenomenon were presented in the following Time Magazine article:

TIME MAGAZINE Friday, Dec. 12, 1969 Nation:
Hippies and Violence

Part of the mystique and the attraction of the hippie movement has always been its invitation to freedom. It beckons young people out of the tense, structured workaday world to a life where each can do "his own thing." The movement has flowered and spread across the U.S. and to many parts of the world. It has drawn all sorts of people: the rebellious, the lonely, the poets, the disaffected, and worse.

Some two years ago, says Dr. Lewis Yablonsky, a close student of the phenomenon, criminals and psychotics began infiltrating the scene. They were readily accepted, as anyone can be who is willing to let his hair grow and don a few beads; they found, just as do runaway teenagers, that it is a good world in which they can disappear from law and society. "Hippiedom became a magnet for severely emotionally disturbed people," Yablonsky says.

A few of them, like Manson, also found other advantages to being a hippie. The true gentle folk were relatively defenseless. Leaderless, they responded readily to strong leaders. But how could children who had dropped out for the sake of kindness and sharing, love and beauty, be enjoined to kill? Yablonsky thinks that the answer may lie in the fact that so many hippies are actually "lonely, alienated people." He says: "They have had so few love models that even when they act as if they love, they can be totally devoid of true compassion. That is the reason why they can kill so matter-of-factly."

Yablonsky believes that there has been far more violence among the hippies than most people realize. "There has always been a potential for murder," he says. "Many hippies are socially almost dead inside. Some require massive emotions to feel anything at all. They need bizarre, intensive acts to feel alive—sexual acts, acts of violence, nudity, every kind of Dionysian thrill..."

When I was researching the HIPPIE TRIP I became good friends with David Smith. I acquired some great interviews with Dave at the Haight-Ashbury Clinic he founded. One day we were discussing the scene in a room at the clinic when I heard a belligerent booming voice saying, "Fuck you man. These are my girls, and you better take care of them right now!"

I went out in the hall and saw the guy yelling. It was Charles Manson and he was yelling at a doctor because he had to wait for his girls to be given care. This, of course, predated his becoming famous for his later murders. As stated in the Time article, quite a few violent criminals put on a peace necklace, came into the Haight, used drugs, had sex with the Hippie girls, and many committed acts of violence.

In total, my trip into hippieland and writing the book was a fascinating experience. In addition to encountering Gridley, Leary and Manson I met many interesting people who were attempting tu unshackle themselves from a conventional life. I recall asking one 16 year old who had runaway to Haight-Ashbury walling around with a full beard and stoned on a daily base, why he was there. He succinctly said, "My parents have made it in America. They have everything you could possible have materially, and they are not happy. Maybe there is an answer to a better life here in the Haight."

Chapter 6

George Raft, Hollywood and Psychodrama (1970 to 1980)
Researching and Writing About Raft

Around 1970, after my trip into hippieland, I had become somewhat disinterested in crime, delinquency, hippies and directing therapeutic sessions. I wanted to strike out in another direction.

I was always a movie buff and, growing up in Newark admiring mobsters of the 1920s, found George Raft a tough role-model of a man in his many movies. When I was around 10 or 11 I recall yelling up to my mom on the 3d floor of the 6 apartment building we were living in at that time asking for her to throw down a dime. This would get me into the Hawthorne movie. There were usually 2 films playing back to back and a bunch of short subjects like Popeye, Betty Boop (who was a very sexy cartoon character) and Flash Gordon. I saw most of the movies that are now being shown on TCM when they originally came out. I especially liked the gangster movies like the original "Scarface."

One of my favorite actors was George Raft. Not the greatest actor of his time but certainly, by todays terminology "the coolest." A real man, who took no crap from anyone. And I felt real terrible when I saw him in the original and best movie of SCARFACE (1932) when Paul Muni playing an Al Capone character killed him for messing with his sister played by Ann Dvorak. Forget Al Pacino's imitation Scarface. Raft and Paul Muni were the real McCoy.

I had a good agent around 1974--the Reece Halsey Agency. Reece and his wife Dorris who ran the agency on Sunset were great people, good friends, and helped me publish several book. In reviewing the old movie heros I liked, I had mulled over the 3 actors whose biography I wanted to write about, and sociologically covered the old Hollywood in the process. There, of course, was Cagney, Bogart, and Raft. Cagney was a great actor--but his personal life was dull. Bogart's bio had been done. Raft, according to some reports, had been a genuine rum-running gangster in NY before coming to Hollywood. I thought wouldn't it be great to do his bio.

One day I called Reece and said, I would like to do George Raft's bio. Given my prior book subjects, I thought he would say, "Lew, what have you been smoking". Instead he said, I deal with Ray Milland's agent who also manages Raft--I'll get back to you."

A few days later Reece called me and said, "I have a meeting set up with you Raft and his agent." I was excited to go to the agents office on Beverley Boulevard in Beverley Hills--and meet one of my movie heroes.

It was a weird meeting because as we were introduced and discussed the possibility of my doing Raft's bio he seemed unhappy and not really interested. In fact Raft kind of glowered at me like he did to enemies in his movies. I thought I was in one of his old movies. Being the way I am, very direct, I interrupted the discussion and said, "George what's the problem." He said, "why would you set up that guy downstairs to keep tossing a coin up in the air like I did in SCARFACE? I told him I never did that.

I later found out that some guy downstairs from the office saw Raft getting out of his Cadillac and though he would perform a good gag by flipping a coin like Raft did in SCARFACE. After I cleared up the fact that I had nothing to do with the gangster, we went on to make a 50-50 deal for me to write Raft's biography.

From that point on George and I hit it off and I met with him many times for around 2 years in writing the biography. He was around 80 at the time and lived in a Condo, probably set up for him by the mob, in Century City. He had blown most of the money he made in films on good times and bad investments. He not only cooperated with me on the book--we became good friends. We hung out together at his place, restaurants, and he came to my home several times.

One time he invited me to a ceremony with Mae West at the unveiling of her statute at the Buena Park Wax Museum near Disneyland. There I met luminaries like Lloyd Nolan, Rock Hudson--and the several other leading men from Mae West's films. It was a memorable day for the star struck kid from Newark to meet some of my old movie heros.

Another time I recall George invited me to a gala celebrity ceremony which included Gregory Peck and other stars at the Beverley Wilshire Hotel. George had a job at that time with the Riviera Vegas Hotel that had an office across from the Hotel. A columnist Walter Winchell once asked George what his job was with the Vegas Riviera Hotel, "My job is to tell people like you that I work for the Riviera Hotel."

George invited me to attend his "roast" for the Friar's Club. There were around 500 people in the ballroom at the Beverley Hilton Hotel It was a most entertaining evening. All the top comedians were there and other celebrities on the diaz including Frank Sinatra, Dean Martin, and Cary Grant. I don't recall which comics who were roasting Raft told the following gags--but they were funny. One was to the best of my recollection, "George in a movie played a terrorist who was suppose to blow up a car. He's so dumb he burned his mouth on the exhaust pipe.

The other gag I remember was a comic who became very somber and serious in his delivery. He turned to the crowd and said something like the following: "Frankly I'm disgusted with all of you and the penis jokes being told here about George. You are grown men and this is an adult audience, and yet the presenters keep talking about the size of this man's penis!" The audience did squirm a little, and were quiet. The comic than said, "I'm not going to mention Georges penis---However, I would like to say a few words about his balls." You had to be there.

It was a gala night for me to meet one of my movie idols Carey Grant. He was a regular guy, and joined in with the evenings nonsense. Somehow, he and I talked briefly about my doing Raft's biography. I, of course, in a nice way asked him if he would be interested in my doing his bio. I gave him my card with my phone number.

About a week later, I picked up the phone, and there was the elegant voice of Carey Grant! My first reaction was someone was imitating Grant and putting me on. However it was really him thanking me for asking about doing his bio--but he was too busy, etc. What a mensh to call me back!

Raft's sidekick, and gofer Mack Grey, a friend from George's New York days, told me the following story about Raft's generosity during his days of stardom. They were on an elevator going to visit someone. The elevator man commented on what a sharp suit Raft was wearing. According to Mack, "George whipped off the jacket, and told the guy to stop in later for the pants. George was a soft touch for his old friends from New York, and squandered most the large amount of money he made giving loans to old friends.

Mack was nicknamed "the Killer." I asked Mack, whose real name was Greenberg, "how did you get that name."

I expected some sinister violent story from his past. He told me he once visited George's then girlfriend Betty Grable, and he was limping. She asked what was wrong? Mack had just received a hernia operation, and told her the Yiddishe word for hernia--a "I have a killa." From then on Grable would laughingly call him the killer.

I met many celebrities, who were friends of Raft in the process of my writing the biography GEORGE RAFT. George would call and set me up with interviews with many stars who had something to say about him. In my interview with her, Lucille Ball told me how George had helped her out financially when she first came to Hollywood and was broke. Mae West was grateful to George, who knew her in N.Y. for insisting on having her first movie appearance in a speakeasy drama he was in called "Night After Night."

Other stars I interviewed through Raft's introduction included Fred Astaire, Walter Mathau, Frank Sinatra, and Edward G. Robinson. He would call them up and usually say something like "Lew Yablonsky is writing my biography and maybe you would meet with him and give him a few stories about our relationship." They were always happy to comply because everyone liked Raft. Unlike like some of his movie roles, he was a kind and generous man.

George had brought Mae West to Hollywood for her first movie which launched her stardom. In this first movie a dowager at a party says to Mae as they are sashayin along at a party "Goodness--what beautiful diamonds you are wearing." And Mae's reply was "Goodness had nothing to do with it." That line and others she coined like: "Is that a gun in your pocket, or are you just glad to see me" became famous. Or her line, Too much of a good thing is great."

I thoroughly enjoyed several meetings with Mae West. She owned among other properties in Malibu and LA the Ravenswood apartments just south of Vine in Hollywood. It was a tall apartment complex. After Raft called her she invited me over for an interview.

I arrived breathless on the top floor apartment for our first meeting. It was in the afternoon. I was shooed into the all-white apartment by a weightlifter (who I later found out was in her Vegas act) and serviced her sexually. He was wearing a cutaway bankers coat with striped grey pants--like a butler.

This was in mid-afternoon. Inside the apartment everything was in white. There was a white nude statute of Mae from her earlier days. I sat down on a plush white chair only to be quickly told "Miss West sits there--you sit over there."

Around 5 minutes later she came sashaying into the room in a peach negligee. She was very cordial, and her screen sexy self. Few people now remember what a sex symbol she was in the 1930s when I saw her in her many movies. At 84 she still had it for this 50 year old sociologist.

During the interview we started talking about how Raft who knew her in NY had brought her to Hollywood to star in George's early movie "Night After Night." George played a speakeasy owner and Mae played a sexy Mae West. The conversation quickly veered from Raft to West. This, I found was true about most celebrities I interviewed. They would talk briefly about Raft then they switched over to talking about themselves.

Mae still had "it" for me. I thought it was a possibility that she had more in mind when she ushered me into her plush bedroom to show me where the ghost of her former pet monkey still hovered over the bed. Mae was into believing in ghosts. While in the bedroom, we were interrupted several times by her jealous butler weight lifter--so the sexual event of my teenage dreams never came to pass.

Mae liked me, and I was invited back several times to meet with her. One time she invited me to a seance with a psychic named Kenney Kingston who at that time was the psychic to the stars. The highlight of one of my meetings with Mae was the day she sat across from me and began singing in her inimitable voice "Frankie and Johnny were sweethearts,etc..." She was a great lady.

Among other stars I met and interviewed through the auspices of George Raft for the biography was Lucille Ball--who told me how she was loaned money by Raft when she began working in Hollywood. At the time of my interview with Lucy--she was in bed with a broken ankle from a ski accident. She was charming and told me several stories of the old Hollywood. Of all people, when I was interviewing Lucy, Patty Andrews of the famous Andrew sister also visited the bedroom.

Another fascinating interview for me was with one of my idols the fantastic movie star and dancer Fred Astaire. He was as he appeared on screen a nice sweet guy. I kvelled about how I had seen and loved all of his movies with Ginger Rogers. I asked him if he knew when they were making the Astaire-Rogers movies that they would be classics? He demurred and said: "When we were making those movies we never thought they were that great. One time when I did this dance with Ginger she was wearing a heavy beaded dress. The reason I was dancing so fast was to get away from being hit by the beads on her dress."

A most interesting interview for me was with movie tough guy "Little Caesar" Edward G. Robinson. He had co-starred in a movie called MANPOWER with Marlene Dietrich and Raft. After the movie was made there had been gossip columns and screen magazine stories stating they had competed and actually fought each other for the love and affection of Marlene--off screen.

In my interview which obviously was many years after the movie I noticed that this great star seemed very nervous. I said, "Mr. Robinson is something wrong? He replied, "Is George still mad at me? I then found out they had a scene in the MANPOWER movie where Raft took his friend Robinson forcefullY out of a bar. This scene had resulted in an off-screen fist fight after the cameras stopped rolling.

Now years later, the great actor, Robinson was still worried that Raft was mad at him. I later told George about Robinson's question. He called Robinson and they laughed about the incident and again were good friends.

My Raft book was quite successful and Robert Kirsh's review in the LA Times 6/23/74 was very positive. Kirsch wrote:

"George Raft has assured 'himself a place in the pantheon of film personality through his one brilliant role: George Raft. Coot, elegant,

assured. offscreen and on masked passion, turbulence,. sensitivity." Class was his ideal.and he believed in a gambler's luck.

That Lewis Yablonsky has-written a biographical study of the actor, "George Raft" (Mc'Graw-Hill, 1974) is ·a piece of luck for him and for the reader. Yablonsky,' a sociologist and one of the foremost authorities on psychodrama, raises the book from ordinary showbiz profile to a penetrating insight into the relationship between personality and screen image. Like much about Raft the book has class...

He made a living as a male taxi dancer, little more than a gigolo. became an entertainer, a Broadway character, came out. to Hollywood. where he began to play the roles which he had observed in real life.

Raft's acting often could not remain within the boundaries of make believe. He seemed to' be carried away. Edward G. Robinson, who was to became a friend and booster of Raft, told of a screen fight in which 'Raft could not , stop even after the director yelled, "Cut!" "It was as if the role bad taken over the man...As an actor Raft's range was limited-he always 'played George Raft...

His later life proved difficult and he would have more than his share of troubles. These be met and is meeting with poise and grace. This surely accounts. for "his continuing presence in the mythos of America; films are the projection of the national psyche and Raft has an enduring place. In this book, we see why."

My Raft book was a best seller. My publisher McGraw-Hill received and placed the following comments on the book jacket:

"The-story of my good friend George's climb from the roudy speakeasy clubs on Broadway in the twenties to the top of Hollywood stardom is an exciting American -saga. Reading George's biography by Lew Yablonsky is the next best thing to being there." -**FRANK SINATRA**

"The most roguishly appealing movie bio since Errol Flynn's My Wicked, Wicked Ways." **Kirkus Reviews**

"A richly documented·biography. Drawing on the reminiscences of major Hollywood figures who knew Raft well, Yablonsky probes deep!y into Raft's early life-his emergence from New York's Hell's Kitchen, his career as a dancer, boxer, friend and associate of gangsters, ladiesman and finally a major Hollywood star. There *is-a vast nostalgia appeal here. Yablonsky's writing is sensitive; his portrait of Raft firmly set in his era ..... Publishers Weekly*

A great story. George was an important and exciting star. When better men like George are made-then I'll make 'em:'-MAE WEST

When the book was published I visited with George at his home. He was pleased with the book, although he never read the final manuscript. He did have one weird comment about the book. He said, Meyer [Lansky the mob boss}called me after he read the book. He didn't like what you said about him and Bugsy Siegal stealing cars." I told George, "there's nothing I can do about that--the book is printed and out." When I got home I looked up the section George was referring to. In one paragraph, I had written based on my research that Siegal and Lansky had an auto theft racket at one time. Further down, I mentioned that Lansky and Siegal ran "Murder, Inc." in New York. That apparently didn't bother Lansky but the small time stuff like auto theft bothered him.

On another occasion, after the book was out, George had an illness and I visited him in the hospital. It was shortly before he died. There were quite a few of his old pals from his earlier years at his bedside. They were very cordial when he introduced me as the author of his biography. Then George said, "You know Lew's brother heads up the FBI office in Vegas." There was a marked change in their attitude toward me, and they clammed up and viewed me with suspicion.

George died on November 24, 1980 the day after my birthday. I was in New York at the time with my family, and regretted not being at a large memorial for him in Vegas. I have very pleasant memories of him and the times we spent together. I often see his old movies like "Manpower" and "They Drive by Night" with great pleasure on TVs Turner Classic Movies. In the latter movie Raft had the leading role, and Bogart was in a co-staring role as his kid brother. Bogart is, of course, in the history of film considered the more versatile and bigger star. However, for me, my friend George was a major star who I will always remember with great fondness. Writing his biography was a significant part of my life.

Reflections on Raft, Acting and Getting Psychodrama on Television

In Kirsch's review of my book he accurately pointed out that Raft always played the same movie character "Raft." The image he had created on screen was George Raft. Other actors, like Spencer Tracey or Lawrence Olivier played many different roles that were not their own personna.

Moreno in his writings always accurately pointed out that we were actors in our many life roles. The relationship between acting in a movie or play, and acting in reality always intrigued me, and was a significant aspect of my work in psychodrama.

Researching Raft for his biography caused me to think about various issues related to acting, role-playing in real life and psychodrama. Raft was an interesting case study on this subject. Without question despite his earlier life personas as a dancer or sometime gangster, Raft was in over a 100 movies, and acted out over 100 screen roles. They were always Raft.

In the process of writing Raft's biography, I spent over a hundred hours in personal discussions with George. I found him to be a man who had a profound problem most of his life with what Moreno in his writings on psychodrama termed the "histrionic syndrome." Essentially this is a situation where the role an actor is asked to portray conflicts with his self-image and his life in reality and this causes a personal problem.

When Raft worked at Warner Brothers in the thirties and forties, he became part of a star system that included many fine actors such as Edward G. Robinson, Bette Davis, Paul Muni, and James Cagney. For these actors, unlike Raft, there was usually a limited confusion between the roles they played on screen and their personal identity. They had their own personal identity outside of the roles they enacted in movies.

Most actors can throw themselves into their role and understand this is simply a role they are playing for theatrical purposes. Some maintain the role 24 hours a day during the making of the film. At a recent Kennedy honors ceremony (2009), most of the commentary on Robert DiNiro stated that he became the person he was playing. Although he personally was an artist and an articulate intelligent man off screen--on screen he became "the raging bull" fighter Jake LaMotta or a psychotic taxi driver.

This was not true of George Raft. He invariably played himself on the screen, and this fostered his histrionic syndrome. In brief, the other actors used an acting skill to portray a role, whereas Raft tended to portray a character based to a great extent on roles he had actually played in life. Raft's personal relationship to his theatrical roles was complex.

As a psychodramatist and therapist I noted that Raft's cool screen facade masked a man plagued by phobias, nervous habits, and hidden fears. His feelings about himself were sometimes so negative that he looked into a mirror only when he combed his hair, and then he rushed the process.

Since his earliest movies, Raft consistently refused to view himself on the screen. After he saw his first movies, he refused to see the rushes, rough cuts, or even the final prints of any of his subsequent films.

I was with George when he appeared on the Johnny Carson show to plug our book. It was an interesting experience for me and Raft. In addition I enjoyed meeting Johnny Carson. When interviewing Raft, Carson showed an old film clip of Raft's movie "Bolero" where he danced with Carol Lombard. Carson was amazed to see Raft turn away when the clip was being shown. When Carson questioned him about this avoidance, Raft replied, "I'm afraid to look, because I'm probably awful."

Most actors do not see their "self," when they looked at themselves on the screen; they see a performance. But Raft's involvement with the roles he played and his self-concept made it painful for him to see his actual "self" on the screen.

In my interviews I found that in real life, Raft had battled his way to stardom from a childhood of poverty in Hell's Kitchen, New York. In Raft's later years, when he became an affluent Hollywood film star, he was like the "Golden Boy" of Clifford Odets' great play.

In a commentary on this play, about a fighter who rose up from poverty, Smith Clurman made a penetrating comment on what might be called The Golden Boy Syndrome. It characterizes George Raft's life and is revealing about what later led to his personal problems of role confusion on and off the screen.

Clurman writes, "The story of this play is not so much the story of a prizefighter as the picture of a great fight-a fight in which we are all involved, whatever our profession or craft. What the golden boy of this allegory is fighting for is a place in the world as an individual; what he wants is to free his ego from the scorn that attaches to "nobodies" in a society in which every activity is viewed in the light of a competition. He wants success not simply for the soft life-automobiles, etc.-which he talks about, but because the acclaim that goes with it promises him acceptance by the world."

In the play, the heroe became a fighter to achieve his goals--Raft became an actor to achieve stardom.

I can't resist here inserting Marlon Brando's classic comment as Terry Malloy in the movie
"On the Waterfront" when he discussing with his brother how he threw a fight he could have won. He tells his brother, "I could have taken that guy any time. He became a contender and I got a one way ticket to Pallookavile. Your my brother you should have taken care of me. I could have been a contender. Instead I'm a bum, which is what I am."

In Raft's case, the actor's main attribute was his tough-guy looks, his style, and his flip-of-the-coin gambler attitude on the screen. This he had acquired from being a dancer on Broadway, hanging out with reallife gangsters, and being a part-time hood himself, involved with bootlegging during Prohibition.

In a peculiar way, Raft believed that the roles he was asked to play represented his personal self. He once told me, "I was offered this part of a judge who is so corrupt he pushes dope. I couldn't play that role."

George's personal and screen role-conflict manifested itself in another parallel situation. He was asked by film mogul Samuel Goldwyn to play the part of Baby Face Martin in the film called Dead End. In the role, he was to portray a psychopathic killer sought by the police who hides out in the New York slum where he was raised as a boy. Raft balked at one particular facet of Martin's character: He told me "In the part I am, on the lam, hiding out around this neighborhood in cellars and places like that and I meet this gang of kids . One gang member recognizes me as this killer, Baby Face Martin. The gang begins to idolize me-and I'm supposed to teach these kids how to be tough and how to be a criminal. I couldn't bring myself to do that." Raft turned the part down, and it went to Bogart.

In one situation, in his role he was suppose to play the role of a man who lost his mother, and was to place flowers on her grave. Raft told the director he couldn't do it he, The director asked "Why." Raft's answer was "because my mother is still alive." The director insisted, and a fist fight ensued between Raft and the director.

Raft's insistence at not playing these roles reveals his histrionic syndrome. He tended to confuse his own self with the theatrical roles he was asked to perform for film.

This type of histrionic syndrome problem emerges when an actor's self-identity becomes schizoid. A role conflict about who the person really is becomes confused with his theatrical identity. As an actor's wife who had the problem with her husband once told me, "When my husband comes home, I don't know whether it's going to be my husband Joe, King Lear, or John Dillinger."

Doing the time I was writing the Raft book my comprehension of the relationship between acting and my role as a psychodramatist was enhanced.

During this period, I continued my work in psychodrama at my Institute, and the issue of the complexity of role-playing" became clearer. Doing the Raft's book enlarged my understanding of psychodrama.

PSYCHODRAMA ON TELEVISION

Around that time a TV producer from PBS contacted me about doing psychodrama project on TV. The Project was to be filmed in Public Broadcasting System studio in Pittsburgh. Consequently, before the enormous number of "reality shows" now shown on TV, I was able through PBS to develop and put on the screen a number of reality shows of average people in their psychodramas.

Over the years I have directed a number of psychodrama sessions that were videotaped or filmed and later projected to a mass audience. The one I directed on PBS network television was the best one. The production I directed involved over fifty hours of psychodrama in a television studio with a "repertory" group of people who were randomly auditioned and cast from the community. The people selected were told, if they were willing, they would be presenting their personal dramas on TV. This was in 1972 more than 35 years before Dr. Phil, and other reality shows on TV

The group selected for the PBS series was composed of a cross-section of people recruited for the show. The group included old, young, black, brown, and white, with varying political positions.

All of the sessions were videotaped over ten days of psychodrama sessions that I directed, and the best sessions were edited and utilized for the 12 programs that were aired on 226 PBS stations around the country.

The sessions were slices of Americana and included: a black woman whose militant activities against racism and the oppression of women produced complex family problems; an articulate and creative man in a robot job who felt he had wasted his life; a poor gas station attendant who fervently believed in and defended a society that had obviously given him the short end; a young black man who believed on a deep level that the death of his "Uncle Tom" father would end an era, liberate him and his own son from experiencing racism; a young woman who vacillated and commuted between a hip, communal life and a "straight" existence; a young gay man into gay liberation who was having "marital problems" with his wife, Bill; and other, more standard lifestyle problems.

The programs shown on the PBS stations around the country seemed to reach some deep levels of human experience and had an impact on many people beyond the immediate group. This was evidenced by the audience response in thousands of letters that indicated a personal identification with the problems and conflicts presented on television sessions I directed.

The program also received positive critical reviews on this perspective of mass impact from over a hundred media sources. Several specific critics (in addition to many others) analyzed and reflected a positive response to the intent and meaning of the programs. Following are some of the critical reviews:

Lewis Yablonsky Ph.D

Newsweek, November 6, 1972

Psychodramas: 'The Family Game" offers an entirely different family line. The twelve-week series, produced by WQED in Pittsburgh for the Public Broadcasting Service's network of 226 stations, presents real parents and children in a taped, groupencounter session, in the hope that viewers will apply the psychodramas to their own problems. Guided by sociologist Lewis Yablonsky, participants act out their most intense feelings about freedom and authority, sex, drugs and race prejudice.

On a recent segment, a middle-aged gas-station manager named Tony angrily tangled with several counterculturists in the group. "You need mental treatment!" he exploded after learning that a young girl panelist was shacking up in a commune. Another searing moment came when a troubled young black pointed an imaginary gun at his middle-class father and spewed out a lifetime of loathing for the way his father was "playing' whitey's game." At the close of each show, the leader urges viewers to adapt the discussions to their own hangups.

The New York Times
Sunday, October 1, 1972

. . . a young black man, encounters his own despair. He rages against his father for allowing white society to humiliate him. He rages against that society for forcing his father, and him, to play its game. And he rages at the knowledge that it will do the same to his son. With the help of another participant, he acts out a confrontation with his father in which he threatens to kill him. He affirms violent revolt. "A pistol puts you in charge." And through it all, he cries.

It is a rage and a pain black people-particularly black people with children-must deal with somehow. But it is not a parlor game. Even with the gently controlling presence~e of master psychodramatist, Dr. Lewis Yablonsky, the reassuring social director of the psyche who set up these episodes, George's responses are personally explosive. -

Buffalo Courier Express October 10, 1972 (Buffalo, New York)

Accustomed to stagnant spectator roles before the big eye in the living room, we've gone a long way toward losing the art of conversation and, more particularly, the art of communicating meaningfully with each other. "The Family Game" hopes to start us on the way back. Subtitled "Identities for Young and Old," the half-hour programs enable us to watch real people-not movie stars-act out their feelings on subjects that touch their daily lives. There is real drama here. It is not soap suds. The series deals realistically with fathers and sons, drugs, sex, religion, what real patriotism is, and other gut issues troubling us today in all our homes.

Around 8 years later after the THE FAMILY GAME appeared on TV I was approached by an ABC producer to be a consultant on doing a TV series on psychodrama. I was hired as a consultant, not the director, because the producer want "a younger host." I was around 50,The producer hired a psychologist David Viscount who at that time was a talk radio star. He claimed to be a knowledgeable psychodrama director. We had weeklong rehearsals for the Project. I directed them as a warmup for the actual filming because Viscount had not directed many psychodramas. I was to was hired as a consultant and part of the production staff to teach Viscount more about the method.

I directed a number of preliminary sessions. We filmed in a Hollywood studio with Viscount learning. Some of the sessions I directed I recalled involved a young man from NY who had a problem with his father; a divorced woman having difficulty raising her children, and some other prototypical problems. Among the many sessions we filmed, for me, the most interesting one involved a woman who had been a prostitute for 20 years, and wanted to quit her profession. I remember playing the role of a "trick" who was imploring her not to quit since she was an important person in my life. When I viewed the screening of the film, like Raft, I thought I was awful.

Average citizens were solicited as subjects; and people who had worked with me at my psychodrama Institute as auxiliary egos were hired as regulars. They were a kind of repertory group. I had an actor who played leading man role; a lady who a mother figure, and some others who were excellent at role-playing. The rehearsal psychodrama were really a prelude to the current (in my opinion awful) reality shows that now pillute television.

Dr. David Viscount was dredged up to do the psychodramas for the pilot that we made. He was not a good psychodramatist. Viscount was flamboyant but he really did not understand the hardcore meaning of psychodrama as a method for helping people. He saw psychodrama as a theatrical TV production for entertainment. However, we did get people to participate as subjects, and filmed around 10 programs in one week. The pilot was shown on ABC; however, it was not picked up by the network as a series.

My work in psychodrama in my classes at California State University and on TV caught the attention of many people. I was popular enough at that time to catch the editors of "PEOPLE" magazine.

The following article appeared in PEOPLE on 8/8/77 by writer Eleonore Hoover. The article with pictures went as follows:

"In the last 27 years California sociology professor Lewis Yablonsky has directed more than 3,000 psychodramas, playing "every role in Western civilization from pimp to President."

"Most people are locked into an image which dominates their life," Yablonsky observes. "Psychodrama allows them to be somebody else. Best of all, it provides an opportunity for them to act out their violence without hurting anyone. Few people know how angry they are." Psychodrama was pioneered in the 1920s by Yablonsky's mentor and friend, the late Viennese trained psychiatrist J. L. Moreno.

Yablonsky, 53, and his wife, Donna, operate a weekend workshop in Los Angeles called the California Institute of Psychodrama. Participants are given soft paddles, or Batacas, and encouraged to pummel one another to let out repressed anger.

On a typical Friday evening Yablonsky began with about 25 men and women, who paid $75 to attend. Myra, a quiet housewife in her mid-40s, who was attending with her therapist, complained that her husband was cold and rejecting. Yablonsky quickly set up a "dialogue" with another participant who played the husband. At

Yablonsky's suggestion, Myra (not her real name) hit the man with a Bataca and screamed out why she was angry. Soon she was sobbing in rage while the group chanted encouragement. Then, in a reverse, she was cast in the role of the husband to try to understand his view of the situation.

By the end of the second day Myra was clear-eyed and smiling. She had learned from the group that her complaint was a common one, shared by most of the women there. Yablonsky summed up: "She was able to get out her feelings and explore her worst fears in a safe environment." Her therapist believes that the session helped Myra avoid a breakdown.

At the state university in Northridge where he teaches, Yablonsky has assigned students to reenact such chilling events as Jack Ruby's killing of Lee Harvey Oswald, the Manson family's murder of Sharon Tate and the suicide of Freddie Prinze. The purpose: to feel what it's like to "be inside the other guy's skin," an experience which is "the first law of psychodrama."

Through psychodrama, Yablonsky, whose academic specialty is criminology, has helped talk street gangs out of murder and despondent people out of suicide. He even fell in love with Donna during a psychodrama at Synanon in Santa Monica 16 years ago, when she was acting out a teenage drug episode. She is, Yablonsky says lovingly, "My NO.1 associate and best friend." They often solve family problems by trading roles-"mediating and moderating our extreme positions. It is a profound learning experience."

The author of 10 books, including The Violent Gang, a highly praised 1962 study of urban delinquents, and the recently published Psychodrama, Yablonsky grew up In Newark where his immigrant father drove a laundry truck. As a boy young Lew was beaten by blacks because he was white and by Nazi Bundists because he was Jewish.

When his best friend went to prison for hijacking, Yablonsky decided, "We had to get on one side of the law or the other." His brother joined the FBI, and Yablonsky went to Rutgers, took his doctorate at NYU and taught at the University of Massachusetts and UCLA. Four years after coming to Northridge in 1963, he was voted the "outstanding professor" among 9,000 faculty members in the state system...

Chapter 7

My Research into the Extra Sex

Factor

Despite the positive news reports, Donna and I were having our problems. To the outside observer my marriage to Donna was idyllic. We worked together in psychodrama, and were loving parents to Mitch However, there were chinks in the armour. I was always very researching and writing my books, directing psychodrama and teaching. Donna began to get bored and go out. I recall discussing the situation with a psychologist friend of mine--at the time when I had several books being published in one year. He said, "Possibly Donna finds it hard to live with you. She is an aspiring actress who isn't getting very far with her dreams. You on the other hand are doing great. She might be jealous of your success. You tell me that she rations sex with you. That may be the only power she feels she has." His diagnosis was apparently correct, and slowly but surely we drifted into a secret but open marriage.

Since this book is in part a confessional I must admit to several affairs at that time that society would view as incorrect. One was with a very beautiful 22 year old student who I will call Maria.

During the period of the criminology course she took with me she was straight A student, and very sharp in class discussion. I could tell she was enamored with me. At the final day of the class, I told her that I thoroughly enjoyed her A paper, and invited her to my office to discuss it. (How crass can a Professor be.) She was happy to accompany me, and we, as the kids called it necked. This later became a regular sexual tryst--where we met once a week for several weeks at a local hotel. She was terrific and we both enjoyed the affair. It ended on a sad note since I was married at the time, and she wanted to go further with our relationship. I always remember Maria and the affair as sweet and beautiful.

In my some 50 years as a Professor, I only had a few affairs with students. Another memorable one was with an extremely beautiful 20 year old I will call Meg. She came to my office often to discuss the criminology theories we had discussed in class. I was around 50 at the time and did have some moral scruples on getting involved with a young girl like Meg. The affair was launched in a ridiculous way.

I often had special guest speakers at my criminology classes. One was a guy who became a friend named Albie Baker. He was a well known jewel thief who had authored a book called STOLEN SWEETS. His book was the foundation for the great Carey Grant Hitchcok film "To Catch a Thief." At Albies lecture to my class to my class he brought a friend who was a man named Green who had been famous photographer of Marilyn Monroe. After class we had coffee, and they talked about nothing but the beautiful Meg. Albie, who had sociopathic tendencies could not understand why I would not pluck this gorgeous girl from the vine. Albie inspired my weaker side.

Around this time Donna and I were separated. Meg lived in a campus apartment. During the break, at the next class I asked Meg about her apartment--lying that I was interested in renting and moving on campus. She jumped at the cue, and invited me to look at her apartment. I did and we did. She was quite sensational. She earned an A in the class, and when the semester ended--she ended our relationship. OY!

Around that time I had a few other affairs that were not with students. The beginnings of the breakup with my wife motivated my participation in several extra-marital affairs. My extra-sex, as I called it, piqued my interest in the subject. I started to do some research along these lines--read Kinsey's books and became somewhat involved "for research reasons" in some of the sex scenes that were taking place in Los Angeles at that time. I became heavily into the research and developed sufficient material for a book proposal. Through my agent Reece Halsey I acquired a contract with NY Times Books for a book on extramarital sex.

Los Angeles Magazine heard about my research project and after I was interviewed published the following article appeared in the Magazine. Los Angeles Magazine 8/78 "Sex and the Married Professor"

In 1948 Alfred Kinsey found that over half of all married men played around; today, 30 years later, a Cal State Northridge sociology professor has found that that figure still holds-but also that the men who are doing it are doing it more often and with much less guilt.

This fall, Lewis Yablonsky will be publishing his findings in The Extra-Sex Factor: Why Over Half of America's Married Men Play Around for New York Times Books and hopes that it may "vitiate many wives' pain at discovering their husbands' affairs-because it really has nothing to do with them."

Yablonsky, who lives in Marina Del Rey, says that 80 per cent of the over 800 men surveyed "love their wives, have satisfying sex lives with them and in no way want to leave their marriages. They have enormous motivation to keep the home together-what I call a strong homing instinct." The mustachioed professor found it "surprising" that the most frequent reason cited for extramarital sex was "I enjoy relationships with other women, and sex is part of that" rather than reasons having to do with dissatisfaction in the marriage.

Yablonsky, who's also authored books on delinquency, criminology, Synanon and role playing, is hard at work on his next "extra-sex" book this one focusing on women. So far, he's found that extramarital sex for women "is much more related to lifestyle dissatisfaction-there's much more agony of monogamy."

My personal sexuality has always been an important factor in my life--possibly too important. My sexual obsessions started in my early years with Ruthie, my excitement by the flamboyant strippers in my youth at the Empire Burlesque, and my sexual activity in the Navy. It's no mystery that I married a lady who had been a "loose-lady" when she had been involved in drugs. My assumption about Donna based on our hot pre-marital sex was that I was going to have all the great sex with her my active libido desired.

Given these elements of my life my motivation for writing a book on the subject of sex was a foregone conclusion. Doing the book gave me the cover for becoming what we term in sociology a "participant-observer. This gave me the license, and enabled me, as a function of my research, to became involved in the sex scenes that were going on in LA at that time.

Two of the experiences I had, among others are notable. One was with an older woman. When the article in LA Magazine came out I received a number of phone calls inviting me to what might be termed sex parties. One call was from a woman who told me she had participated in many sexual orgies. What was especially interesting about her was that her son was a Rabbi. He knew about her sexual activities and I later found out that he was vehemently opposed to her behavior.

At my current ripe old age it is somewhat embarrassing to describe one of the parties she took me to. It was a relatively young crowd of around 40 people in their 30s with a few older folks present. It was in the Valley, and the setup was that it was like a cocktail party with bedrooms in the back of the large house for sexual activities. When someone partnered up with someone else in the group they would go to one of the backrooms for sex.

To carry out my direct research and join the party I approached an attractive lady--spoke briefly to her, and then invited her to join me in a sex room. She angrily said, "I don't know you and who do you think you are? I went back to my escort the Rabbi's mother and reported my hurt feelings of rejection. She told me to not worry about it and try again.

I picked out a beautiful blonde around 30 and made my proposal. She responded after some small talk by saying, "I thought you would never ask!" We went into one of the rooms and I had a great experience.

My viewpoint on "cheating" in marriage at that time based on my research was presented in a Q&A article published in the SAN FRANCISCO CHRONICLE, UPS (UNIVERSAL PRESS SYNDICATE) 2/3/79 By Philip Nobile.

Extramarital sex is fast becomIng a popular pastime. The rate of adultery among married men is better than 50 percent, and American wives are doing their best to catch up. Blessed by cliurch, state and 2000 years of Judeo-Christian tradition, monogamy won't die easily. ! But a growing number of analysts insist that the condition is unnatural and deserving of death.

Sociologist Lewis Yablonsky is one of them. A professor at California State University here, Yablonsky felt that adultery was dysfunctional and anti-social until he interviewed approximately BOO married men, whose average age was 36.

To his surprise, he said, he found that extramarital sex seldom led to divorce and actually improved marriages. Yablonsky's study, "The Extra·SexFactor: Why Over Half of America's Married Men Play Around," raises the question: Why not?

Despite changing times, the rate ,of adultery among married men hasn't changed significantly since the '40s. You came up with the same 50 percent figure that Kinsey found, didn't you?

"Yes, men are wide open to other sexual arrangements. Jealousy, hostility and guilt about extra sex are culturally induced."

Is exclusive monogamy;a stressful condition? To put the question another way, is playing around better for your health?

"Marriage can be happier with sexual freedom. For instance, many of the men I Interviewed felt hostile toward their wives when they could not meet their sexual expectations. But when these men began having affairs, they grew to love their wives more because the source of their discontent dissolved.

I doubt that any intellectual argument in favor of extra sex will persuade the jealous wife or husband that fooling around is harmless. What do you do about the naked emotion of jealousy?

From many psychodrama sessions I have conducted on this very subject, I can say that when a wife realizes that her "husband loves, honors and respects her despite the extra sex, she doesn't feel rejected and therefore her jealousy may be diminished.

Have you noticed whether wandering husbands are ready to grant their wives the same freedom for extra sex?

"I found a very strong possessiveness among these men. Most men are "closet machos" who resist sexual freedom for their spouse. They feel that their wives would somehow betray their socialization role as mothers and nurturers by playing around as the men do."

Around that time Donna and I lived in the same house but had an open relationship that we seldom discussed. She began "stepping-out" and later I found out had been drinking and smoking marijuana. I decided to do the same, minus drugs and alcohol, and had several affairs apart from my "research."

These activities didn't bode well for the continuation of our marriage. I recall, we consulted a therapist. The idiot recommended that I smoke marijuana with Donna to help fix the relationship. Given my inability to inhale (like Clinton) the marijuana I tried had no effect on me. Donna, however, would get high. Our marriage was to put it mildly--faltering.

One positive result of our marriage disruption was that I did complete my research and publish my book THE EXTRA-SEX FACTOR: WHY OVER HALF OF AMERICA'S MEN PLAY AROUND (New York Times Books, 1979. The book has been republished in 2009 with IUniverse Books.)

As I write this review of my earlier opinions on E-S the media has exploded because it has been revealed that the revered golf athlete Tiger Woods had a number of extra=sex affairs. He has been pilloried by the press, and his extraordinary successful career and image has been severely damaged.

From my viewpoint from then (1979) when I published my research findings in the book to now as I write my memoirs extra-sex and the response to it has not changed. Following are some excerpts derived from my 2009 edition of my book THE EXTRA-SEX FACTOR that indicate the continuing complexity of extra-marital sex in 2010:

In my preface to the IUniverse 2009 edition I wrote--most people are not open to discuss their sex lives. The recent film "KINSEY" presents insights into the difficulties of obtaining accurate information on people's sex lives. When I carried out my research into the extra-sex behavior of people outside of their marital or "committed" relationship people were more open about discussing the subject than when Kinsey did his research back in the 1940s.

Since the EXTRA-SEX FACTOR was originally published by New York Times Books (1979), I have kept up with the research and literature on the subject of what is varying called "cheating or extra marital sex. There has been no marked change in the basic statistics on the subject. Around 50% of men have sexual relations outside of their marriage or "committed" relationship; and around 40% of women do the same.

A major change has apparently been in the types of sexual relationships people enact. There appears to be more diverse sexual behavior. Some of this activity may be due to the increased freedom of explicit sex in the media and sexual activity presented freely on the internet.

There appears to be no new explanations and rationales for "extra-sex" than the data I have delineated in my book. In general, men participate in E-S essentially for their sexual satisfaction. Whereas women participate in extra-sex primarily for relationship needs and sex is secondary.

My Extra-Sex book, when first published, was serialized in 3 Editions of the New York Daily News with the title "Cheating." Following are some of the mainpoints covered in the serialization that are as relevant today as they were when my book was originally published based on my research. My viewpoint, in part explains the breakup of my marriage to Donna.

In general the concept of "romantic love" dominates our culture in literature, on the mass media" and in popular music. The sa]e of romantic paperbacks and the viewing of romantic daytime soap operas have soared. Despite the cynical and intellectual cover that many sophisticated people present, on a deep emotional level most men and women still seek romance.

Several myths have endured: Everyone can find an Ideal mate Only one person in the world exists Ior you. That certain someone is easily and immedi· lately recognized. Finding That someone is the only basis for true love and happiness in marriage.

Many sophisticated men and women believe that a relationship short of these ideals is defective; and, in fact at the beginning of some marriages a methodical effort is made to shape reality to fit and perpetuate these romantic ideals.

When reality Intrudes in a marriage same men feel shortchanged as I did in my marriage. Their lovebirds begin to shriek at them and disagree with them. I, as many other men I interviewed for my book became outraged by the women who used to be a passionate and understanding lover-girlfriend. They begin to feel they made a gross error.

At first, they may try to revitalize the romance with their wives, who in many cases have assumed the sexually unromantic role of mothers. If this fails, they may once again embark on a pursuit of their romantic dream. And to some degree they may find themseives treated better sexually and often emo· tionally by seeking and finding a new other woman or women.

The new woman only sees the man for short periods, and usually in a romantic haze. The sexual affair is not encumbered by problems with children, financial issues, or long-standing personal conflicts. If the other woman wants the relationship to work. she can easily role-play the ideal woman for her married man for the brief periods of time required for her performances. As they deepen their relationship, she can relax and be herself. The mistress, however, who relaxes her romantic approach and becomes more demanding is often replaced.

Today, even swinging has become institutionalized.

Prostitution has become an open sexual playland, with girls on the streets of most large cities and all kinds of possibilities on the internet. Men can obtain recreational sex with prostitutes almost at any hour and any way they want off the internet. More than half of the men who purchase this sex are married.

For some married men sex is a secondary factor. Though married, they are lonely and desire another worman to openly talk to without consequences for what they say. In this context, many high-priced prostitutes point out that many men are less interested in sex than they are in a conversation with a non-judgemental understanding woman.

The wife who finds out about her husbands E-S may drive their husband back Into extrasexual action or resolve his need to explore further. One wife who learned about her husband'. affairs never stopped throwing it up to him and being suspicious. His response was, "I'm getting blamed anyway, I may as well do, and I don't want to hear about it anymore."

In another case. a wife responded to the discovery of her husband's extra·sex with more sex. "I had no idea he wanted more sex than we had until I found out he was going to massage parlors, with prostitutes, and had had a few lengthy affairs. He never told me he was unsatisfied with our sex life. Now I do like that old song: 'I love him in the morning, love him every night, because a good man nowadays is hard to find.' I'm not mad at him and I'm sure our life together is fuller."

The husband of this woman told me that he no longer had any reason or time for extra sex.

Many men admit they'd be more tempted by an extramarital affair if it weren't for the dangers of discovery and the resulting impact of family conflict. As one man put it. "I would like to have more sex, but I'm afraid to run the risk. 1 could lose my wife, the kids, my friends. our house--everything I've worked for all my life." In this pattern, the man has no moral or ethical resistance. He simply fears being caught. The price is too high.

Many men I interviewed felt that lying to their wives and guilty feelings caused more pain than the pleasure that was derived from the;r extra sex.

One man put it this way: "I'm a coward. I'm afraid of rejection, and I'm afraid of my wife catching me. Those are the only reasons I don't play around."

A factor that deters the extra sex of many men Is that they are highly selective. These men have a unique sexual relationship with their wives where their ideal pattern is enacted andthey have no motivation for extra sex. As one man category commented: "My wife knows how to press all of my buttons sexually, and I know exactly what she likes. Where could I find another woman who could do me right?"

Many husbands, especially those who are religious, say that extra sex goes against their ethical grain. One typical man in this category remarked, "I wouldn't do it because it goes against God's law, and I believe in the sanctity of my marriage vows." This concept was foreign to me in my marriage.

Some psychologists believe that monogamy is maintained in contemporary society at a great personal expense because the normal physiological proclivity for men is to participate in sexual activity with more than one woman. This was apparently the case in the early days of humankind

The traditional marital state is in conflict with a male's earlier training as a teenager to become a "sexual warrior." However, if he pursues this proclivity in his married life, he is generally considered promiscuous and feels guilty or ashamed.

When a man is sexually frustrated in his marriage he may act out his anger on his wife in the extreme with wife-battering. Extra sex also may be partial revenge in a system that trains a man to be a sexual warrior in adolescence and then traps him in a restrIctive form of conventional marriage.

My restrictions with my wife are embarrassing. I would come on to her, and too often she was not interested. Finally we agreed on a 3 times a week schedule. Then, we would sometimes get into an argument of whether or not it was from viewpoint only twice that week, and she would argue we had reached our quota. This was not good for our marriage--consequently on my many business trips at that time I would find other sources for my sexual drives.

All my life, to put it mildly I have had a strong libido. It occurs to me since I don't believe my father had as much sex as he wanted with my mother. A man's sex pattern or the lack of it is determined as much by his socialization and values apart from his marriage as by his marital relationship.

Following are two extreme cases from my research that illustrate this factor. Bill and Arnie were opposites with regard to their sexual drives.

Bill is a deeply religions mali who lives in a suburban "sexual hell" because he believes he will "go to the actual hell," as be puts it, "if I sin through adultery." His wife believes "sex is dirty, painful, and unnecessary except to procreate." Consequently she reluctantly rations it out on Saturday nights. Despite tis situation, Bill restricts himself to a monogamous relationShip because of the structure of his personality. his inner and religious values, and the bck of opportunity that goes witH his life style.

Arnie is a sociopathic swinger. Life to him is "one big ball," with no ethical, moral or spiritual restrictions. His motto is, "If it feels good, do it." He happens to have a loyal, devoted wife.

Both men claim to be happily married, yet they remain enthusiastic advocates of their extrasexual double life.

Celebrities are in a different life situation related to their sexual drives and availability as compared to the average male. Women relate to their power and are more available. This obviously true of sports and other celebrity figures with regard to "groupies" of all types.

The recent exposes of people like Tiger Woods, Mel Gibson, John Edwards, and several governors makes this point. Women are easily available, and they are utilized for the star's pleasure with little concern for the consequences. That is until they are exposed. They then become, in my opinion unnecessarily contrite and apologetic.

If you put food in front of a hungry man he will eat it. They are not necessarily at total fault for their escapades. The public tends to invest cultural stars with a certain piety and make them into role-models. When their secrets are found out their is a certain perverse joy in the "outing" for the general public. And if it is a low-level unexciting news week when their extra-sex issue explodes--it appears in all forms of media

The other woman in married man's extra-sex is of interest. She may be a sexual object limited to a one-night stand, a prostitute, a brief affair, or a mistress toward whom the man has deep loving feelings that last for many years. Any one of these factors makes it a ripe media plum

In general, my data reveals that most men have a limited involvement with their other women. The objective is often an uncomplicated recreational form of sex or a socially satisfying brief relationship. Prostitutes are the most efficient sex object for a married man who wants this type of short-term noninvolved sex. Yet many men find brief one-night stands inadequate to their needs. In some cases the relationship involves a second home with a mistress for the man where he is "understood" and valued. The mistress situation goes beyond the simple sexual activity described, and often encompasses a reciprocal romantic love and friendship relationship.

The mistress situation often develops out of a business association. Typical examples are secretaryboss, pilot-stewardess, director-actress, or male-female colleagues. More often than not, the married man has a superior position and influence over the woman who gets involved. As one man put it, "she really goes to bed with my money, status, and accomplishments in the world, not with me.

But so what." As one Hugh Hefner type very rich man responded to my comment about one of his mistresses "all she wants is your money." His quick response was, "I couldn't care less why she fucks me as long as she fucks me."

The female response toward becoming a mistress is often simply being attracted to the man involved, unrelated to or in spite of the fact that he's married. Some women, however, seem to be especially attracted to married men. As one divorced woman who had been her bosses mistress for more than two years commented: "1 have no intention of ever marrying Jack. But for me right now my relationship with him is very useful. He has no hold on me and I don't have any claims on him. It's just good sex."

In general, my study of E-S reveals that monogamy is an idealized myth in contemporary society.

More than half of America's married men have affairs, and among those who do not, a significant percentage feel frustrated in being restricted to one spouse.

As I write about E-S in the year 2010, given the rapid changes in sex roles, women seem to exhibit the same emotional posture as men do about the constraints of monogamy on their real feelings. A more honest acceptance, therefore, of the true emotional, sexual, and relationship needs is in order and would help relieve some of the emotional pain that both married men and women experience on the discovery of so-called cheating by their partner.

Here is a quick summary of my over-all research and analysis.

1. Total monogamy in contemporary society is a myth restricted to religious idiots and hypocrites ala Jimmy Swagart who enjoyed relieving himself in the sight of a naked hooker, and the gay minister who was a customer of a male hooker. More than half of all married men have extramarital affairs during their marriage, and about 75% of this group report that their extrasexual activity is pleasurable and emotionally gratifying.
2. Most married men who have extrasexual affairs find most aspects of their marriage satisfactory.
3. Most men (about 80%) who have extrasexual affairs have a strong "homing drive," place a high value on their wives

and family. and have no intention of leaving their home situation.
4. Extrasexual behavior about 80% of the time is clandestine. Very few married people live out an open pattern of extras ex because of the emotional impacts of recriminations, and a degree of self-deception for emotional reasons.
5. About 85% of extrasexual activity is short-lived. In fact, a two-night stand comprises the extrasexual acting of most married men. In only about 16% of the cases do men carryon a relationship beyond a year.
6. Most men participate in extrasex because they desire and enjoy the companionship of other women. This. I believe, is one of the most significant findings of my study. Men. and to a large extent women, seem to have a hunger for and are developing an increasing need to have relationships with others beyond the boundaries of their marriage.

Despite the effect of these social and erotic forces. it is a wise couple that does not lose contact with the positive dimensions of their marriage. In brief. if one mate or the other does have an extrasexual affair, and it is relaled, a judicious handling of the situation, after the fact, can produce positive rather than negative effects.

Without advocating extrasex, if a couple understand why it happens, it can help strengthen rather than destroy their marriage. In my case toward the end of my marriage to Donna we were fairly open with each other about the E-S we were participating in. We stayed together for a few years after the romance was gone because we did enjoy being with our son, and various trips we took together.

Chapter 8

Divorce & a Father/Son Book (1980 To 1994)

Donna and I had a loving relationship and marriage for almost 20 years. The day she gave birth to my beloved son Mitch at St. Johns Hospital in Santa Monica on March 4, 1964, was without any doubt the happiest day of my life. Mitch and I have always shared our lives with each other.

It's a long and sad story, however, in brief, around 1980 about 20 years into our relationship and marriage my extra-sex factor "research", Donna drinking, and other issues led to a final agreement to divorce.

Another factor in our divorce was that Donna, believed, as in Isben's play, "The Doll House" something more was "out there" that was better than the cozy relationship I thought we had as a family. She wouldn't stop going out--so finally we divorced. She was smart enough, however, to agree at the separation to have Mitch, who was then a teenager, live with me. I wa now a single man and father with a 15 year old son. My personal interest turned to becoming the best father I could be, and I became intrigued with the sociological issue of the relationship between fathers and sons.

MITCH

My son Mitch was the inspiration for my my later book on the relationship between fathers and sons. When I was divorced Mitch and I lived in the Palisades, then I was able to buy a small house on Boone Ave. In Venice California. Mitch and I were closer than ever. The 2 of us alone in one house without Donna. She faded out of our lives, and I continued to support her in an apartment in her favorite ritzy place Beverly Hills.

Mitch is the clear love of my life. We shared many wonderful experiences together. Everything including Little League. Many of our experiences together are documented in 2 books I wrote that were inspired by Mitch FATHERS AND SONS, and THE LITTLE LEAGUE GAME. I participated as an involved father in the Brentwood Little League and one season as the coach of Mitch's team. That year he was voted best player in the League.

I partially retired in a plan at the University that enabled me to continue teaching one Semester a year. I continued directing directing psychodrama in the U.S. and in Italy. We needed the money and it was fun.

Mitch did well and graduated from Palisades High School. After graduation, he enrolled at Cal State-Northridge of course in sociology. During his student days he was in my criminology and psychodrama classes at CSUN.

I usually stayed away from graduation ceremonies at CSUN--as I did at NYU. The only day I put on my Doctorate robes and went to a CSUN graduation was when Mitch graduated CSUN in 1982. I filed in with the Professors and he filed in with students. By a strange coincidence in a crowd of several thousand at the graduation he wound up sitting one chair in back of me.

It was a great day for the 3 of us when Mitch graduated CSUN. Donna happily attended the Commencement Ceremony. Mitch went on to acquire a position as a Los Angeles County Probation Officer. As I write this in 2010 he has served with distinction as a Probation Officer for almost 30 years.

Around the time when Mitch graduated CSUN, I direct many training workshops in Therapeutic Community projects in Rome, Turin, London, Paris, and Amsterdam. Mitch accompanied me on many trips to Europe. One day as we were flying across the Atlantic toward a week-long psychodrama workshop in Turin, Italy I had to direct.--I told Mitch how tired I was. He promptly said, "Dad cheer up you only do a half of a week workshop." I said, "what are you talking about?" He responded, "You say whatever in English, then your translator repeats it in Italian. You only do half a session." Mitch was a smart kid--who was always helpful to me in many ways. We have dearly loved each other all of his life.

In 1980 I had signed a contract with Simon & Schuster to do a book about the relationship between fathers and sons. As with my earlier books the subject intrigued me. I became heavily involved my research for my book by interviewing fathers and sons and reading whatever I could on the subject.

During this research period, among the many books I read was an interesting book by Kathy Cronkite who reflecting on the children of famous parents including her father Walter Cronkite. She came to a number of conclusions about the positive and negative impacts of having a powerful father. Not that I was anywhere near the class of Walter, I became fairly well known and appeared on 100+ programs touting my books. Part of my doing the F/S research was to learn more about properly carrying out my own role as a father.

What especially interested me about Kathy Cronkite's book was that it was written in memory of Paul Newman's son, Scott Newman. He died in 1978 of a self-inflicted drug overdose. I was interested in how one of my favorite actors Paul Newman dealt with this enormous loss of his son.

In her book Kronkite wrote about how she had became friends with Scott who was an aspiring actor himself after she moved to Hollywood to start her acting career. According to Cronkites book the relationship between Scott and Paul Newman was rocky because of Scott's apparent drug addiction.

In the book Kronkite wrote about an interesting experience she had at a party with Scott. She wrote: "One evening I heard Scott drunkenly accuse someone of being interested in him only because of his father, when in fact the 'antagonist' did not even know who his father was. Later at the same party he said belligerently to someone else, 'Don't you know who my father is?'

When Mitch was a student at Northridge he had similar interactions with people about his Sociology Professor father. I never considered myself famous--although through my books I am somewhat known. This issue was of concern to me in my relationship to Mitch. I always attempted to avoid my power position with him as my son. It probably was helpful in his later job as a probation office, however, it might also be annoying to be somewhat in the shadow of your father.

Under unusual circumstances I was able to get some inside data on Scott and Paul Newman on this issue directly from Newman's daughter. In the process of doing my book I completed a first draft of the book and was on a plane bound for NY to meet with my publisher at Simon & Schuster. I crouched in a window seat on the plane working on a final editing of the manuscript. The lady to my right kept asking me annoying questions about the manuscript and what it was about. I finally told her

In reponse, she whispered to me you know who is sitting next to us." With annoyance, I said "Who?" She then told me it was Scott Newman's sister. We shuffled our seats and on the plane I got a terrific interview with Paul Newman's daughter about Scott and Paul Newman's relationship for my book.

Scott Newman's tragedy was a partial result of his being on the edge of the spotlight. He worked sporadically as a stunt man in the movies but wanted to become a full-fledged actor. The sister felt a deep involvement with her brother's problems as the son of a celebrity father.

She felt she had many of the same problems experienced by her brother. Her comments about the relationship between Scott and Paul Newman are of value in understanding the general problems that a celebrity father automatically acquires, and how this can affect his son's life. She provided me with an interesting interview on the plane. I later used the interview in my FATHER AND SON book: She commented as follows in my impromptu interview with her:

"One night we were all having dinner in our home in Brentwood. Dad and Mom were there and two of my sisters. After dinner I went to the back of the house to wash some clothes and I saw this face with glasses behind the locked gate. At first it scared me-then I saw who it was. It was Scott.

"It was kind of eerie to see him behind this big iron gate, because it reminded me of how he had put himself out there, really outside our family, looking in. It was about a year before he died of an overdose of drugs and alcohol.

"I remember we talked for a long time that night sitting out by the back door. The thing I remember most about our conversation was that one minute he was saying how much he loved me, Dad and the family, and how bad he felt about the way things were, and how he couldn't seem to get it together and stop shooting drugs. The next minute his face would get cold and angry and he would become insulting and almost violent.

That night as we talked he became hostile and got pretty loud. My father must have heard him because around that time my dad came to the back door and said, 'What's going on out there?'

"Dad really wanted to talk to him. I know Dad loved him a lot and really wanted to help, but somehow it didn't work. At that time Scott said that he didn't want to talk to him. I remember Scott told me that all the talking he had done with Dad and to shrinks had done him no good.

"Dad did his best. I remember when I was younger they would go a lot of places together. And Dad would talk to him a lot. But, of course, Dad was always superbusy as an actor. And when he was making a movie he just wasn't available. I'm sure Scott wanted a lot more time with him than he got. ,.

"When someone you love and need can only see you now and then for just a few hours, you feel love and hate. When you really love someone as Scott loved Dad, you hate the fact that he can't be with you more. I think that's the reason Scott was a drug addict and had a lot of anger in him.

"There are many good things about being in Paul Newman's family. One thing is that you know there is always a hand or a safety net to catch you if you fall. There's always money, and then there's the name. You always go to the limit of anything you do, because you think how far that name can take you. Scott maybe figured he would be rescued at the last minute. But the hand didn't appear.

"All my life-and I'm sure this was true of Scott too-I felt I had to be famous and successful. It's only recently that I figured out, 'Hey, you really don't have to be famous if you don't want to.' Figuring that out has relaxed me and made me feel happier. Maybe Scott never figured that out. And he died trying to be another Paul Newman. He could never succeed because my dad is one of a kind."

Scott Newman lived in the shadow of his father's public image, and no doubt this always affected their relationship. Although I am certainly not a Newman being a Professor of Sociology who writes books--I always worried that this issue might bother Mitch. He would often be greeted with the question of whether he was my son.

Fortunately, although I was interested in the subject of fathering, Mitch never had a problem with my role. He has had his own great career as a probation officer.

In my research for the book and also in my effort to learn how to best enact the single father role I developed some theories about fathering roles. Most fathers develop some basic modality of a father style. The following are my theory on the basic types of father roles that I determined based on my research and personal experience:

CATEGORY ONE. Compassionate Loving-Doubling Fathers.

A father of this type is generally an emotionally healthy man. He is capable, when it is appropriate, of placing his son's needs ahead of his own. He is able to give of himself and place his son in a central role in his life. His son's needs usually take precedence over his own needs, and this reveals the intensity of his compassion and love for his son.

He is capable of doubling with his son. By doubling, I mean the ability of a father to become one with his son's emotions rather intensely in his early years, and to place himself inside his son's self when necessary in his later years. Doubling enables him to feel his son's joy and pain. It is a form of loving that requires an intense kind of empathy-the ability to accurately take the role of his son in significant emotional situations. (I find myself in Category One.)

This father type usually wanted a son in his life plan. He borders on being poetic and lyrical about the birth of his son. He perceives the birth of his son almost as the fulfillment of, or at least as one of the epochal experiences in, this own life.

CATEGORY TWO Peer- Type Fathers: Many overloving-doubling fathers become buddies rather than fathers to their sons. Such men do not assume the proper status of fathers because they do not perceive themselves as superordinate to anyone, or capable of controlling anyone. They remain boys or son-types no matter what their age. They attempt to be "buddies" or peers with their sons rather than fathers. emotionally, they are perpetual children who have not attained sufficient maturity to become fathers or role-models to their sons. This type of father may love his son like a brother, but because of his peers hip behavior he doesn't generate much respect from his son, nor does he offer much of a lofty role model for his son to emulate.

Peer fathers usually feel besieged by their problems and the world around them and are not motivated toward heavy achievements. They tend to share their problems with their sons. In this way they often place unnecessary burdens on their sons at too early an age. They seldom discipline their sons because they don't have a clear position on correct behavior or rules. They are usually dominated by their wives and only serve as agents of their wives in the control and discipline of their sons.

My own father was in this category. He always shared his problems with his sons, thus burdening them with a gloom-and doomed vision of the world. When my father disciplined me, it was only after he had been harassed by my mother to "do something" about me. Then he would in effect tell me my bad behavior (whatever it was) didn't really matter to him. But it did upset my mother and when she was upset he was in the line of fire. Therefore, he told me to "straighten up and fly right" not because of any correct-behavior precepts he held, but because my mother was giving him trouble. In many ways he was not a father figure, but a beaten-down older brother who was another child to my mother.

His role as a "brother" who was unwilling to be my superior was revealed to me in a recent comment: "You know, Lewie, you don't remember, but sometimes when your mother was going to hit you or one of the other boys, I would say, 'Don't hit them, hit me first.' "

A positive characteristic of peer-buddy fathers is that many of them tend to be playmates to their sons. They can sometimes be "good brothers" who supply a friendship that is denied to sons of competitive or macho fathers. My father and I had many positive memorable times together playing baseball. I think he wished he could play with me on my high school team, because he seldom missed a game. He would park the laundry truck, and I would always see him watching me play. It was a wonderful feeling seeing Harry at my games.

A psychologist I interviewed described his own buddy-father as "a man who had no balls at all. He was always puling, whining and complaining about life. My mother totally dominated him. He would only discipline us at her behest. His heart wasn't in it because he had little concern with bringing us up. He was so embittered by his plight in the world. I had the feeling he was always jealous of me because

I was the youngest one in the family. I believed he longed to be the kid brother, because that would automatically get him more affection from our mom. He could then relax and not have to fight the world as hard. He wanted to be one of my mother's sons, not a father."

CATEGORY THREE. Macho Fathers. Macho fathers have an exaggerated idea of the meaning of masculinity. This type of father basically relates to his son as an extension of his own ego, and power in the world. in effect, he is little concerned from a compassionate viewpoint with his son's ego development. The extreme macho father is a man whose personal masculinity and identity is tied to his son's performance, as it relates to his own egocentric needs.

Although fathers of this type are not necessarily physically battering fathers, most brutal fathers tend to fall into this category. Their brutality occurs more often on a subtly emotional verbal level than on a physical level. They are superdirectors of their sons' lives, and their sons seldom develop any personal autonomy, because their fathers' superman judgmental postures are omnipresent.

A big-league ballplayer revealed to me how most of his lifelong problems developed from his conflict with his domineering macho father. The father succeeded in making him into a great big-league baseball star at the expense of the son's emotional rage. A son with a "macho-father often maintains a vendetta that more often than not impairs his son's happiness and produces self-defeating behavior patterns. There was a great movie made on this subject called "Fear Strikes Out." It was the biography of the star baseball player Jimmy Piersall. His father kept pushing him to better even when he was a big-leaguer. Piersall was at various times driven "crazy" by his father.

CATEGORY FOUR Psychopathic Fathers: The dominant personality factor of the psychopathic father is his basic lack of compassion. It is regrettable when a psychopathic man has a child, because as a father he is incapable of training that child to feel human. He is at the opposite extreme from a compassionate loving-doublirig father.

By definition, the psychopathic father's personality exhibits a persistent behavior pattern characterized by an almost total disregard for the rights and feelings of his son. The son doesn't learn how to be compassionate for others.

The following father, who I met during my writing the Father/Son book is for me an example of the Category 4 father. I met him during a period when my wife and I, in our therapeutic work, would take a teenager into our home when the teenager could not get along at home. Social workers would refer the youth to us, and we were paid for the time they spent with us.

This man was the father of a 16 year old who we took into our home because he couldn't get along with him. In my opinion, the man was an abusive albeit very wealthy father. After about a few month the teenager living in our home was doing great. He went to school and was cooperative.

The father was meeting with me to discuss how the boy was doing and to discuss future payments for board and therapy in our home. I told him I needed more than the $150 per month he was paying me.

He was a very successful and wealthy salesman. He told me, "$150 is all I have allocated for my son. That's it. I will not pay any more money for him. I accepted the deal since I didn't want to cause the boy any further problems.

When our business was completed, the father said with a grin, "Come outside with me. I want to show you something nice." It turned out he wanted to show me the new Rolls-Royce he had bought for $150,000 that day. His self-image clearly took precedence over his father role to the detriment of his son's emotional condition.

The man was a prototypical egocentric father who, like many American men in every echelon, was consumed by his own needs for personal validation through extravagant self-centered success. In this case at the expense of his son's personal development.

There are too many egocentric fathers in our society like this father. This type of father, consumed by his quest for upward mobility, like Abraham sacrifices his son to our society's apocryphal God of success.

Darryl and Richard Zanuck

An interesting case I learned about in the process of my interviews for the book was the difficult and interesting father and son relationship between Darryl F. Zanuck the legendary 20th Century Fox movie mogul and his son Richard. I was able to get this lengthy interview with Richard Zanuck through a good friend of mine, Howard Sackler who had written "Jaws" one of the films Richard Zannuck had produced.

The reason I was very interested in this interview was because at one point in the father son relationship Daryll had Richard fired from his position at Fox, and security guards were called by his father to remove him from his office. Richard told me the following story about him and his father in a lengthy interview. Despite his fathers treatment of him (or maybe because of it) Richard became a major film producer in his own right--despite his manipulative and controlling father. Following is part of the story Richard Zanuck told me:

"When I was a kid my dominant reaction to my father was fear. He was a very competitive and flamboyant man who had a short temper when anyone got in his way or disagreed with him. That didn't mean that he wasn't capable of tremendous love, but he still had an explosive short fuse if he didn't get his way.

"I think what I suffered from as a kid was the same thing others suffered from who had to go to his offices and work with him. I don't think I was unnecessarily picked on, any more so than his associates.

His temper was part of his great enthusiasm. When he was positive he could make you feel great. But there was always this feeling that he was a walking time bomb. It was a thin-ice situation and he was liable to explode at any time, especially if he felt you had crossed him or disagreed with him.

"Because of his personality, his success and his enormous ego, he was a distant figure as a father during my childhood years. It was hard for me to go to him and have a father-son conversation on the most basic levels.

He was a distant father.

When I was a kid, before I became a teenager, he and I rarely went anywhere alone. I do remember a couple of hunting trips to Mexico when I was a kid. But there were always a couple of cronies of his around. As a matter of fact, I can't recall one instance where we went on any kind of an outing or anything alone.

My father competed with and dominated everyone with whom he came into contact. This included big shots in the movie business, stars in his studio like Tyrone Power, Henry Fonda, Olivia de

Haviland. Everyone feared him and capitulated to his domination, even tough adversaries like Jack Warner.

One of my special memories as a kid, beginning when I was six or seven, was his showing films at home. We had a big screening room in our house and on Sunday nights a lot of movie people, stars and friends, would come to the screenings. I didn't really see these stars as special.

A handsome leading man would come without his toupee and he would look ordinary. I'd overhear stories about their troubles with their wives or kids. They were my father's friends, and I never saw them as the superstars they were. I remember the star I was most impressed with when he showed up in person was Hopalong Cassidy. I was a fan of his movies. He impressed me.

After dinner Dad would screen a film in our projection room. My two sisters and I seldom ate dinner with the grownups. We ate dinner alone, and then were allowed to come in and see the movie.

My dad and I would usually sit alone in the back so he could be near the controls. He was bored a lot of times when he didn't like the movie, and he would begin to fool around with me. We would inevitably end up wrestling on the couch. Obviously, at that time when I was seven or eight he was a lot bigger and stronger than I was. But for him everyone, including his son, was a competitor. He would get me in a headlock, and then he would make me say the word 'give,' for 'I give up.' He loved to win, and he beat me regularly.

"We went through this ritual for a lot of years. When I was around thirteen there were a few times when I felt I might be able to get him. But he always managed to wriggle out of my headlock and get me.

Then came this fateful night I'll never forget. I was now fourteen, and partly because of my dad's. inspiration, I had become a pretty good athlete. He started his usual stuff of fooling around on the couch. I could just feel for the first time that I was stronger than he was. I got him in a perfect headlock, and I showed him no mercy. His face became all red, and his eyes were almost bulging. I just kept squeezing and asking him the question he had asked me all those years. He finally blurted out, 'give.'"

The crux of the competitive relationship between the two came when Darryl was in Europe playing around for a few years with his mistress, and Richard took over the studio as president. In brief the macho father Darryl came back, fired his son. Not only did he fire him, he had security throw him off of the 20th Century Fox lot.

My own father Harry was the exact opposite of Zanuck in terms of any power in the world. He was in essence a loving compassionate father. In all of his adult life he was low-level truck driver with limited power in the world. He had a continual struggle to pay the rent and put food on the table. He never exerted any power over me. Perhaps if he would have I would not have become as arrogant as I sometimes am.

A man's style of fathering obviously has significant impacts on his son's basic personality and approach to life. Because of their fathers, some sons approach life with joy and zest. Others, those who are in search of fathers, become locked in self-defeating competitive struggles with their fathers and other men. In my work and relationship to Synanon, I noticed that a lot of "square" who were not drug addicts related to Chuck Dederich, as if he was the father they never had.

Psychopathic fathers seldom change; however, egocentric fathers can be converted into loving, compassionate fathers. A key to change is a self-recognition of their problem. Fathers, like Daryl Zanuck, and the Rolls-Royce father miss out on having the best friend they can ever have in their life.

A factor that I determined was valuable to fathers and sons was in later years to winding up as "best friends." Obviously a father can love his young son--but there isn't enough there for a friendship on the part of the son that went two ways. Also when the son is a naturally rebellious teenager--he is not as interested in having fun with his Dad as he is with his teenage buddies and girls. In brief their are normal phases and abnormal phases in the development of the father and son relationship.

Based on my research I determined that a good father/son relationship goes through 3 definitive phases. I delineated these phases in an article I wrote for the National Family Magazine (6/19/82) that appeared in newspapers around the country; and in my book FATHERS AND SONS.

The essentials of my opinions derived from the article are based on my interviews with more then 500 fathers and of course my effort to understand my own relationship with my father Harry. I have observed three basic evolutionary phases in the lifetime father-son relationship. Following is a summary of what I believe should essentially occurs during each phase in order for the father and son to reach an epiphany of friendship when they are both grownups:

1. "'What Do You Think. Dad?" (Birth through age 12)

The early nurturing period has long been considered the the role of the mother. However, there is ample evidence that this time does not belong solely to the mother. Fathers need to relate to the basic care of their sons from infancy on. Sons at an early age are interested in caring from their fathers and the opinions of their fathers.

This period in his son's life is also of great consequence to a father's own personal growth. A man who immerses himself in his young son's develop· meant is bound to become a more compassionate and loving person.

2.The Struggle for Individuality (ages 13 through 19)

The teen years are very significant in the father/son relationship. It is during thIs period that the son begins to develop his own identity to the world in general.

During his teen years the son will most likely become difficult as he struggles to develop his own identity. During this phase many fathers (especially macho and psychopathic fathers) perceive the struggle of their son for his own identity as an attack on their power and masculinity and react with over-control and sometimes punitive violent reactions. As a result of of this natural conflict some fathers and sons foolishly become estranged for a lifetime.

3. Man-to-Man Friendship (age 20 through adulthood)

If all goes well during these early phases a father and son can achieve the desired goal of a loving and wonderful lifelong friendship.

I am personally extremely lucky to have achieved this kind of relationship with my son Mitch. In my later years this loving and caring friendship has been a total joy. I never call my son Mitch. I always call him "sunny" because he has brought sunshine into my life. And no doubt has helped me live to an old age.

In contrast my relationship to my Dad Harry was kind of a straight line. We loved each other and he was always good to me but he was so consumed with being a workaholic that he never opened up to me. When I rode with him on the laundry truck we never talked about anything of relevance.

Also, regrettably, he never disciplined me. My discipline in my early and teenage years came from my mom Fannie. Nothing harsh but loud and in the moment. I only remember one time when I had done something wrong taking me aside and saying to me: "You know she's mad at you. Don't do it [whatever it was] again. In my later years after developing some insights as a therapist I concluded that my father was only distressed with my bad behavior when it made my mother mad. My intuitive belief is that when she was mad it diminished his sex life.

In general the 1980s had been a significant time in my life. I was now in my mid years of 50 a recognized Professor of Sociology and Criminology. I had researched some important social issues and had written some useful books. Personally I had once again a single man, and had several girlfriends during this period. The main positive development in my life was my great relationship with my son Mitch. We were truly good friends and lived happily together.

Around that time, a reporter for the LA Times, Marshall Berges did several lengthy interviews with me and attended several of my criminology lectures at the California State University, where I taught, for an article that I believe summarized my life at that time. My interviews with reporter Marshall Berges were interesting to me because they forced me to summarize my life situation during this period; and I was enabled to read a very salutary and encouraging perspective on my life written by a talented reporter. The article made me feel that I had done something positive with my life and achieved a degree of recognition for the nutty kid from Newark

Los Angeles Times--View Sunday January 6, 1985
A Sociologist With Street Smarts
Professor Draws on His Own Experience in Youth Gangs By MARSHALL BERGES,
Times Staff Writer

"Standing before a university' class and delivering a lecture on criminal behavior, the professor betrays considerably more than mere textbook knowledge of the subject. Small wonder. Lewis Yablonsky leads a life at the edge of crime. He grew up among East Coast gangs and he came within hijacking distance of going their way. He chose instead to become a sociologist who probes and deals with a range of difficult personalitiesóantisocial, abnormal, threatening bizarre.

A sturdy and blunt-speaking six-footer who looks as if he could give a good account of himself in a gang slugfest, he delivers his findings regularly in lectures at Cal State Northridge, where Yablonsky was once awarded trustees' recognition as "outstanding professor" among 9,000 faculty members in the state universe system.

Authentic Lessons

Occasionally he calls on his students to relate their experiences with crime, and because not only police officers but ex-offenders have signed up at times for Yablonsky's courses in criminology, "We tend to get some authentic lessons into the classroom," he-says with deadpan understatement.

Most of the lessons come from Yablonsky's close encounters with crime. "Gangs are infected by a neurotic phenomenon of machismo," he told a class recently. "The hard core at the center of the gang is probably beyond reach, but it's possible to take an artichoke approach to the peripheral or marginal members of the gang. They can be peeled away and redirected into more socially acceptable activities if we convince them that they are men without having to prove their manhood by chopping each other up every time they strut down the street."

Yablonsky, has also gained insights to the riddles of behavior and a measure of fame for himself as an expert in psychodrama.

"Very few people know how angry they are," he said in an interview. "Psychodrama allows them to act out their feelings of violence without hurting anyone. The idea is to get inside the other guys skin, to develop empathy "

In addition to lectures on criminology, he conducts a class in psychodrama at Cal State Northridge, where the object, Yablonsky said, is "to explore social problems on a direct emotional level. In some sessions we deal with current events like a living newspaper." His students have reenacted through role-playing the crimes of the Hillside Strangler, John Hinckley's attempted assassination of President Reagan, and other chilling events.

Yablonsky's work does not stop there. Three times a week he holds group therapy and psychodrama sessions with troubled adolescents at a private hospital in Van Nuys. "It's not exactly fun and games," he told a reporter who accompanied him on a visit to the hospital. "With kids who have OD'd on pills, life or death is only a matter of degree. Just imagine a 14-year-old who has reached a state of depression where there seems no option but suicide." To help the youngsters see that there are alternatives, Yablonsky occasionally brings in youthful ex-addicts from such anti-drug groups as Synanon, Cocaine Anonymous, Alcoholics Anonymous and Delancey Street, the latter a therapeutic community for young veterans of drug involvement.

"The person who can talk most convincingly to a mixed-up 14year-old is someone who's had the drug disease, has had some kind of treatment, has gone through whatever it takes to change from addiction to non-addiction, is still faced with certain kinds of temptations and has to deal with those temptations."

Training Workshops

Separately, for therapists who are studying the techniques of psychodrama, he holds monthly training workshops in his Marina del Rey apartment. In these sessions the therapists are encouraged to work on difficult situations in their own lives, and occasionally the participants are urged to scream shout and even to pound each o;her with a battoca, a foam rubber paddle, to let out their anger. "The total experience becomes cathartic for everyone involved," Yablonsky said. *I can give you a close-to-home example of how psychodrama opened up my life. When I was a youngster I felt that my mother was oppressive and over-involved with me. But in psychodrama I saw that many more people had the opposite problem mother they resented for not loving them enough. It gave me perspective and mellowed my resentment."*

Surrounded by poverty, anger and crime Yablonsky grew up in Newark. ¡To call it a tough environment doesn't begin to describe it," he said. *"My father drove a laundry truck 10 hours a day and he earned about $30 a week. On Saturdays I helped him with deliveries. His paycheck put us a tiny notch above lots of neighbors who lived in cellars, got drunk on their welfare checks and shot off guns routinely to celebrate the weekend.*

"As a boy I was beaten up by Nazi bundists because I'm a Jew, and by blacks because I'm white. On the streets I'd hang around with dice hustlers and get involved in gang wars. Some of my pals were real psychopaths. I was raw, skinny and scared, but I tried to keep a cool, hip image. It was the only way to survive. But in school I began reading in a serious way, wolfing through Shakespeare and other great writers, trying to find out what made people tick. I led a strange kind of double life, keeping one foot on the streets and another in school. For some time I wasn't sure where I belonged. But when my best friend went to prison for hijacking a fur truck, a really stupid experience where the truck ran out of gas in the Holland Tunnel I realized I had to get on one side of the law or the other.

After a hitch in the Navy, Lew Yablonsky entered Rutgers University on the GI Bill, and there ¡ picked up my first book on sociology. *The subject really knocked me out, because It opened doors to all the things I was interested in: why people do what they do, what motivates them to violence and crime. It also became the beginning of a lifelong inquiry into the role of the victim.*

Eventually earning a doctorate in criminology at New York University, Yablonsky helped pay his way by working as counselor at a juvenile jail in Newark.

Lots of social workers came from a sterile background. They'd practically faint at the sight of a knife or gun. But I felt right at home with jailed kids. I could understand their fury. I figured it was my responsibility to tell society why these kids were violent, and at the same time to explain the attitudes of civilized people to the kids in jail. I began to see my role In life as sort of a translator between these two very separate worlds.

Crime Prevention Program

Subsequently hired to direct a crime prevention program In New York City, Yablonsky spent five years working with street gangs and gaining insights to the cause- and-effect relationship between drugs and crime. I would rather do live research than depend on questionnaires, he said, and his findings led him to write a book, The Violent Gang, a widely acclaimed study of urban delinquents.

Yablonsky also worked first as a student, later as a colleague with Dr. J. L. Moreno, a psychiatrist and founder of psychodrama. Yablonsky gradually came to see psychodrama as LA theater of life in which human scenarios can be raised to a higher level of consciousness and comprehension for the purpose of enlarging humanistic communication and compassion.

Yablonsky is by temperament a searcher and innovator rather than an evangelist. When in 1961 another criminologist alerted him to Synanon a then-new center for drug therapy in Santa MonicaYablonsky headed for the West Coast. He introduced psychodrama to Synanonís drug addicts, and he later wrote a book about the experience, "Synanon: The Tunnel Back."

I've always been busy with, among other projects, writing books, and I keep too much of the pleasure and pain to myself. The pleasure Is doing research, going out and interviewing people, exploring situations in depth, reading books, collecting data. The painful part comes when I close the door to my study, and for another year sit there alone, collating material, abstracting data, defining themes and writing the book. The walls of my study are a prison where I am both the warden and the prisoner. I don't want any visitors and I can't stop to make civilized conversation with another person

Following the book on Synanon, he spent three years visiting hippie communes around the country, including Haight-Ashbury and Big Sour, gathering firsthand research for another drug-related book, "The Hippie Trip." Yablonsky said: A friend once told me that

I have a knack for putting myself into the middle of a complex social situation and then writing my way out of it. Its true. For example, one time when there was a typical father-son strain In the relationship between Mitch and me, I began asking questions of other fathers and other sons. I interviewed hundreds, and various prototypes began to take shape: autocratic, egocentric and distant fathers, compliant and rebellious sons.

My interviews led me into the emotional ties between others and sons; their interactions and interdependencies; their indivIdual rights and duties and their obligations to each other; the normal and pathological conflicts between them and how mothers and daughters can intervene constructively in such conflicts; the degree to which a fathers status in the world can affect his sons aspirations. After exploring in depth a great many dimensions of this complex relationship, I put it all together into a book, "Fathers & Sons." And in personal terms let me say that. my son, Mitch, who is now 20, is majoring in sociology and criminology at Cal State Northridge.î

Currently, Lew Yablonsky is writing a book on victims. My interest in the subject began way back when I took my first course in sociology, he said, and I've been involved with victims all my life. But now my focus is on the victims role why people play it and how to avoid it.

My research Indicates there are actually three basic categories of victims. One group consists of those who are non-participants. An example of this is the adult harmed by an unknown assailant, or a child who might know the offender but has no power to resist. A second category consists of victim-prone people. An example here is the person who participates on some level in victimization by failing to take realistic or obvious precautions and thus makes himself or herself vulnerable. A third and by far the largest group consists of victim precipitators and participants. These are people who consciously or unconsciously set themselves up as victims; they are often people in search of victimizers. In this group you will find people of low self-esteem, including the battered wife or battered husband, whose attitude is, I don't deserve any better.

Rescuer Syndrome

in this group there are people who have delusions about a relationship that encourages victimization, an attitude of He really loves me, even if he treats me badly. And it includes the person afflicted with a rescuer syndrome, an attitude of I'll help him overcome his alcoholism. He'll change and then we'll both be happy. And still others who, having been abused as children, take part In a vicious circle: Filled with rage that is not understood, they act out the consequences of their own victimization on other victims as they grow older.

Therapists take various approaches to try to help victims; my own way is often psychodrama, and I've seen it help many times. But there is also a real need to structure places to which victims such as a battered wife who does not know where to turn for help can escape and become devictimized.

Yablonsky himself is occasionally a victim of overwork. "At times I'm just plain exhausted, and it's as If I'm re-enacting my father's role, those 10-hour days on a laundry truck, six days a week. But what I'm doing is not a job. Being a professor and a therapist and a writer of books is, altogether, one hell of an interesting and exciting life."

Chapter 9

Spinoffs: Psychodrama and Therapeutic Community Workshops In The U.S. And Europe

I am very grateful to Marshall Berges for his excellent interviews, and the time he took to write this lengthy article. In effect it was a mini-biography of my work and me at that time. Around the late 1980s and early 1990s based on the foundation of my work at that time and my books in various languages, I was invited to do workshops on psychodrama and therapeutic communities around the United States and in Europe.

When I researched THE TUNNEL BACK: SYNANON back in the early 1960s I had a special relationship with Synanon founder Chuck Dederick. The discussions I had with him were intellectually stimulating. We had spent endless hours discussing the "process" of Synanon, Chuck envisioning at that time that the Synanon approach would be emulated in various ways on a world-wide basis. I believed him at the time, and it has come to pass. There is an organization called the World Federation of Therapeutic Communities; and there are 100+ countries that belong to the WFTC.

Chuck and the early people in Synanon were, from my viewpoint, pioneers of the method. Some of the notable spinoff TC organizations from Synanon include Phoenix House, Amity, Daytop, Delancey Street in the United States and a variety of Synanon-type organizations in Europe and around the world

My books on Synanon and Psychodrama were translated into several languages including German, Italian, and Dutch. My books, along with all of the national and international media on Synanon was instrumental in facilitating many therapeutic community spinoffs from Synanon. Based on Synanon and my book in the 1970s through the 1990s I was invited and directed over 30 lectures on Synanon, and psychodrama workshops in TCs in Europe--especially Italy.

The Nevada State Prison project became a prototype for hundreds of prison projects utilizing the Synanon methodology in the U.S. and around the world.

The TC method began to be used widely in prisons in the United States by various TCs like Amity and Phoenix House. Cell blocks would be set aside by the prison administration for prisoners being treated while incarcerated. (In 2009 California had around 12 programs of this type in several of its prisons. I visited, gave lectures and directed psychodramas in these program, especially in Texas, California, and Italy.)

As an example of my psychodramas in prisons I will here briefly describe one of my prototypical psychodrama sessions. It was with a prisoner named Eddie at the Donavan Prison in California. He was doing time for a violent act and had been in the Amity Prison Program.

At the session, as always, after a brief description of psychodrama I would open the session by saying, "Who would like a session today." Eddie raised his hand and said, "I'm getting out of here soon and I have a plan to kill this phony minister." He was serious. A potential murder was of interest to me in possibly deterring the murder, and he had the attention of the group. Many of them harbored similar thoughts about getting someone when they were released back into the community.

Eddie came forward to have a session. At first he rambled on about some situation where a "minister" who was the head of some devil cult had taken his pregnant girlfriend's embryo. I understood from him that unborn child was going to be part of some cult ceremony. I never full understood Eddies story or what his anger stemmed from. However, it was clear to me he was preparing to kill this "minister" when he was released from prison.

Eddie became the subject of the psychodrama confronting the man with a fake psychodramatic gun in the session. Two of the prisoners were his auxiliary-egos doubling for Eddie, who in the role-playing session spewed out all sorts of insults and anger at the "minister."

Long story short the session (which was videotaped) ended with Eddie fully clearly recognizing that if he went through with his planned murder he would be in prison for life or executed. Later on Eddie became what I have termed an "experience-therapist" and became the Director in a few years of another Amity prison program fn the California Department of Corrections. Periodically over the past decade I run into Eddie who is now a solid citizen and as an "experience therapist" was helping other from continuing their criminal life.

The "Experience Therapist" Concept

The "experience-therapist concept was a central aspect of the lectures and workshops I worked on at that time. Therefore, I am here going to go into detail derived from my later book on the Synanon approach THE THERAPEUTIC COMMUNITY (Gardner Press, 1994). Following is a summary of the concept. of the role of an "experience-therapist" like Eddie became:

Former criminal/addicts are uniquely qualified to become effective ETs for three important reasons.

1. First, they have been through the throes and conflicts of their original problems as criminals or drug addicts. They know many of the rationalizations and self-deceptions that keep a person on the criminal/addict merry-go-round: from the streets, to jail, to prison, and back. They comprehend on a deep emotional level, from their own experience, what a criminal life is like. They have "been there" themselves. I refer to their affliction as criminal aids--"addiction to incarceration and death syndrome"
2. Second, they have gone through the complex resocialization process of personal change in a TC program. They know, on a firsthand basis, the painful emotional crises and traumas of confronting their own lives more directly without the cloud of drugs to ease their pain. They have experienced the various phases of reorganizing their relationships with their families and friends.
In this process they have developed valuable coping mechanisms for dealing with the temptations of sliding back into their former states of existence and for breaking

off relationships with former partners in crime. They have learned how to stay away from crime, drugs, and gangs and are succeeding as responsible citizens.
3. Third, as a result of these two sets of experiences, a past life as a criminal and firsthand knowledge about their recovery process, former offenders have usually developed some special insights and skills.

They are not easily outmaneuvered or conned by the people they are trying to help. They quickly acquire the respect of their clients because the clients know the person "treating" them has been there and back. They can see through the rationalizations and ploys that they once used themselves.

The result is a communication that has more therapeutic power than that usually achieved by more traditional professional therapists. These paraprofessionals also know from their day-to-day experiences the self-discipline required to continue to lead a crime- and drug-free life.This, in brief was what I taught professionals and potential "experience-therapist" in my lectures and workshops.

I especially enjoyed a presentation I made in Germany on the subject of therapeutic communities and "experience therapists" at a TC international Conference in 1990. Among other things I did did at the Conference was visit at the Berlin TC. It was specifically called "Synanon House." It was near the famous Wall in Berlin that stood between East and West Germany.

I remember the emotional joy I felt standing in front of this place when I visited Synanon in Berlin for an International Conference where I was a featured speaker at the World Federation of Therapeutic Communities. It gave me a sense of accomplishment about the many years and books I had contributed to this field that helped many people.

The highlight of my trip was meeting TC people from all over the world who developed this methodology in their countries. After my speech at the WFTC, I gave a special presentation at the Berlin Synanon House.

It was a special honor for me to hear, the founder of the Berlin Synanon--Ingo Warnke tell the following story of how he founded the organization:

"I was a heroine addict in Berlin along with my then wife. I use to score various drugs from medical doctors who would write me prescriptions. One day I went to this doctor to con him out of a prescription for demarol to help me with my habit. He wrote on the prescription blank 'Lewis Yablonsky The Tunnel Back.'

I was totally pissed off because the doctor ruined a perfectly good prescription! I finally found Lew's book on Synanon. I read it several times and used it as a bible for forming the Berlin Synanon House."

At the Conference, I was honored and thoroughly enjoyed presenting a special lecture with Ingo to the group of several hundred in Synanon House Berlin. I recall that the group was seated in plush red antigue-looking arm chairs that had been donated to the organization.

As stated the original basic TC Synanon approach to criminal/addicts continued to be duplicated in various forms into countries around the world. (Recently I emailed the World TC organization to determine this fact.) Although I lectured on the TC method in many countries including Japan, Germany, and Holland, most of my European lectures and psychodramas were in Rome and Turin Italy.

In the early 1990s I gave one of my a presentations at an international TC conference in Rome. It was, in part, sponsored by a TC organization called CEIS. At that time there were around 20 TCs in Italy that were based on the Synanon approach as delineated in my book PSYCHODRAMA which had been translated into Italian (Astolabio Press, Rome.)

At the conference in Rome, I became especially intrigued with the enormous TC developments in Italy. The Italian organization, Centro Italiano di Solidarieta or as they are known worldwide "Ce.I.S." (pronounced "chase"), was responsible for the management of many TCs throughout Italy.

In addition to its TCs that worked directly with addicts, CE.I.S. had developed a significant educational center that trained not only Italian TC leaders but professional and ex-addict counselors who were TC leaders from other countries.

This Italian TC movement, was founded by Father Mario PicI with the support of Pope John Paul II. It was sparked by the leadership of 2 individual Juan Carelli and a former criminal/addict

Tony Gelormino. Tony, who in my opinion was an outstanding "experience therapist" was sent from the New York Daytop TC to Rome to help Picci and Corellie develop the Italian TCs.

CEIS became a prototype, and served as the innovative cutting edge of the worldwide TC movement. Building on the inherent cultural strength of the Italian family, CE.I.S developed new significant approaches for the addict that incorporated their resident addict's family into the TC process in a unique way. The family was brought into the therapeutic process in Rome at their Educational Training Center at the Castel Gandolfo Institute north of Rome.

Castel Gandolfo was the Summer home of the Pope. It was rumored that the then Pope who attended CEIS drug addict graduation ceremonies helped finance the organization. It become a most valuable and important core educational system for the burgeoning world movement.

I directed over 10 week long training workshops at the Ce.I.S. facility on the "social structure of TCs," the concept of the "experience therapist" psychodramas, and group therapy for TC leaders and mental health professionals from Europe and other countries. Given the axiom that the best teaching engenders the most learning, my work at Castel Gandolfo and several Ce.I.S. TCs produced, for me, considerable new research findings and energized my long-standing interest in the TC process.

CEIS, as stated was founded by Father Mario PiccI. The story I heard about the founding was that Picci had been attempting to treat criminal/addicts at the crime ridden central train station in Rome. He heard about Daytop in New York, a spinoff from Synanon, and directed by a Priest William O'Brien. Picci negotiated with Father O'Brien and he sent Tony Gellormino, from my viewpoint a seasoned "experience therapist" to Rome to assist in the development of the Rome TC.

I recall an interesting meeting with Tony who assisted me with my workshops in Rome. Tony would pick me up at my hotel to go to work with the groups at Castel Gandolfo in a new red Cadillac convertible. The beautiful car puzzled me and I asked Tony how he got it. He told me that the TC received the Cadillac as a donation from a Mafia boss whose son was a heroine addict being treated in the Castel Gandolfo facility.

In our trips he would reminisce about his criminal activities in NYC. One of his stories is notable and to the best of my recollection it was told to me by Tony as follows: "In New York, my partner and me in those days did a lot of armed robberies to support our heroine habits. One day we heard there was a lot of money to be stolen at this loft apartment in Chelsea. We went to the place and to our surprise there were about 15 people and a lot of art paintings in this large kind of loft. We pulled our guns, lined them all against the wall, and took their money and any valuables they had on them. As we were leaving, one of the group said, 'This was fun, come back again.' I thought this remark was ridiculous until I later found out that this was Andy Warhol's loft." The Warhol gang apparently enjoyed the armed robbery thinking it was "performance art!"

My reputation in Italy as a psychodramatist and as the author of my book PSYCHODRAMA, translated into Italian, resulted in my performing additional workshops.

Many of them were at the Italian TC in Turin. The priest who sponsored my work in Turin, Don Paolo attended my psychodrama training sessions and was very helpful. Also my friend and psychodramatist Leonard Manzella was vital to my work in both Rome and Turin.

Leonard, was an actor, who had appeared in 30+ films in Italy and the U.S. He had a leading role in one of Marcello Mastriano's movies. He had heard of my psychodrama classes at CSUN and became a student of mine. He became an outstanding auxiliary ego and psychodramatist. He later acquired a social work degree at the University of Southern California, and has performed significant work in prisons in Mid-California.

My main man in Turin was my translator Chris Owen. He would translate my words from lectures and assist me as a role-player in psychodramas. Chris was from England but lived in Turin where he was and is a teacher. I said many times that after I had completed around 5 weeklong workshops--Chris could direct the sessions without me.

Notable to my work in Turin was a Synanon-like prison program in a cellblock in a Turin Prison where I ran several psychodrama sessions. The program was directed by a female who clearly commanded respect from the prisoners and helped them therapeutically in the program.

I recall, the guards were a blast with their colorful uniforms and hats that I saw as a spinoff from the Mussolini fascist era. They did however have heart and were emotional. I recall a session with an Italian prisoner who had family problems. One of the guards broke down in the middle of a session crying. I sent Leonard to the prison hallway to calm and help him with his problem. Leonard later told me the guard blurted out, "I had the same problem with my family when I left for duty in the prison today."

All of the sessions in Turin were great and emotional. The social issues were very much like the problems we have in the U.S. In one session I recall directing a special group, that was comprised of 8 individuals who were diagnosed with HIV and AIDS. Their problem, no doubt, stemmed from their drug use. We had a number of sessions confronting the possibilities of dying. At that time I had was around 65, and the subject of death and dying had become of great personal interest to me. I recall telling the group with AIDS that I empathized with them since I had around the same amount of time to live out my life as they did. The sessions were helpful to the group, and also personally to me. In particular, a member of the group named Mario spent many hours after a session discussing life and death issues. Some of the psychodrama sessions that I recall involved the issues of married men, who were obviously fearful of passing their malady on to their wives--and their concerns about impregnating their wives.

All in all, my experiences directing psychodrama and Synanon training sessions in Europe were important in my life. On a personal levet, being single, at one of the Conferences in Rome where I was an invited lecturer, I met and formed a laison with a beautiful and brilliant lady psychiatrist from Portugal who was attending the workshops. Although we were together very briefly--I fell in love with her and had thoughts of marrying her. We enjoyed a brief time together in Rome and Castel Gandolfo.

I recall the sad day when I was leaving to fly home. She was up at 6AM in the yard of where we were staying in Rome to send me off with a warm hug and kiss--as I boarded the car for the airport. I also recall, that the 2 occupants of the car, were recovering addicts who probably wouldn't be there if it wasn't for the influence of Chuck, Synanon, and my Italian book.

I later tried to follow up and see the lovely lady again but it never happened. We met one more time by chance at a psychodrama workshop I directed at a psychiatric conference in Vienna around 5 years later. I saw her in a restaurant at the Vienna Conference Center. We had coffee together with her new husband. I regret that I had not pursued a relationship with her when I had the chance.

At the same time I was directing session in Europe, I was teaching at CSUN and directing therapy sessions at my Psychodrama Institute in LA. I was doing lot of psychodrama sessions and group therapy both in the U.S. and abroad. I didn't know a great deal about the need for a therapy license.

Around 1985 a friend psychologist Les Sommerfield surprised me one day when he told me I really needed a license to do therapy. Over the years, I had helped many of my students acquire therapy licenses in California. However, I never thought I needed a license until Les told me I needed one.

After doing therapy for many years I decided to get what is called a California Behavioral Sciences "Marriage Family Therapist" license. I studied for over 2 years and then in 1986 took both an oral and written examination. It was ironic that some of the questions and possible answers on the written exam were derived from my books. I passed the exams and have been a licensed therapist in California since 1986

My MFT was helpful in my psychodrama work--but I also have performed many interesting individual sessions. One individual session I did was especially memorable. The therapy session was with one of the American astronauts who walked on the moon.

This came about through an affair I had with a wonderful lady named Marilyn. I hooked up with Marilyn when she called me out of the blue and said: "I have written a book called SEXUAL ETIQUETTE and several people have told me your a guy who can help get me get my manuscript published. I was reluctant. However, after several phone calls that I dismissed she said: "Look, I will pick you up, and cook you a nice dinner--if you will help me out." That did it.

Marilyn was a beautiful blonde, at that time around 35. I did go to her home, had a delicious dinner and we had a good time discussing her project. I gave her some good advice on publishing. Around midnight as I was taking leave I said half-joking "I would like to go to bed with you. What is the sexual ettiguette in this situation?" She led me into her bedroom .Very shortly we were making wonderful love. My relationship with Marilyn went on for some time.

Where Mr. Moonwalker comes into my story was shortly after Marilyn and I had broken up. We became good friends and were no longer lovers. She called me several times telling me that this famous astronaut had moved in with her and they were lovers.

Around that time he apparently had an alcohol problem. Marilyn told me "I enjoyed my relationship at first, now he hardly gets out out of bed. Frankly I want to help him and get him out of my house. Can you help me?" Marilyn knew I was, among other things, a licensed therapist. She asked me to help her handle the situation. I said, if he is agreeable I would give him one 2 hour session.

Marilyn set it up and the 3 of us had a nice dinner at Marilyn's house. Then I told Marilyn to leave the two of us alone. The astronaut and I went into the next room and had a one-on-one session. Marilyn phoned me later after the session and happily told me that I had helped resolve the situation, and he was moving out.

The pertinent finding in my session with the astronaut was his relationship to his father--who was an apparent controlling taskmaster. This was the most interesting element in my encounter with the man, and for him a major insight into his problems.

The insight was revealed in the following exchange. At one point, near the end of our session I asked him "What was the first thing your father said to you when you came back from the moon." Without missing a beat he told me, "My father said, why weren't you first man on the moon." OyVey.

By the way, Marilyn received a $100,000 advance on her book and it was published. To the best of my knowledge from the media

I learned that the astronaut cleaned up his problems and became a significant lecturer who provided the government many new ideas about space science.

When I full retired from teaching in 1994 I was equipped for and fortunately discover the role of "expert-witness" work in the courts. This opened up a whole new and fascinating profession. It was a role in which all of my criminological background and experience came together.

Chapter 10

Expert-Witness Work and Gangs (1994 To 2010)

In 1990 I acquired "early-retirement" from my teaching at CSUN. The "early-retirement plan involved teaching one semester per year and at the end of 5 years the system placed me in full retirement from my University teaching role. My "retirement" plan enabled me to work on my various lectures in the U.S. and Europe and write my books. In 1994 I became Emeritus Professor of sociology and criminology which meant I was fully retired and they didn't pay me anymore.

I wanted to continue in my role as a Professor; however, the bureaucracy blocked this possibility at CSUN. I was fortunate to find an opening and accepted an appointment as a Distinguished Professor of Criminology at Texas A&M University-Commerce. It was an interesting experience for 2 years. The faculty in the Department was very cordial and since I was in a small university town I spent time with my colleagues. They were all involved in interesting sociological subject, and my students seemed to enjoy my lectures. In addition to criminology courses--I taught a course in psychodrama.

In addition to my European trips, I was invited by the Minister of Justice of Japan to come to Tokyo to lecture on TCs and gangs. I also directed a weeklong psychodrama at a University in Nagoya.

In Nagoya, when I first arrived, at the first session everyone was bowing to me but no one wanted to become the subject of a psychodrama session and reveal their personal life. At the first session I said, "If no one wants to open up--I am catching the next plane to California." After that there were a deluge of very intense and emotional sessions. One I recall was a stereotype situation of a macho man who controlled his girlfriend. The lady had a good session, and the group seemed to benefit from an attack on Japanese male chauvinism.

While a professor at Texas A&M I kept my condo in LA and commuted regularly between Dallas, and LA. During that time I also directed my workshops in Europe and continued my writing. I later completed and published a new edition of JUVENILE DELINQUENCY (Wadsworth, 2000).

Around that time I was contacted by a number of lawyers who engaged me as an expert-witness in several gang cases in LA. I found the E-W work most interesting, in part, because it integrated my 50 years of work as a criminologist. I became fascinated with directly working in the courts on real cases. My work as an E-W was also an eye-opening new education for me on the real dynamics of the criminal justice system.

The first time I was ever hired as an expert-witness was back in 1962. The lawyer who engaged my services was assisting the parents of the 16 year old Michaels Farmer who had been murdered by the Egyptian King gang in a NYC park. The civil case alleged that the City of New York failed to provide sufficient police security to preventing the murder. The attorney had read my book THE VIOLENT GANG that described the incident, and I flew to NY and testified. I believe the parents of Michael Farmer received a settlement of $50,000.

Since 1994, I have been very active in my role as an expert-witness. All of my early personal experiences, and my years as a criminologist and social psychologist researching and directing therapeutic projects with gangsters and gangs in prisons, came together in my expert-witness work.

As of this year 2010 I have worked as an E-W on 300+ gang cases and around 20 civil cases. All of my past experience has provided the foundation for my expertise for consultations with lawyers interviewing defendants and my court testimony.

Many of the gang cases I have worked on are related to a law in California entitled 186.22. If a youth commits a "gang-related" crime and he is a member of a gang he can be enhanced to 25 years to life. Consequently when I testify as an E-W my testimony is often about whether a youth is in a gang and the offense is gang-related. In my overall experience I have found that prosecutor tend to overcharge on the 186.22 law more than half the time.

This is why in my gang E-W work in court cases I began to use more precise terms that are consistent with my research findings on gangs. For example, I prefer not to refer to a youth as a "gang member" when he is marginally connected to a gang. The term "member" connotes a more precise and definitive participation in a gang than my research reveals about adolescents and young adults. Many simply hangout with alleged gangsters who live in their hood.

The following theories relating to "gang membership" and "gang structure" serve as a foundation for my viewpoints and opinion expressed in my Reports and in court testimony as an E-W. I often place these theories on a placard in the courtroom and explain them to the judge and jury as they relate to the defendant, the alleged crime, and the overall case being adjudicated. This is often helpful to the defense of a youth who is alleged to be a gangster--but is not.

In my first book THE VIOLENT GANG (Macmillan, 1962 I presented my basic theory on gangs "Near-Group Theory." Based on my 50 years of work in the field I have seen no reason to change my theory on gangs. The foundation of my perspective and testimony in court as an E-W on street gangs is my basic near-group theory.

My theory of the violent gang as a "near-group" posits that street gangs, unlike the popular viewpoint and the police perspective, vary with regard to their degree of organization. Some gangs are cohesive, closely-knit and well organized. In contrast, gangs that fit the model of a near-group are very loosely structured, and the concept of "membership" as found in most coherent groups is unclear. Gang near-groups are characterized by diffuse role definition, limited cohesion, impermanence, minimal consensus of norms, shifting membership, emotionally disturbed leadership and, a limited definition of membership expectations.

This factor of near-group gang organization is a significant in criminal trials I have participated in, since many defendants I represented were either core participants in a gang, on the periphery, or not involved with a gang. . The gang defendants status on the degree of cohesiveness of the relevant gang and his role in the gang is often critical to the gangsters defense. My consultations with the attorneys, reports, and testimony often has a significant impact on whether the youth is convicted, and if he is--the extent of his sentence. Also, in many cases I have worked on the defendant may be in a gang; however, the offense was not related to his role in the gang.

In my E-W gang work, my main testimony on a youth being charged is the Issue of "Gang Membership. After interviewing the defendant, reading various discover, and consulting with the attorney I would testify as to where the defendant belonged in the gang.

Based on my extensive research on gangs, I have delineated six basic types of gang active-roles and nonactive roles that are pertinent in identifying levels of participation in a gang. These roles are vital in determining a gangster's status as a foundation for ascertaining the defendants innocence or guilt in an alleged gang crime and whether or not the crime was gang-related. Following are the roles:

Active gang roles

1. OGs or Veteranos are longtime core gangsters dedicated to their gang. They are individuals who have "put in work" (committed crimes) and earned their status in the illegal behavior aspect of the gang;
2. Gs are gangsters who comprise the general troops or soldiers in the gang;
3. Wannabes are young "interns" aspiring to become full-fledged gangsters, and they often commit illegal acts including acts of violence to gain gang status.

Nonactive gang roles

4. Gangster groupies comprise a relatively new category of youths who do not ordinarily participate in criminal gang activity but gravitate to, and apparently enjoy hanging out with, gangsters out of their own ego needs, and intrigue with the gangster lifestyle. They tend to dress and talk like Gs, and are enamored with "gangsta rap" music.
5. Residents in a G neighborhood are young men who have grown up and live in a gang neighborhood, and find it necessary for their survival to identify with the gang, even though they do

not participate intensively in the gang's criminal activities. They are often arrested for being in the wrong place at the wrong time, even when they are innocent of participating in a crime.
6. Former gangsters are individuals who in their earlier years were participants in a gang. However, as they become older and wiser, they determine that gangbanging and crimes related to being in a gang involves stupid behavior; and they "mature out" of the gang and its criminal activities.

In my work, I find that when some defendant are given a 2nd chance in an effective treatment program like a therapeutic community, many gangsters can change into good citizens. Many Individuals who started down the delinquent or criminal path have turned their life around and become valuable citizens.

As a case in point I recently wrote a letter to the California parole board on behalf of a prisoner who I knew from my work in the Amity TC at the Donavan Prison. He was up for parole and requested a letter from me based on his helpful work in my therapy sessions at the prison.

The prisoner, Reyes had committed murder, and had been sentenced to a life term. In my groups at the prison Reyes was very helpful as an auxiliary ego in a number of my sessions. At the time I met him he had already been in prison for over 20 years. Apparently, my letter on his behalf along with other positive recommendations helped to get him paroled. He was paroled and sent across the border into Tijuana.

He sent me the following Email about his "freedom" from Tijuana. I found his Email to be most gratifying, and I responded:

"Dear Dr. Yablonsky first let me wish the best and good health, I am fine and trying to deal with my new life in Tijuana. At times it seems like I'm back in the war zone like in prison but I look around and I quickly find plenty of open spaces where my sight and thoughts can drift into. Where as before all I saw were walls and barbwired fences. Yes being free beats anything. I'm finding out slowly that even though I am alone over here, I can uplift myself just by knowing that I've been blessed by God with another opportunity at life. Thank you Lewfor giving me a chance to walk into your world and learn from you, and thank you from the bottom of my heart for the letters you wrote for me in my battle with the Parole Board. I pray that this mail gets to you, I didn't know you had so many web sites, that's really cool I always knew you were the real deal. Lew, I wrote some stuff through out the years I participated in Amity. Different subjects, a 3 year journal, about my board hearings, the Governors denials and a lot of other personal observations that I experienced. Plus, what remains in my memory which is a lot. Lew I want to tell the story of my experience with Amity, from 1991 to the year 2000, can you help me, it should be interesting reading if not educational. Well dear friend it was nice talking to you and may God bless you. With love and respect always, Reyes.

Jose, I was glad to hear from you and that you are doing well. You are clearly a positive role-model to a lot of guys who would like to be in your status of freedom. If I can be of help in your writing--send me an outline of your work or around 10 pages. I am 84 and semi-retired; however, if I can be of help to your possible manuscript--email me some part of it. Your writing and experience could result in a valuable document that, as I have indicated, could be a hopeful path for some guys who are stuck in the prison system. Hang in there, and keep in touch. Your friend, Lew

Jose is only one example, albeit, an unusual one where I believe I have helped a former offender reform.

I believe that my testimony in court, in this regard has been helpful to many youths who have erroneously been identified as gangsters or overcharged by prosecutors for a crime.

Defense attorneys do not have the services of a police officer, and seldom have the benefit of a criminologist gang expert. On top of this inequity in the trial process, in order to attempt to indicate to the judge and jury that I have a bias for the defense, prosecutors almost always prosecutors ask me the percentage of times I have testified for the defense. Of course, my answer is "around 95 percent of the time"—and, as I like to add to my response, "You [prosecutors] seldom, if ever hire, me."

In my work as an E-W I have developed a clinical judgment with regard to how forthright and honest—or not—a defendant is in responding to my questioning. Most of the time defendants, even in homicide cases, are cooperative since they perceive me as someone who might be helpful to their defense.

Only on one occasion was my interview rebuked by a defendant who was in jail awaiting trial because he had allegedly committed a gang murder. He was brought to the interview room of the jail in handcuffs, leg and waist irons. He was then handcuffed to the interview table across from me. The incident is of interest since the defendant was, for no good reason, surly, defensive and resistant to answering my questions about his life situation and the crime he had allegedly committed.

His was a tough case since the evidence and the witnesses against him were strong. He had been offered a fifteen-year plea bargain deal. His lawyer told me that it was a good deal, considering the evidence against him, and that the client had rejected the plea bargain. The lawyer suggested to me that I should bring it up with him and recommend that he take the deal.

After some preliminary discussion, I gingerly broached the subject and recommended that it was a reasonable plea bargain. At this point he ended our conversation by angrily saying, "Fuck you man! You're suppose to be helping me and you fucking think I'm guilty. I'm out of here!" He tried to stand up but his handcuffs would not permit it. In the context of dark and sad humor I thought it was ironic for him to say this—since he was obviously going nowhere. I was the one who would go through the sliding double doors out of the joint to freedom, and he was going back to his cell. I apparently had some influence on him since the next day the attorney informed me that the defendant had taken the deal.

My preparation as an E-W for a case generally involves 4 phases of analysis and action: (1) the reading and analysis of various legal documents—including the preliminary hearing, police reports and the theory of the case from the point of view of both the prosecution and the defense; (2) interviews with the defendant (usually in jail), his family and others; (3) consultations with the attorney; and then (4) the testimony of my opinions in court.

Some of My Most Interesting Cases

My current work as an E-W is one of the most important aspects of my life. Consequently, in this autobiography, I believe it is important to go into some detail about my work over the past decade. To provide the reader with some understanding of what my gang expert-witness work involves I have selected the following 6 cases. They are for me the most interesting cases selected out of the 300+ case I have worked on for the defense. These cases reveal the kind of work I perform for the court and for the community.

Following are 6 example case reports that I have summarized. These cases delineate how I prepare the lawyer and myself in these cases in my expert-witness work. In all of these cases I was able to integrate my interviews with the defendants, interviews with the attorneys, and the large amount of police and other discovery in the cases into my opinions and Reports. The following summaries of actual case Reports I have written for the court provide some insight into my current life's work

1. A Gang Massacre and the Death Penalty

Twenty year old Lorenzo was, in my opinion, involved in the most horrific gang murder case in American history. He was with 4 gangsters who went to party in San Bernardino and shot 4 other gangsters to death, and left one wounded individual feigning that he was dead. The attorneys for the defendant Lorenzo hired me as an expert-witness. After reviewing all of the data in the case, and an interview with the defendant I wrote my opinions that are stated in the following summarized Report:

My opinion is that Lorenzo is best described as a "Socialized Criminal." His criminal orientation over his teenage years was fostered by his participation in the culture of the gangs that existed in his neighborhood. In most respects youths like Lorenzo growing up in a hood and propelled by a dysfunctional family, often for their survival and a search for a family participate in gangs.

The foregoing comment is significant factor to be considered in the sentencing involving an alleged gang member like Lorenzo. Is he a core or marginal gang member? It is my opinion, based on the evidence I have reviewed that Lorenzo was a marginal gang participant prior to the incident in this case--and in the process of the crime at the murder scene. Some corroboration of his marginal gang participation is the fact that he is not mentioned in the gang injunction for the "7th Street gang" enacted by a Judge Wilde in 1999.

Also, in the testimony of a gang member Ramirez, the prosecution's star witness and an admitted participant in the crime, there is no indication that Lorenzo had any "gang policy" role. He essentially, knew the homies in his hood, and the 3 participants in the crime because he grew up with them. He was a marginal participant in the gang, and had no role in the gang's "policies."

Basically he was "at the wrong place at the wrong time" when the crime in this case was committed. As indicated in the testimony of Ramirez, like Lorenzo, he was just "hanging out at a barbecue party." Lorenzo had a peripheral role and not a "membership" or leadership role in the gang involved in this case.

I would place Lorenzo in the category of a Resident in a G Hood. He grew up in the hood with many of the youths he knew who were active gangsters--but to the best of my information and analysis was never specifically arrested for gang activity. He had been for a time incarcerated at the California Youth Authority for robbery and a carjacking, and was only out for a brief time prior to the incident in this case. To the best of my information, prior to the offense in this case, other than the one for which he was convicted and imprisoned at CYA, Lorenzo has a limited prior offense record that would call for the death penalty he is facing.

His prior limited offense record, the brief period he was out of CYA prior to this offense would indicate that he had a minimal, if any involvement in gang politics which was cited by the prosecution as the motive for the 4 murders. In brief, it was alleged that the murders were committed for taking over the gang from the victims who were killed.

These factors coupled with the fact that during the period in Colorado, where he ran away to after the incident, he was a model lawabiding citizen for over a year. In Colorado he worked steadily and this factor should influence the Court for a more lenient sentence of life in prison rather than death by lethal injection.

In brief it is my opinion that Lorenzo was marginally involved, if at all, in the gang politics that is alleged to be the causal factor for the murders in this case. These factors, in my opinion mitigate his culpability in the crime in this case--and should constitute strong mitigators for the lesser sentence.

"NEAR-GROUP" GANG THEORY AS IT RELATED TO LORENZO, AND THE GANG IN THIS CASE

Based on my extensive research of gangs since 1950 for my books I have developed a general theory of street gangs as "near-groups." Most street gangs, are neither tightly knit sociological "groups" or at the other extreme random mobs of individuals. In this context Lorenzo was a marginal non-active Category 5 residential gang participant. He mainly knew and grew up with the more core gang members--and in my opinion was not an active participant in the murders. I believe he was as I have stated in the proverbial "wrong place at the wrong time" and was not involved in any of the gang's leadership politics or alleged preplanning of the incident.

In my interview with Lorenzo he gave the following description of his situation the night of the crimes;

"I had been up for 2 nights and had been doing a lot of drugs. I had no idea of any gang mission that was to take place that night. All of the guys at the party knew each other and were friends. I grew up with many of these guys and they were my friends. From the drugs and the drinking I did before the crime, I was kind of out of it just hanging out. I was inside the house laying on a couch, and then I heard this pop pop outside the house. I knew what the sound was and I just ran from the scene."

"I later thought that the guys were all loaded and got into some dumb fight over money owed or some drug deal that went bad. I had already told my parole officer that I planned to go to Colorado. I then took off for Colorado around 3 months after the murders. I didn't even know they were looking for me.

After the incident I went to Colorado with my girlfriend Nicole. We were happy together, and she became pregnant. Our daughter was born in California after I was arrested about 14 months after being in Colorado.

I paid no attention to what had happened when I was in Colorado until I was arrested. In jail for these 7 years prior to the trial, facing a possible death sentence made me think long and hard about my past life and the stupid shit I was involved in. I feel I have really changed my attitude about life and certainly the stupidity of "gang life." My review of the evidence indicates that there were some witnesses who corroborate Lorenzo's limited participation in the violence and his account of the event.

Despite my Report and testimony Lorenzo was given the death penalty and sent to death row at San Quentin Prison.

2. The Gay Caballero Bank Robber

I was hired as an expert-witness in this case by an attorney Ken Behzadi who had hired me in several other federal cases in the past. This case involved a 22 year old man who was gay and cross dressed in women's cloths. He had robbed a bank in his hood and had been identified on a bank surveillance tape on the day he robbed the bank. He was later identified and arrested. As a bank robbery it was a federal case. The attorney wanted "A Social-Psychological Analysis" of the defendant Jose Flores for use in possibly mitigating his sentencing. My focus in this Report is on the "mitigators" that might be helpful in determining Flores's sentencing process.

OPINION. Flores is a "Socialized Criminal" who is not motivated to commit crimes by any special personality pathology. To the best of my information on his background, he is a non-violent offender who has been essentially involved with drugs and prostitution to support his drug habit. His criminal act in this case tends to stem from his family background, his drug addiction and his need for money to supply his habit. It is in this context that Flores has committed his offenses of prostitution and robbery for profit--in this case the bank robbery.

PERSONALITY AND FAMILY ISSUES

In the context of my roles as a criminologist, a social psychologist and a Board of Behavioral Sciences Licensed Marriage Family Therapist I feel competent to analyze Flores's emotional situation that led to his crime. Based on my review of the data in his case and my interview with him I did not find any marked personality characteristics that would indicate any special personality defect in Flores. Having said this, I feel compelled to comment on his homosexuality and his marked behavior and appearance as a woman rather than a man.

In general social scientists are divided on whether an individual become a homosexual because of their socialization process or the physiological components they are born with. I have no clear viewpoint on this issue. I do note, however, based on my interview with Flores and my analysis of his family background that this is the gender decision he has made. In brief, he appears very feminine with long hair, feminine mannerisms, and choses to dress as a female. Of course, none of this behavior is criminal.

He indicates, that as a child he knew he had more feminine impulses than masculine emotions. As he told me, "When I was around 4, if you placed a doll and a racing car in front of me, I would pick the doll." In this context, in addition to his natural proclivities he was apparently sexually abused by his mother's live-in alcoholic boyfriend for several years.

According to Flores, "It began when I was 5 to around the age of 8. When my mother went off to work as a housekeeper, he would take me into his bed, and commit various sexual acts on me. He threatened me with physical harm if I told, and I was sworn to secrecy."

As is typical in cases like this his mother, had some knowledge of what was going on; however, in the prototypical manner that parents are complicit in the sexual abuse of their child, she did nothing about it and remained in denial. The family secret was kept, and Flores went to school and lived in this dysfunctional family environment until he was 14. At that time, for whatever reasons his mother acknowledged his homosexuality and angrily kicked him out of the house. This combined with his past abuse propelled him out into the streets with none of the usual support accorded a teenager.

Being on the streets, alone, and without any family support drove Flores into becoming a teenage prostitute and drug addict. He found that if he appeared as and dressed as a female he could earn more money. Given this factor, his homosexual proclivities were reinforced.

The drug abuse factor increased from crack-cocaine to meth amphetamines, and finally to heroin addiction. Based on my experience in working with heroin addicts, I would characterize his substance abuse as an effort at "self-medication" in order to act-out the sexual prostitution behavior that was repugnant to Flores.

He decided to try another method for acquiring money, and turned to the bank robbery. He described the motivation for his crime as follows: "I woke up strungout that morning very depressed. I needed a fix, and I was broke. I had abscesses on my arms and legs from shooting drugs. The thought of getting in a car with a trick and giving him a blowjob made me feel more sick. That's when I thought I will try something else. So I went to this bank and handed the teller a note telling him to give me money. I felt bad for the teller when I saw his face turn scared after I handed him the note. In a way, I wish I had been arrested then; however, the security guard was flirting with an attractive woman and paid no attention to me. I got $1000 dollars and left the bank."

At this stage in Flores's life he dressed and acted as a woman. A friend of his showed him the news article where his picture had been taken on the bank's security camera, dressed as a woman robbing the bank. He was traced to his home at that time and arrested. Flores told me that he was glad he was arrested. "Being in jail, I am drug-free, feel better, and looking forward to a better life than the miserable one in my past. I have begun a drug rehab program here in the jail, and am looking forward to furthering my education in prison and when I am released."

SUMMARY OPINION

Flores appears to be personable, in touch with reality, and in my opinion very contrite about his past behavior. He has remorse, and to the best of his ability, in the jail, he is a model prisoner. He is participating in a program to deal with his drug abuse problem, and plans to enroll in any available educational and treatment programs when he goes to prison.

Flores is by no means a hard-core criminal. His crime is explained by his past difficult family life and his addiction problems. He is not a confirmed criminal or bank robber. It is my opinion, that if he receives leniency in his sentencing, and is sent to a correctional facility where he can be helped--he has a real potential for rehabilitating himself.

Flores is well-spoken, effectively bilingual in English and Spanish, and has aspirations to work in some capacity where he can use this ability as a translator. In my opinion, based on my 50 years of working with offenders, I believe Flores is in the upper 10% of individuals who can change their lives, become rehabilitated, and become responsible law-abiding citizens. The criminal justice system can effectively aid in Flores's rehabilitation at this juncture in his life. Toward this end I would recommend that Flores receives a minimal sentence.

I believe Flores received a sentence of 2 years in a federal prison.

3. Cain and Abel. A Man Murdered His Brother on the Possible Assumption that His Brother Was Going to Kill Him.

This case involves a 30 year old defendant who killed his brother in the real or paranoid belief--that his brother was going to have him killed by the Mexican Mafia. After he shot and killed his brother he went to a police station and fully confessed that he committed the murder. The interview and the confession were videotaped, I viewed the videotape, and also read and analyzed various data on the case. I interviewed the defendant in the LA County Jail. Following is my Report to the attorney.

BASIC OPINIONS Some of the facts in the case are clearer than others. Millan does have a background as a gang member in his earlier years, and was incarcerated for around 12 years. During this period he no doubt had some relationship or dealings with the so-called Mexican Mafia or as they called Eme. (I have had several cases related to the Eme gang, and am familiar with their violent behavior.) It is a fact that Eme does "green-light" a hit on some individuals who cross them. Beyond this factor, the Millan case is difficult to assess in terms of the clarity of the motive for Millan shooting and killing his brother.

In Millan's statements made on videotape during the police interrogation after he had admittedly shot and killed his brother he described his motive. In summary, according to his statement, he believed that Eme was out to kill him; and he killed his brother because he believed his brother was trying to "set him up." Millan also rambled on about how prior to the meeting with his brother Eme had stalked him through several individuals that he knew from his past gang experience.

My background and experience (as cited in my resume) includes my being licensed as a California Board of Behavioral Sciences Therapist. In my work as a therapist I have directed group therapy sessions with several hundred criminals. I find it difficult to clearly determine whether Millan's statements in his police interview are real or hallucinations. He attributes his motive for killing his brother to his belief, real or paranoid, that he was being "set-up" to be killed by the Mexican Mafia.

I attempted to pursue the issue of "fact" or "paranoia" with Millan in my interview with him at the County Jail. My opinion remains inconclusive. During my interview, he was resistant to discuss the issue of Eme. This might very well be due to his fear of being assaulted in the Jail by the gang.

I regret not being more definitive in my opinions; however, I have found this to be a difficult case in determining exactly what Millan's motive was for shooting and killing his brother.

Addendum on 1/26/09 for my possible testimony
There are two possibilities in this case:

1. Defendant had relevant and accurate information that he was being set up to be killed. Or utilizing my concept of victim-precipitated-homicide he responded by killing his brother who he truly believed was setting him up.
2. Based on my experience and training as a California licensed therapist Millan, at the time of the killing, was in a mental state of paranoid delusion; and believed his brother was out to get him killed. As a potential victim he responded in self-defense.

In either scenario his response with his act of murder was mitigated by either his reality assessment as a former gangster; or by his emotional state at the time of the crime.

There was no trial or need for me to testify. The defendant took a deal and I believe received a 15 year prison sentence.

4. A Jag Case: The United States Airforce Vs "The Gangster Disciples." The Emulation of a Chicago Gang.

This was a JAG case I was hired to work on for 3 JAG attorneys with the U.S. Airforce. I was an expert-witness on behalf of one of the participants in what I believed was a pseudo-gang that was created by servicemen who were stationed in the U.S. Airforce in germany. The defendant Jones was being tried at the Air Force Base in Little Rock, Arkansas. I traveled to Arkansas twice and interviewed Jones at the Base, and had numerous consultations with the 3 JAG attorneys assigned to his defense.

The Basic Facts In The Incident.

On the night of July 3, 2005 around ten AF servicemen joined together to initiate MSgt. Juwan Johnson into their "gang." They called themselves the "Gangster Disciples", the name of a notorious Chicago gang that they copied but in my opinion had no connection to. Their hangout for several years was a bar called the Black Sounds a Hip-hop nightclub in Kaiserslaughtern Germany.

The rag-tag group of around 10 included one AF woman Sgt. who became part of the gang by being, in the gang's words, "sexed into the gang." To get into the gang she admittedly in her testimony said that she had sex with around half of the gang "members" in order to join and be a member of the gang.

The group, in fact, on the night of the incident what is known in gang lexicon as a criminal street gang "jumping-in." The gang gathered with the potential new member at a remote place near the small town in Germany. The servicemen were from various cities in the U.S. Some of them had recently returned from duty in Iraq, and were no strangers to violence.

They encircled Johnson, and then the leader of the gang, known as "the Governor" Rico Williams began by asking Johnson if he was sure he wanted to join. Johnson said, "Yes."

Williams, in my opinion, a "Jim Jones" type of charismatic leader, then punched Johnson in the mouth knocking him out. When he came too, others began to hit Johnson while he was on the ground. An AF Sgt. named Sims, who was William's second in command became a more ferocious assailant. Half way through the "beat-down" Williams asked Johnson if he still wanted to join the gang. Again, he said, "Yes." The defendant Jones was apparently in the group that did the beating.

Right after the beating the group knew Johnson was in bad shape and should have gone to a hospital. However, Williams, the victim Johnson and the group agreed that all they would do was take him back to the barracks. He was dumped on his bed. The next morning he was found dead.

The group had a meeting the following day to discuss a cover-up. After the meeting, Rico Williams left the country, and has not been found to this date. Others, including Sims were tried--and Sims received 12 years. The woman, Ellis, was granted immunity and testified against the others. Several have yet to be tried.

I was hired as an expert-witness in October of 2008 by JAG defense attorneys Majors Veronique Anderson, Major Conrad Huegen, and Captain Jeremy Emmert to assist in the defense of the defendant Jerome Jones. The three are defense attorneys for JAG.

The AF JAG trial took place at the AF base in Little Rock, Arkansas In January, 2009. I interviewed Jones twice on the base, consulted with the attorneys, read and analyzed several thousand pages of data on the case, wrote a Report, and testified in the JAG Military Court on January 22, 2009. [At the trial when I was testifying in the military court I felt like I was in the movie "A Few Good Men."]

Most of the other defendants received sentence from 5 to 12 years. I believe based, in part on my testimony Jones received a 2 year prison sentence and a dishonorable discharge.

5. A CASE OF NECROPHILIA

I testified for the defendant, a juvenile named Curnette in this case which involved nicrophelia. The following news article is a good description of the offense committed by the 3 involved individuals

. My analysis and Report based on interviewing Curnette and the analysis of police reports and other data follows the article.

10/26/2004 San Bernardino County Sun

Necrophilia inspired killing. Prosecutor says

Stephens had sex with Victim McKendall's corpse,

By JOE NELSON , Staff Writer

SAN BERNARDINO - Necrophilia inspired Joshua Curnutte to lure a 16-year-old Highland girl to Little Sand Canyon, where she was beaten to death before Curnutte and his friend had sex with her body, a prosecutor said Monday in Superior Court. "What you will hear may seem very disturbing. There's violence of the worst kind,' Deputy District Attorney Lewis Cope told the jury during opening statements of Curnutte's murder trial.

He said Curnutte, 17, and Jonathan Stephens, 21, of Highland, formed their own gang, the North Side Necrophiliacs. On April 2, 2002. They and Highland resident Luke Miller, 16, lured Christy McKendall to remote Little Sand Canyon on the pretense of looking at a marijuana garden Stephens had planted. Near a natural spring well and an old dam in the mouth of the canyon, Curnutte and Miller held down Christy's arms and legs while Stephens choked her into unconsciousness, Cope said. "It was not enough that Jonathan Stephens would squeeze the life out of Christy McKendall,' said Cope, adding that Stephens picked up a eucalyptus log from the ground, one of many from a stack of cut logs. "With that log in his hands, he brought it down on her face again, and again, and again, and again."

Stephens and Curnutte then had sex with her body, Cope said. Curnutte's attorney, Julian Ducre, argued that Curnutte and Miller were caught off guard by Stephens' actions and had no idea he planned to kill Christy.

After Stephens had sex with Christy's corpse, Curnutte did the same out of fear of getting hurt, Ducre said. Ducre said the evidence will show that Miller refused to go along with the necrophilia. A hiker found Christy's body on April 7, 2002, when he tossed a cigarette butt in the well.

A Metropolitan Water District worker at the well on April 5 to monitor its water level testified Monday that he spotted something in the well at the time, but didn't report it because he thought it was a mannequin. Daniel Cabrera, now a private in the U.S. Marine Corps, testified that he and three friends were in the parking lot of Cajon High School the day after the killing and were approached by Curnutte, who asked for a cigarette from them and struck up a conversation.

'For some reason, I don't know if he had to prove himself to us. ... He told us that him and two of his friends had murdered a girl, and he had to get away, he was squatting,' Cabrera testified. Cabrera said Curnutte appeared "out of it,' as if high on drugs...

My Report to the Defense Attorney and the Court

Following are my viewpoints and opinions on the dynamics of the relationship of Josh to Jon Stevens in answer to the question of why older youths like Stevens hang out and associate with younger boys like Josh. These opinions were written in a Report to the defense attorney Julian Ducre who had me court appointed in the case.

1. The older person in this type of group is usually emotionally and socially inadequate and has difficulty developing relationships in his peer group. Consequently, he finds that younger boys will listen to him, and to a certain degree, respect him, and follow his direction From these younger boys that he controls he receives the attention and affection--he doesn't get from his peers. His peers tend to view him as a disturbed person and they usually have no interest in associating with him. (Cite Stevens racism nazi tattoos, drug use, bizarre behavior, etc.) Consequently he is alienated from most normal relationships with his peers. In the older person--young boy dyad the older person can command control and manipulate the young boys with whom he associates. In brief, with young kids he has a degree of power and acceptance, that he does not have with other people.

2. WHY DO SOME YOUNGER BOYS LIKE JOSH SEEK OUT AND RELATE TO THIS TYPE OF EMOTIONALLY DISTURBED OLDER YOUTH?

My research and therapeutic experience indicates that many adolescent boys who have an absentee father problem, like Josh, tend to associate with older individuals who may misguide them-- but do give them their attention. Their father is either ineffectual in the father role, an addict or alcoholic, abusive, or not available. (For example, my estimate is that around 80 to 90 percent of the 160,000 prisoners in the California Department of Corrections prisons have this kind of problem with their father and this issue has had a significant impact on their criminal behavior.)

As a result of this factor, typically their socialization process is "fatherless." They are in search of an older person who can fulfill their lives with a father figure--even if this person is an ineffectual and deviant human being. He is all there is, and for the father hungry youth better than nothing. This older individual who has taken an interest in him is paid back with compliance to his control and direction--even if the behavior required is deviant and bizarre and goes against the younger persons moral compass.

3. HOW DOES THIS TYPE OF PATHOLOGICAL RELATIONSHIP BETWEEN JOSH AND JONATHAN AFFECT THE SCENARIO OF THIS MURDER?

The best way for me to answer this question is to briefly note several factors involved in the incident.

FACTOR 1. Jon Stevens is the controlling boss in the relationship and Josh is the follower On the evening of the murder, Jon is able to manipulate his 3 young followers, including the victim to the place of the incident in order to "ostensibly" show them his marijuana stash--and smoke some dope.

He probably had a premeditated idea about the "choking sex game" and the pathological fantasy of a more severe crime he has had in mind for some time. Given his controlling Svengali ability he gets the victim and his 2 dominated cohorts to go along with the game.

FACTOR 2. With the help of his manipulated young "friends" he initiates the choking of the victim. He goes into a state of murderous fugue, a characteristic of sociopathic killers and brutally murders Christy. In order to make sure the two youths are part of his insanity he commands them to participate in the incident.

FACTOR 3. After Josh sees the brutal assault by Jon on Christy he becomes severely emotionally distressed and frightened. The whole playful deviant and bizarre scenario has changed into a brutal homicide. In my interview, he keeps referring to this factor of the situation as a horrible nightmare.

He is now, with good reason, fearful of Jon who he now perceives as a maniac who has committed this brutal and unanticipated act of homicidal violence. Josh is now in a state of shock and disbelief about what has happened. He complies with Jon's commands out of a fear that if he doesn't do what Jon has told him to do--he will be killed by Jon. With good reason, he now perceives Jon as a homicidal maniac capable of any atrocity--and fears for his own life. Out of his fear that he too might be killed, Josh goes into a partial state of blackout and emotional shock and follows Jon's bizarre orders.

FACTOR 4. THE AFTERMATH-POST-TRAUMATIC STRESS-DISORDER, DEPRESSION AND A SUICIDAL IDEATION. According to Josh--Jon, Josh, and Luke leave the scene of the crime, and silently walk home. Neither of them is in a state of emotional exultation. Josh is in a state of severe depression--as he told me, "a good friend of mine Christy was dead." He had great remorse and was in a state of Post-Traumatic-Stress-Disorder caused by the horrendous situation he had participated in and experienced. These emotions were still present in him and visible during my interview with him some 2 years after the incident. He had remorse for his behavior and felt extremely guilty about what was done to her, Part of his remorse was related to his comment "I didn't help my friend Christy. She was a nice person and I really liked her. I can't stop seeing her face--after Jon had beat her up."

In brief, Josh suffered from post traumatic stress disorder, a deep depression and regrettably acted out his suicidal tendencies In many ways, although he was a participant in the horrendous incident, he will very likely remember the trauma of this event for the rest of his life and will avoid his ever being in this type of situation again. I see this most regrettable incident as an aberration in Josh's life. Unlike Jon Stevens Josh is not sociopathic or psychotic, and has a conscience. This is partially indicated by his understandable remorse, and depression for being part of a horrendous incident. He is an intelligent young man with a conscience; and my prediction is that he will serve his time, utilize whatever positive educational facilities are available in prison and leave prison to lead a reasonable life. Based on my analysis of the incident, his emotional history and my interview with him I don't see him as ever repeating a crime like this one again in the future. I believe justice would be served for all parties involved if he given a reasonable sentence that will give some hope for a positive future life.

FACTOR 5. THE AFTERMATH-POST-TRAUMATIC STRESS-DISORDER, DEPRESSION AND A SUICIDAL IDEATION. According to Josh--Jon, Josh, and Luke leave the scene of the crime, and silently walk home. Neither of them is in a state of emotional exultation. Josh is in a state of severe depression--as he told me, "a good friend of mine Christy was dead." He had great remorse and was in a state of Post-Traumatic-Stress-Disorder caused by the horrendous situation he had participated in and experienced. These emotions were still present in him and visible during my interview with him some 2 years after the incident. He had enormous remorse for his behavior and felt guilty about what was done to the victim.

6. A Young Woman "Sexed Into A Gang" That Involved 2 Murders

The defendant, a white 18 year old girl, "fell in love" with a neighbor who happened to be a Hispanic gangster. On 2 occasions she drove her boyfriend and his 2 homie co-defendants to 2 houses where they murdered 2 individuals. She was arrested along with the 3 alleged murderers. She was charged under 186.22 with being a "gang member." The prosecutor's expert-witness a police officer testified in the preliminary hearing that she was a gangster because, in his words "she was sexed into the gang." Following is my verbatim Report for the attorney and my possible Court testimony

To: Attorney John Chacker

Subject: Report on the Jane Smith case.

As you know, I was appointed as a gang expert in the Smith case. Since then I have reviewed and analyzed the various data you provided me including: various Police Reports, the Preliminary Hearing in this case, other data, and my interview with Smith. In my Report I will attempt to provide my opinion on some of the basic issues and questions in this case.

1. IS SMITH A "GANG MEMBER"?

[Here I have eliminated repeating my 6 basic types of active and inactive gang roles that are pertinent in identifying whether or not an individual is a gangster.]

OPINION: based on all of the data I have reviewed to date, it is my opinion that Smith does not fit into any of these categories and is not a gang member.

Based on analysis of the data and my interview with Smith following are the 8 characteristics I have used, in part, to determine that, in my opinion, she was not a gang member:

(1) GENERAL EMOTIONAL ASSESSMENT. Smith is now an 18 year old white girl, and her boyfriend is a Hispanic gangster. She is well spoken, and based on my clinical ability as a California Licensed Therapist, I found her to respond coherently to me in our interview. Unlike most bona-fide gangsters I also believed she was telling me the truth.

Given her appearance in my interview she apparently had a bout with anorexia--a problem often associated with low self-esteem. This accounts in part for her association with individuals who are apparently in a gang. In addition to the anorexic issue she had a drug problem--which no doubt affected her better judgment.

For about one month Smith was hospitalized at UCLA for her anorexic problem. In my role as therapist, I have directed group therapy sessions in a psychiatric hospital with anorexic girls. It is a serious life or death situation, and Smith has all of the emotional characteristics of a continuing anorexic patient. The fact that she is locked up on a 23 out of 24 hour basis at the jail is a dangerous situation for her health, and could possibly contribute to some suicidal tendencies.

This regrettable situation, plus the fact that the other inmates label her a "snitch" when she is only telling the truth about a most regrettable situation she was in could lead to a dire episode. If not letting her back into the community, where she should be since she is a harmless person, the least the system could do for her is have her in a hospital situation as a patient and not as an accused felon in a dangerous jail situation.

Although I am hired in this situation by the courts to serve as an expert-witness I am obligated as a California licensed therapist to point out the danger of her current custodial situation. In her current dangerous jail situation, If anything harmful happened to her health or her physical person by another inmate, in my opinion, LA County would be responsible.

(2) PRIOR GANG OFFENSE RECORD. Unlike her co-defendant gangsters, Smith has no prior offense record of any kind.

(3) SUBSTANCE ABUSE. During approximately an 8 month period Smith was addicted to methamphetamine. The gang individuals she associated with at this time were her connection. This accounts, in large measure, for her association with these individuals. During this period her decision-making ability was severely impaired by her addiction and need for drugs. Given her addiction she was often manipulated into being with the individuals involved in this case in order to acquire drugs for her addiction.

(4) TATTOOS. Smith does have one non-gang related tattoo--a rose.

(5) EDUCATIONAL BACKGROUND. Smith graduated high school, and went on to study for 2 years at a California State University. Her educational background is unlike almost all individuals who participate in gangs.

(6) WORK RECORD. After Smith graduated from high school she worked at a fast food establishment.

(7) FAMILY BACKGROUND Smith lived with her parents. However, during the period of this case incident she lived in a situation with her boyfriend. During her teen years she had some problems with her parents.

(8) GANG PARTICIPATION As previously indicated there is no record of any gang involvement on the part of Smith. It is my opinion that she was "in the wrong place at the wrong time" in the incidents in this case.

Recommendation: Jane is not a gang member and is innocent of murder and should be given a reasonable plea deal. According to my best information she received "time served" and probation.

About My Expert-Witness Work

As an expert witness, my testimony clearly has had an impact on the disposition of the many cases I have worked on. Although I am usually involved with the gang ramifications of the case. I am always aware that the most significant factor in any case I work on is that the defendant's life is on the line for a long or short sentence—or possible acquittal for the innocent. Given my research and work in "correctional" institutions, I know that a few years of prison "education" can turn an innocent youth into a recalcitrant criminal.

Consequently, sentencing a defendant who is innocent to prison can turn a law-abiding person into a criminal. In addition, incarceration in a prison costs the taxpayer, on the average, $40,000 a year for housing, food, and medical services for each prisoner. As an E-W, If, for sound legal reasons I can help reduce a defendant's sentence by 10 years this cuts down a cost of around $400,000 for the state, and reduces the possibility of a minor offender becoming a major criminal.

One of the main elements in gang cases is related to a law 186.22 that enhances the defendant penalty. If a crime is "gang-related" the defendant can get sentenced to 25 years to life in prison. I have often testified that the defendant was guilty of the crime that he was charged with, however, it was not gang-related.

As one case in point, I worked on a case for a defendant who had robbed a victim of around $50 on a parking lot. Based on the evidence I received and my interview with the defendant I concluded that he was a marginal gangster, and the crime was not gang-related. It was an individualistic crime. It would be ludicrous to speculate that the defendant would split up the $50 with a gang, or deposit in a Wells Fargo gang account. He did the robbery for his personal profit, and should be sentenced for this crime. He should not, and based on my testimony did not get a 25 to life gang sentence for this individualistic crime.

Certainly, gangsters who commit gang-related crimes should be found guilty in the judicial process. However, alleged gangsters and youths who are innocent of a gang-related crime deserve a fair day in court. In my work as an expert witness I attempt, to the best of my ability, to enter factual viewpoints and opinions into the judicial process.

In my work as an E-W I have mostly defended individuals I felt were unfairly or overly charged by the prosecution. I have also defended some guilty clients who, in my opinion deserved to have their sentences reduced in a plea bargain. In around 20% of the cases brought to my attention for appointment, when I felt the defendant was clearly guilty I rejected working on the case. There were some cases where a lawyer wanted to hire me that I refused because, in my opinion, the defendant was clearly guilty and was deserving of a long prison sentence.

In part, my efforts at judicial fairness in gang cases are basically generated by my heartfelt and sympathetic emotions for the human waste and destructiveness that violent gangs produce. In my work as an expert witness almost always for the defense, I am also aware of the large financial cost of sending an innocent youth to prison for ten to twenty years.

My work as an expert witness, over the past decade, is also guided by a deeply affecting emotional situation in my life with regard to this difficult social problem. Perhaps I can explain my intensely felt emotions on this subject, more specifically, by describing the following recurring scenario that I observe when I enter a large California prison to direct group psychotherapy and psychodrama sessions with the prisoners.

After undergoing a tight security check at the front gate of this prison that incarcerates around 5,000 men, I have to walk almost a mile through several depressing "big yards" to the hopeful therapeutic community cellblock where 200 prisoners who are in the program reside.

As I pass through these prison big yards I can't help observing hundreds of prisoners along the way. They are usually engaged in typical negative prison activities including small group secretive discussions on crimes they have committed or will commit. Some prisoners are simply strutting around the big yard displaying their absurd macho posturing.

Most of these young men are intelligent Black and Chicano youths who are wasting away in the cold-storage of prison life.

My heartfelt and emotional reaction is that the current judicial and prison systems too often destroys the valuable human potential that exists in these unfortunate men. All of them, even the worst-behaving sociopath, has a spark of motivation and compassion in him and, if given a chance through a humanistic judicial process, this positive spark can be ignited into a flame that would lead him into a law-abiding and satisfying lifestyle. Their plight is characteristic of the over 2 million prisoners incarcerated in the United States,

In this regard, some of my viewpoints and my strong commitment with regard to my work as an expert witness, after she interview me, was presented by reporter Allison Cohen in the following Los Angeles Times article.

Expert Witness: Lewis Yablonsky Has Devoted His Life to Studying Youth Crime

By Allison Cohen, Los Angeles Times December 11, 2000

Their faces are etched in his memory. Sometimes they appear in his dreams: gangbangers he has saved from the death penalty, those he's put behind bars and the wrongly accused who have been freed based on his testimony. From his lost days as a teenage dice hustler on the streets of New Jersey to working inside juvenile detention centers, in jails and behind a professor's lectern for 31 years at Cal State Northridge, Lewis Yablonsky has devoted a half-century of his life to understanding gangs. When he started, they toted homemade "zip guns" fashioned of wood, pipe and rubber bands; today's carry AK-47s.

Since he gained emeritus status as a professor of sociology and criminology at Northridge in 1994, Yablonsky's sights have turned from the classroom to the courtroom, where he is putting to use "50 years of wisdom" as an expert witness in criminal cases from here to Florida.

"You are dealing with a lot of realities here," he said recently of the many cases he has worked on. If he believes in a case, he will pore over court records and police reports and interview defendants and their families to find something, anything, to sway a judge or jury that they might not have the right guy, or if they do, to spare his life. "About 5% of [murderers] are Jeffrey Dahmers," Yablonsky said, referring to the serial killer. "But most of these guys can be turned around. That's what I'm about."

He has saved one Tucson gangbanger from the death penalty, arguing that the 24-year-old turned to a life of gangs as an adolescent only after his father murdered his mother. And he has freed another boy—named Geraldo-who was wrongly accused of a

drive-by shooting in Sacramento after shots were fired from a truck in which he was a passenger. Yablonsky on a rare occasion has testified for the prosecution—earning thanks from former Dist. Atty. Gil Garcetti for testimony that helped put Damien Williams behind bars for the brutal beating of Reginald Denny after the 1992 Rodney King verdict.

"In the case of Lewis, we are talking about someone who is saving lives and helping shape the court system," said sociologist Andrew Scott Ziner, who helped select Yablonsky for this year's William Foote Whyte Career Award for Sociological Practice, presented by the American Sociological Assn. "It's a great swan song for him," said former student and current social worker Mike Boretez, "to take all the years of his work and to be able to effectively incorporate them-the criminal and the therapeutic side." Yablonsky is considered the "most celebrated and distinguished faculty member in the department and the university as a whole," said Jane Prather, chairman of the Northridge sociology department.

"I probably have a lot more to give now than ever before in my life," Yablonsky said of the knowledge gained from the 7,000 to 10,000 interviews he has conducted with gangbangers over the years. As a child in Irvington, N.J., he was beaten by thugs because he was Jewish. He carried a switchblade until he was nearly 18 to protect himself from black gangs in Newark. They beat him routinely, he said, because he was an ofay—a white boy. "I learned what it feels like to be an underdog," he said.

Although he never joined a gang, he befriended kids in trouble with the law, such as his best friend, Davie, who ended up in prison after hijacking a truck. "I went on to do well," Yablonsky said, "and I've always wondered why he went the way he did." After a three-year tour in the Navy, Yablonsky enrolled at Rutgers University on the GI Bill. It was there that he picked up his first book on sociology. In time, he earned master's and doctoral degrees in sociology and criminology at New York University. During those years, he worked full time at a juvenile jail in his hometown, where he ended up face to face with many of the gangsters he knew from the street. He is working on his book, "JUVENILE DELINQUENCY: Into the 21st Century," and reviewing stacks of paperwork for upcoming cases...

Endnote-2010

At 85, I am grateful for the opportunity to be called upon to continue my work as an expert-witness and continue writing about my research and life. It is not only rewarding emotionally--it keeps my brain active.

A student of mine, with whom I had lunch and discussed this autobiography commented, "You certainly have had an interesting life." I responded, "no, I have had several different lives and enjoyed and personally benefited from all of them. These lives include psychodrama, Synanon, therapeutic work, extra-sex, crime, and sociological observations--not necessarily in that order. I have many fond memories of my various work projects around the world. My past and current life is clearly enhanced by my close relationship to my son Mitch. We get together almost everyday. At this time in my life-- every day is a holiday.

For further information contact:
Dr. Lewis Yablonsky
2311 4th St. Suite 312, Santa Monica, Ca. 90405
Phone & Fax (310) 450-3697.
E-Mail: expertwitness@lewyablonsky.com
Website: http://www.lewyablonsky.com

Books Published By Lewis Yablonsky

1. The Violent Gang (Macmillan 1962, Penguin 1966 and IUniverse, 2009)
2. Synanon The Tunnel Back (Macmillan 1965, Penguin 1967, Ernst Klett-German Edition)
3. The Hippie Trip (Pegasus 1968 and Penguin 1973). And IUnivers 2009
4. Robopaths: People As Machines (Bobbs-Merrill 1972,) Penguin,1973, Dutch and Japanese Editions).
5. Crime and Delinquency (Rand-McNally, 1970, 3rd Ed., (Houghton-Mifflin 1982)
6. Criminology, 4th Ed. (HarperCollins 1990) New Edition in process.
7. Juvenile Delinquency, 4th Ed. (HarperCollins,1988)
8. George Raft A Biography of Hollywood and Stardom, (McGraw-Hill, 1974; Mercury Press 1989). And IUniverse 2007
9. Psychodrama: Resolving Emotional Problems Through Role-Playing (Basic Books-HarperCollins1976, Brunner/Mazel 1992, Translated into German, Italian, &Spanish).
10. The Extra Sex Factor (New York-Times Books 1979 and IUniverse 2009).
11. The Little League Game (New York-Times Books 1979).
12. Fathers and Sons (Simon and Schuster 1982, Fireside Press 1984, Gardner Press, 1990. Translated into German, Italian, Dutch, Spanish, Czech and Portuguese Editions). And I Universe 2009
13. The Therapeutic Community: A Successful Approach For Treating Substance Abusers (Gardner Press,1989 & Paperback1994, German and Italian Editions)

14. The Emotional Meaning of Money (Gardner Press 1991 and IUniverse, 2009). Chinese & German Editions)
15. Gangsters: 50 Years of Madness, Drugs and Death on the Streets 0f America (New York University Press, 1997).and IUniverse 2009
16. Juvenile Delinquency: Into the 21st Century. (Wadsworth Press, 2000.)
17. Gangs In Court (Lawyers & Judges Publishers, 2005 and Second Edition 2009.)
18. Numerous articles published in professional journals on sociology, criminology and criminal justice.

THE YABLONSKY'S AT MOM AND DAD'S 50TH WEDDING ANNIVERSARY: Harry, Fannie, Morris, Lew, and Joe

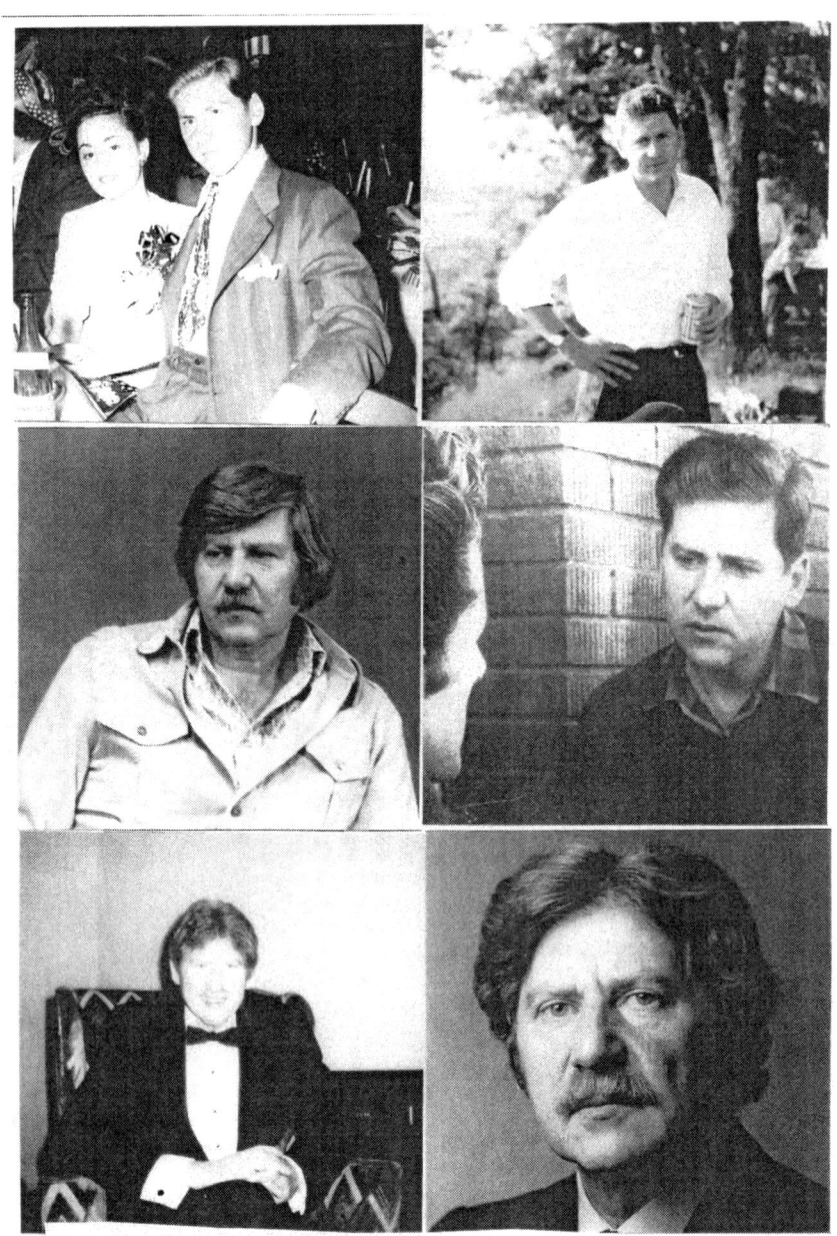

1. LEW'S FACES AND PHASES; FROM "HIPSTER" AT H.S. PROM TO PROFESSOR.

LEW IN THE U.S NAVY & FRIENDS

DONNA, MITCH & LEW

PSYCHODRAMA: THE BOOK, IN TREATMENT & ON TV

SYNANON: 1961-I'm Top Right with Donna; Frankie Lago & me; Senior Senator Dodd, Chuck & me (Dodd called Synanon "The miracle on the beach"): The Synanon band with Donna singing.

CRIME TREATMENT PROJECTS

NEW YORK CITY GANG PROJECT (1953-1958): Gang in baseball uniforms. L. To R. Robert Harron, (V.P. Columbia University); Lew Yablonsky; Captain Herb Koehler, (New York Police Department); (2 unknowns); and Harry Yablonsky (My Father).

The following photo and commentary excerpted from my textbook JUVENILE DELINQUENCY (Wadsworth, 2000). I directed around 20 psychodramas with prisoners in the Amity Project in the Donavan Prison.

This photo of a cellblock at the California Department of Corrections Donovan Prison depicts 200 men who are in the most avant-garde and effective treatment program for criminal/addicts of the 20th century: the Amity Project. The usual recidivist (repeat offense) rate in the United States for released prisoners is around 65%. The Amity Project rate for prisoners who have completed the program, after release, is around 20%! As a consequence of the program these men develop therapeutic skills as "experience-therapists," and many are employed after completeing the Amity Program to work with gangs and juvenile delinquents in the community. This positive experiment portends a hopeful future for criminal/addict treatment in the 21st century.

GEORGE RAFT: The Book, Raft & me; with co-stars Carol Lombard ("Bolero"), Marlene Dietrich ("Manpower") & Humphrey Bogart ("They Drive By Night")

THE VIOLENT GANG

Lewis Yablonsky

An inside report on the minds and lives of the youth gangs that kill—dramatically documented with real cases and recorded interviews

LEWIS YABLONSKY
GANGSTERS

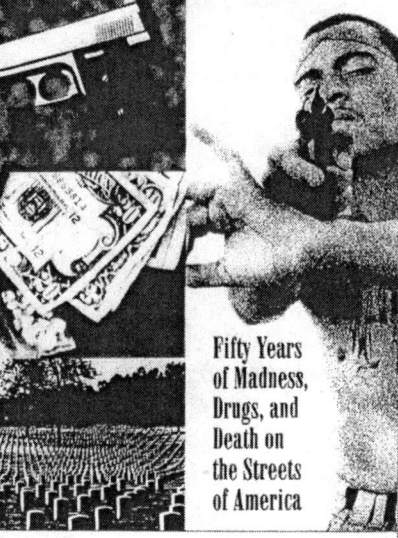

Fifty Years of Madness, Drugs, and Death on the Streets of America

GANGS IN COURT

Lewis Yablonsky

Lawyers & Judges Publishing Company, Inc.

The Therapeutic Community

A Successful Approach For Treating Substance Abusers

LEWIS YABLONSKY, PH.D.